A History of
Preston

David Hunt

Carnegie Publishing,
in conjunction with Preston Borough Council, 1992

A History of Preston
by David Hunt

Text copyright, © David Hunt, 1992

Published by Carnegie Publishing Ltd., 18 Maynard Street, Preston PR2 2AL
Designed and typeset in 10½/12 Times and Bodoni by Carnegie Publishing Ltd.
Printed and bound in the UK by the Bath Press, Bath

British Library Cataloguing-in-Publication Data

Hunt, David,
  History of Preston
  I. Title
  942.7665

ISBN 0-948789-67-0   **(Casebound)**
ISBN 0-948789-68-9   **(Softback)**

A History of

Preston

by David Hunt

Supported by

National Westminster Bank Plc

National Westminster Bank was privileged to become the founding commercial sponsor of Preston Guild 1992. By supporting *The History of Preston*, the Bank demonstrates its commitment to the community in a lasting and tangible way. The book will be a source of interest and reference for many years to come.

Carnegie Publishing,
in conjunction with Preston Borough Council, 1992

To my parents

Preface and acknowledgements

THE eighty years since the publication of the last large-scale history of Preston have been witness to enormous advances in all the fields of local studies. Each phase of the town's development is now marked by much new and stimulating research, frequently of the highest academic quality. At the same time the public's taste in historical writing has also developed, requiring the modern historian to seek a genuinely popular and open form of presentation, whilst remaining faithful to the greatly expanded field of learning which has opened up.

Through these challenges I have endeavoured to chart a course, seeking to produce an account which will also be familiar to those already well travelled in Preston's past. I have justified or revised the conclusions of the town's great trio of historians, Hardwick, Hewitson and Clemesha, in the light of modern research, and have extended their work towards the close of the twentieth century. This has required the development of entirely new analyses of the economic and social costs of the Industrial Revolution, of the impact of the two world wars, and of the steady march of the town towards metropolitan status. The post-industrial city is surely waiting in the wings. Indeed, future writers might well conclude that recent decades have seen the most remarkable developments, with the wholesale removal and redevelopment of great swathes of the town.

Yet the story of the development of a particular settlement and its community can no longer be contained within the confines of a single book, but extends over the whole sphere of our historical heritage. The marked progress of oral history and sound archives, enabling the people of the past to speak for themselves, has been a major development, whilst modern museums stress the surviving social and physical structures of the past. As early as 1906 Anthony Hewitson clearly anticipated the development of landscape studies, and in Preston something of the atmosphere of the closed medieval town can still be felt in the pattern of weinds between Manchester Road and Cannon Street, whilst the ghost of King Cotton still haunts the district between New Hall Lane and Ribbleton Lane.

The photograph, in particular, has greatly changed our perceptions of the past, providing a visual commentary on the evolution of our modern world. The great local history revival of recent years is surely due in large measure to the interest generated by photo-history, and the realisation of what has been lost in the cause of urban redevelopment. In Preston Stephen Sartin has been in the forefront of this approach.

It follows that the hard-pressed abilities of any one writer must draw heavily on the expertise and research of others in the field. In this respect I have been particularly fortunate, and although specific contributions are thanked in the notes to the text, I acknowledge the encouragement and practical help provided by Sylvia Birtles; Marian Roberts; Margaret Burscough; Ada Blackhurst; Diana Winterbotham; William Waring; Alan Crosby; Nigel Morgan; Aidan Turner-Bishop; Geoff Timmins; John Cook and Chris Aspin. Special thanks are due to the County Archivist and staff of the Lancashire Record Office; Terry Shaw and the staff of the Harris Reference Library; and to Robert Rushton and all at Leyland Library. At Preston Borough Council the Town Clerk's Department kindly gave me access to the town's own archive; and the Economic Development Department made available current analyses of economic trends in the town. The Arts Officer, Stephen Whittle, made available material from the Council's local history collection at the Harris Museum and Art Gallery, and many thanks are due to Frank Carpenter, Myna Trustrun and Sally Coleman. Thanks also to Ben Morgan at Carnegie Publishing for re-drawing my scribbled maps so expertly; and for his help in putting my references in good order.

From earlier days I am most grateful for the encouragement of my parents – to whom this book is dedicated – and to M. A. Murray, Leo Warren, the late E. E. Pickering and Stephen Sartin.

I must also acknowledge the encouragement of the members of the Leyland Historical Society, the friends of the Museum at Leyland, members of my local history classes and colleagues at South Ribble Borough Council. Much work was undertaken by Alistair Hodge and the staff at Carnegie Publishing. My wife Anne, and Derek Edmundson, kindly undertook much of the proof reading.

Finally, I am most grateful to Preston Borough Council, in particular members of its Guild Committee, for recognising the need for an updated history of our town, and for helping to provide the resources to undertake its publication – in the momentous year of the bicentenary of the death of Sir Richard Arkwright, and of the 1992 Preston Guild Merchant.

Contents

CHAPTER ONE

Early Preston

P RESTON and its surroundings are fortunate in having an interesting archaeological heritage which provides clues to the area's earliest history. Some discoveries made purely by chance – such as the Cuerdale Hoard or the Poulton-le-Fylde elk – have proved to be of national importance, but such spectacular finds are all too rare. More often, the evidence available from the pattern of surviving sites and artefacts can only allow general conclusions to be drawn about man's activities in the region as a whole, and it is within this broader context that Preston's own archaeological heritage has to be viewed.[1]

The study of the plant remains preserved in ancient peat deposits has provided a fairly clear picture of the main trends in the woodland history of the North West. To the south of Preston, for example, the construction of the M61 motorway through Red Moss near Horwich revealed a sequence of peat deposits extending over eight thousand years. These deposits reveal that, with the coming of warmer conditions, trees able to withstand low winter temperatures began to colonise the tundra-like environment – mainly birch and pine with some juniper, hazel and willow. Around seven thousand years ago, as temperatures and conditions began to approach those of the present day, the forests became dominated by oak and other deciduous trees, and remained so up to their widespread clearance for house-timber and fuel in Tudor times.[2]

The great forests did not completely dominate the early local landscape. In many areas of the Lancashire moors woodland cover was probably never very extensive, whilst enormous tracts of the ill-drained lowland were covered by mosses. These essentially grassland environments provided seasonal feeding grounds for the animals on which early man's hunting and gathering economy depended. In 1970, during the digging of foundations for a house on the former Great Moss at Poulton, the remains of a bull elk – the now well-known 'Poulton Elk' – were discovered. Three bone samples which have so far been dated using the Carbon 14 method, indicate that the five- or six-year-old animal died between 11,500 and 12,500 years ago. What made this find particularly interesting was the probability that the animal had been the victim of a hunting party; two barbed bone weapons were found with the skeleton, and a number of injuries apparent on the bones may have been caused by similar weapons.[3]

On the fells to the south of Preston very large numbers of flint artefacts have been found, and continue to be found, indicating that the activities of the hunter-gatherer groups extended over a wide area. Though often regarded as 'primitive', this highly mobile economy was well adapted to the seasonal products of the contemporary environment. The large native mammals, such as elk, deer and wild cattle, provided meat which could be supplemented by fish (especially salmon) and a wide range of vegetable foods from the forests. Fuel was widely available and the main rivers provided relatively easy penetration inland.

—— The first farmers ——

Around six thousand years ago hunting and gathering began to be supplemented by the keeping of domestic animals and the growing of cereal crops. Separate farming communities traded extensively, and have left large numbers of burial sites along the coasts of the Irish Sea. These spectacular 'chambered tombs' often continued in use as communal cemeteries for centuries. A local example, Pikestones, can still be seen at 900 feet OD on the moors above Anglezarke. Now much ruined, it had a chamber at least fifteen feet long beneath a stone cairn 150 feet long and sixty feet wide at the entrance.[4]

Using axes with polished stone blades, these early farmers brought about extensive woodland clearance. From the study of the geology of the many surviving axes it is known that a number of distinct quarries or 'axe factories' were in operation, and that axes were traded widely. One of the most important factories was at Langdale in the Lake District, and a number of Langdale axes have been found in the vicinity of Preston, in the bed of the River Ribble at Broadgate, at Freckleton, and at Leagram. Two axes were recovered at Winmarleigh, and an axe possibly from a Cornish factory was found at Pilling. So effective were these implements that even before 2000 BC when bronze artefacts began to become widely used, man had become the most important single factor in determining the scale and speed of environmental change.[5]

In Lancashire, a large number of Bronze Age sites and artefact finds are related to burials. Round stone or turf cairns containing cremation deposits in various types of urn, or stone chests (or 'cists') containing burials have frequently been identified on the moors to the south and east of Preston; a major concentration of about twenty sites occurs to the east of Burnley; and large numbers are found along the southern flank of the Rossendale hills between Bolton and Todmorden. Among the best known are the sites on Winter Hill, which dominates the skyline to the south of Preston where, on the summit, soils preserved below a turf cairn

Side-looped palstave (Bronze Age axe) found at Carleton in 1930. The surviving pattern of sites and chance finds, such as this one, reveals a picture of continuous human occupation of mid-Lancashire from early post-glacial times.

The Bleasdale urns, Bronze Age. Excavation of the enigmatic Bleasdale Circle also revealed evidence of the clearance of the district's primeval oak woodlands, over 4000 years ago.

provided evidence that even this area was once extensively wooded, and lower down the hillside the now-destroyed cairn on Noon Hill revealed the remains of a number of burials when it was excavated in 1958 and 1963.

Directly relevant to Preston is a site at Astley Hall, Chorley, which was found accidentally during the construction of a barn in 1963; excavations undertaken between 1974 and 1977 revealed the remains of a circular ditched area containing cremation deposits and two urns. Bronze Age burials were also recovered during excavations on the enigmatic Bleasdale Circle, which was dug over in 1899–1900 and re-examined in 1933–35. Interpretations of exactly what was found differ, but the site seems to have comprised a timber enclosure 150 feet in diameter, within which a cairn overlay a smaller circle of posts and a pit containing two urned cremations. One of the timber posts has been dated to *c.*2200 BC. There are many possible interpretations for this type of site: as the remains of some sort of building; as a complex burial; or as a henge site – a local variant of Stonehenge. The use of massive timbers at Bleasdale is an indication of the considerable scale of activities and resources of communities to the north of Preston. Recent forensic examination of the burial deposits has produced traces of linen cloth.[6]

Many finds have also been made during the reclamation of the moss-lands to the north and south of Preston. As early as the seventeenth century a large number of timber canoes was found during the drainage of Martin Mere, and traces of a prehistoric trackway – Kates Pad – have been found on Pilling Moss.

Extremely well-preserved bodies from ritual or sacrificial 'Bog Burials' have long been known in Denmark, where Tollund Man is perhaps the

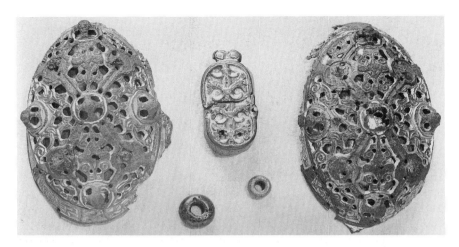

Gilt brooches from the Claughton burial, 830–950 AD. Part of the district's rich Dark Age heritage, which also includes the enormous Cuerdale Hoard, and many settlement names.

best known, and British examples have recently been discovered at Lindow Moss in Cheshire. Two letters written by William Birch of Stalmine and published in the *Preston Chronicle* in 1824–5 suggest that a similar find may have been made at Pilling: 'As some labourers were digging peat, on that part of Pilling Moss contiguous to the road leading to Garstang . . . at a depth of six feet from the surface, a piece of coarse woollen cloth, of a yellow colour was discovered, in which were contained the remains of human skull, with a great abundance of hair of a most beautiful auburn, and two strings of large black glass beads, together with a part of the first vertebra of the neck; the hair was plaited, and of great length'. His description of the amber and jet beads seems to place the burial in a prehistoric context, although all the finds have been lost.[7]

The Preston Dock finds

Prehistoric settlement sites are very rare in Britain, and until recently techniques of archaeological excavation were not sufficiently advanced to record them adequately, even if they were identified. This is particularly true of the finds made during the excavation of Preston docks in the 1880s; no archaeological investigation as such took place, reports of finds were made on a very piecemeal basis, and the finds have been a source of great confusion ever since. A fine display of canoes, antlers and skulls – a range of artefacts found over a huge area of workings and probably extending over a considerable period of time – was a prominent feature for many years in the then new Harris Museum, and so came to be associated together as a single find.[8]

As W. H. Heathcote reported in 1887, the construction of the dock brought to light much that was of interest to the geologist, as well as to the

Hollowed-out canoe, Preston dock excavations 1884–88. The range of animal remains recovered during the construction of Preston dock appears to have been similar to that noted during the building of the main line railway bridge in the 1830s.

antiquary. The river was diverted from its channel along the line of Strand Road into a new course three thousand yards long and three hundred feet wide hard-by Penwortham church, and a huge forty-acre dock was excavated. The geological sequence in the floor of the valley at Penwortham was overlain by peat and gravel which were of particular interest for the remains that they contained: 'The trees in the peat itself are mostly of a small size, 12 ins. or 15 ins. in diameter being about the average. The peat seems to consist mainly of brushwood, and for the most part of hazel, from the large quantity of nuts found. No bones, or anything of interest have been found in the peat'. Many large oak and beech trees were found throughout the gravel deposit, animal bones (red deer, horse, goat or sheep and oxen) occurred in coarse sand usually ten to fifteen feet below the surface, whilst 'Bones, mainly of *urus* [oxen] and antlers of Red deer frequently occur, generally in the lower deposits of sand and gravel about 20 feet from the surface'. Horse and whale-bones were also found in addition to about thirty human skulls which, according to the celebrated Victorian archaeologist Professor Boyd-Dawkins, 'belonged to a people of fairly intellectual development'. Another observer claimed to have seen evidence of some type of piled brushwood structure and a bronze spearhead was found at the entrance to the tidal basin at a depth of twenty feet below the surface.

The significance of these discoveries is unclear. In 1887 E. Dickson warned that there was clear evidence that the River Ribble had changed course frequently, and 'From this fact it would seem that the position of the deposits, or the deposits themselves, are not a sure and certain guide to the age of the bones, etc. found in the deposits'. A century on, and rigorous investigation of the surviving deposits is still needed before the riddle of the Preston Dock finds can be solved.

Of the centuries immediately prior to the coming of the Romans to Lancashire relatively little is known. In the south of England many settlement sites are known, ranging from individual farmsteads to large hillforts and large defended towns. Cereal farming was practised over very large areas with extensive animal husbandry, and recognisable towns began to develop as several of the British Kingdoms began to issue their own coinage and to trade with the Roman world. These trends are much less easy to identify in the North West.

Two hillforts have been excavated, at Portfield near Whalley and

Castercliffe near Nelson. At Portfield, near the confluence of the Ribble and Calder, excavation has revealed a series of ditches and ramparts and the site has produced an important hoard of bronze items including a gold ring and bracelet, perhaps indicating the activities of a local metalworker or trader. Castercliffe, on a hilltop site, revealed traces of three ramparts, including one of box-frame construction, a type found widely throughout Europe at this time. The location of these sites and the indications of continuity from the earlier period point to the continued importance of the lower Ribble Valley and its associated lowlands.[9]

The prehistoric archaeology of the Preston district, though fragmentary, is thus consistent in revealing very ancient patterns of settlement. The more fertile districts of the Fylde, the Lancashire Plain, and the Ribble Valley have probably been exploited by farming communities for over three thousand years, and considerable – if local – tracts of the natural woodland must have been brought into agricultural use. Preston was extremely well located within the region: at a crossing point on important north-south and east-west routes, and situated on a tidal river at the heart of a district with considerable agricultural potential. How far these factors influenced settlement at this time is unknown, but they were implicitly recognised by the degree of subsequent Roman activity in the region apparent at Kirkham, Walton and Ribchester.

—— *The Roman crossroads* ——

For a generation after the Romans' invasion in 43 AD, their sphere of influence comprised only the south-east corner of England, with shifting alliances with the British Kingdoms to the north and west, among them the Brigantes of northern England. This early consolidation came to an end in 78 AD when naval and land forces under the command of Agricola advanced north on both sides of the Pennines. Locally many of the Roman roads, forts and related sites were first established at this time, and rebuilt more permanently in the next half-century.[10]

The strategic importance of the district around Preston was at once recognised: it was critical to the series of roads extending north and west from the arc of military bases at Chester, Manchester and York. To the east the Ribble Valley formed an important route into Yorkshire, and small earthworks at Mellor and Whalley may be the vestiges of a signalling system along it. Near Ribchester this road was crossed by the direct north-south road from Manchester. To the west a coastal road from Wilderspool and Wigan forded the Ribble near the Roman site at Walton-le-Dale and continued through Preston to the fort at Lancaster. A fourth road linked the forts at Ribchester and Kirkham, once again passing through Preston (traditionally on the line of Watling Street Road), to form a crossroads with the Lancaster road somewhere in the vicinity of Fulwood. The River Ribble, tidal to just beyond Walton, may also have been important for seaborne communication. Thus although modern Preston has produced little archaeological evidence of the Roman occupation, the area as a whole was of considerable importance and has a rich Roman heritage.[11]

—— *Ribchester, Walton and Kirkham* ——

The region was dominated by Ribchester, *Bremetennacum*, a site which has long been known to antiquarians. William Camden visited the site in 1582 and 1603: 'Then the Rhibel turning Westward, gives its name to a village called at this day Rhibel Chester, where so many signs of Roman Antiquity, Statues, cairns, Pillors, pedestals of Pillors, Chapiters, Alters, Marbles and Inscriptions, are commonly dug up, that this hobbling Rhyme of the Inhabitants does not altogether seem groundless: It is written upon a Wall in Rome, Ribchester was as Rich as any town in Christendome'. The famous Parade Helmet, one of the treasures of Roman Britain in the British Museum, was discovered with other bronze articles near the river in 1796.[12]

Replica of the cavalry parade helmet found at Ribchester in 1796, the original of which is in the British Museum. Discovered in the bed of the River Ribble, which has eroded through a corner of the Roman fort. Recent excavations have shown that much of the site is still broadly intact beneath modern Ribchester.

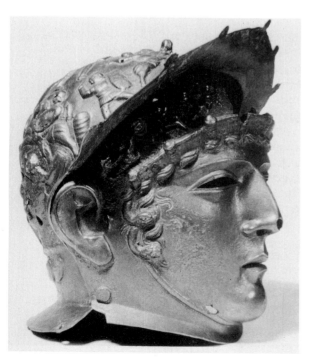

The fort at Ribchester enclosed almost six acres in a rectangle six hundred by four hundred feet, although almost one third of the site in the south-east corner has been washed away by the river. The main stone-walled fort was built *c.*105 AD above an impressive timber and turf structure revealed in recent excavations and dating from at least the period of Agricola's campaign. A short distance beyond the walls lay the bathhouse. Stones from these structures were later quarried for building materials for the modern town, and particularly for the church which was later built over the centre of the fort.

Around this base a considerable civilian settlement grew up. Only a relatively small area of this *vicus* has yet been excavated, to the north-east of the fort beneath modern Ribchester. This indicates a thriving settlement at the end of the first century AD and into the second, which declined in the third, with the expansion and contraction of the garrison. Recent excavation beneath the playing fields

to the north of the church has also revealed a
pattern of streets, perhaps the remains of
wooden houses with shops and workshops.[13]

A short distance to the south of Preston on
the 'flatts' formed between the rivers Darwen
and Ribble lies the site at Walton-le-Dale. To
Charles Hardwick belongs the credit for the
discovery of its Roman origin when he visited
the area on hearing that workmen digging
gravel from the 'plump' had found 'Scotch
pennies' associated with the 'Scotch Warriors'
from the battle of 1648, popularly supposed to
have been buried there. Apart from his
collection of finds and the report of his
unsystematic observations little more was
known of the site until the excavations by the
late E. E. Pickering and the Walton-le-Dale
Archaeological Society in the 1940s and 50s.
Although forced to work only at weekends,
opening trenches between the trees of an
orchard when and where market-gardening
activities would allow, Pickering was able to
clarify Hardwick's discovery, suggest a
chronology, establish the extent of the site
and, most critically, that the site was not
simply of an orthodox military character.[14]

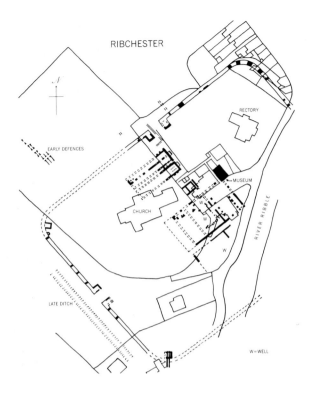

The location of the Roman fort beneath modern-day Ribchester (after B. J. N. Edwards and P. V. Webster Ribchester Excavations Part One*, 1985).*

Larger-scale excavations in the early 1980s revealed that the site had
changed over time. The earliest phase included elements of large timber
buildings. This was followed by a period of intense industrial activity in
streets of long buildings in a grid layout, built end-on to the north-south
road. The 'fronts' of these buildings had a well, with furnaces in the rear,
indicative of some type of large-scale industrial activity tentatively dated
to the late first/early second century AD. At a later date these structures
were replaced on a similar layout by buildings perhaps used for storage.
The final phase at Walton appeared to be very extensive and on a
different layout, but the upper levels of the site had been badly damaged
by ploughing and largely removed. Tentative interpretation of this
material seems to indicate that the site may relate to the early Roman
campaigns, and may have served as a supply base for military activities to
the north. The wider area is not well preserved: the river has been
straightened, and erosion and subsequent land use may have removed
the archaeological data on which a balanced picture of the site could be
based – a site critical to the understanding of the significance of Roman
activity in the Preston district.[15]

The fort on Carr Hill at Kirkham may also have been constructed early
in the Roman period. A structure of turf and timber of late first-century
date was rebuilt in stone and re-aligned in the second century. In 1936 a

small hoard of coins – the Kirkham Hoard – dating from 114–238 AD was found in a small bowl during roadworks. It has been suggested that the road from Ribchester may have continued beyond Kirkham deep into the Fylde to a harbour near the mouth of the river Wyre – the lost *Portos Setantiorum* mentioned by Ptolemy.[16]

Roman pottery is a most resilient product but, despite the extensive and deep excavations for new buildings in Preston since Victorian times, no firm evidence for Roman occupation has ever been found in the town. Isolated finds of coins have been reported, for example single coins of Nerva (96–98 AD) at Ribbleton in 1932, of Gallienus (253–268 AD) behind Haslam Park in 1929, of Tetricus (270–273 AD) at Ribbleton in 1975, and of Licinius (307–323 AD) also at Ribbleton in 1959. Most interesting and frustrating of all is the discovery of a Roman mortarium in a sandpit in Devonshire Place, New Hall Lane in 1925. That so little has been found in Preston is remarkable. With so many sites and roads in the area it is surprising that the town does not seem to have had a Roman presence, but unless new evidence is found that must be the conclusion.

Like other ancient towns Preston is first recorded historically in the Domesday Book (1086), but its origins can probably be traced to the two centuries following the Roman withdrawal, perhaps from c.450–650 AD. Earlier historians traced a direct connection between the decline of Ribchester and the rise of Preston. As Camden wrote, 'But when the Grandeur of the City, having come to its full period, was at last destroyed by either Wars or Earthquakes (for so it is commonly supposed) . . . from the ruins of Ribchester sprang Preston'. And as late as 1836 Edward Baines considered 'It must be allowed Preston was not a Roman station, but that when, by the gradual recession of the waters, or by that mighty convulsion of nature which threw up the huge mass of Pendle . . . Ribchester sunk into decay, Preston rose upon its ruins'.[17] Such a relationship almost certainly did not exist .

Early Preston

With the end of the Roman administration the northwest lost its strategic importance. Its remoteness from the rising Anglo-Saxon kingdoms of Northumbria and Mercia, and the area's natural isolation, meant that the spread of Anglo-Saxon settlement was a much more gradual process here than in other areas, taking the form of a successive filling in of the existing settlement pattern. This is indicated by the survival of a significant number of British place-names; for example the names of the rivers, the Ribble (*Rippel* 710, *Ribbel* 930, 1002), Darwen (*Derewent* 1277), Hodder (*Hoder* 1240), Wyre (*Wir* 1184, *Wyr* 1219) and Calder (*Caldre* 1193) and specific settlement names such as Inskip (*Inscip* 1086, *Inskyp* 1285), Tulketh (*Tulket* 1130, *Tuchut* 1250), Savick (*Savoch*

1190), Treales (*Treueles* 1086) and Preese (*Pres* 1086, *Prees* 1200). It has been suggested that these places 'imply [that] a British population lived on in the interior of the Fylde and was merged gradually in the Anglian population'. Similarly, to the south of Preston one finds Penwortham (*Peneuerdant* 1086, *Penuertham* 1149) and Walton-le-Dale (*Waletune* 1086, *Waleton* 1246) – an Anglo-Saxon name meaning the 'tun of the Wales' or Britons, and presumably applied to them by the early inhabitants of Preston. 'Tun' should not, however, be equated with 'town', a 'tun' being an enclosed area of ground which could surround anything from a single dwelling to the range of buildings associated with a large manor.[18]

Alongside these early British settlements there also developed a number of Anglo-Saxon sites, whose place-names were based not on the ancient Celtic tongue but on Old English. From *c.*700 settlements were organised into estates and ultimately into hundreds, the basic units of Anglo-Saxon administration and particularly tax gathering. Preston is located close-by the junction of three hundreds; the town is part of Amounderness, Walton lies in Blackburn Hundred, and Penwortham in the Leyland Hundred. According to Ekwall Amounderness (*Aghemundesnes* 934, *Agemundrenese* 1086) is literally 'the Ness of (the Norseman) *Agmundr*'.

Although the boundary of the relative influences of Northumbria and Mercia fluctuated over the line of the Ribble, the district around Preston is dominated by Old English (Anglo-Saxon) place-names. As Roy Millward writes, 'The east-west line of Fishergate and Church Street probably lies on the site of the long street of an Anglian village founded some time in the seventh century. The junction of Friargate at the town centre was the crossroad of the short north-south street that led into the common fields on the open fertile bluff above the river. Centuries of town life have almost destroyed this first plan of Preston, but out in the Fylde . . . villages like Kirkham and Freckleton preserve this primitive design of two streets at right angles to each other'.[19]

Several writers have suggested that the town's precise origin may be traced to a grant of lands along the Ribble to St. Wilfrid's Abbey at Ripon in 670. This hypothesis fits the most likely chronological framework and provides the distinctive element of the town's name, whilst St. Wilfrid was long the town's patron saint.

The spelling of 'Preston' is not consistent in early documents: *Prestune* 1086, *Prestonam* 1094, *Prestona* 1160, *Prestone* 1160, *Presteton* 1180 and *Prestun* 1226. The modern spelling occurs in 1094, 1176, 1196, 1212 and 1332. The word is derived from Old English (Anglo-Saxon) *Preosta – Tun*, the 'tun of the Priests'. The Saxon origins of the town are further indicated by the relatively large number of Old English names in the place-names of minor settlements in the district – Fishwick *(Fiscuic* 1086, *Fiswich* 1203); Ashton (*Eston* 1086, *Astuna* 1160); Lea (*Lea* 1086, *Lehe* 1190); Broughton (*Brocton* 1086, *Broctona* 1160); Haighton (*Halctun* 1086, *Aulton* 1201); Barton (*Bartun* 1086, *Barton* 1212) and Newsham (*Neuhuse* 1086, *Newesum* 1249). This is in clear contrast to the wide spread of

Scandinavian place-names in the rest of Amounderness.

From the late ninth century significant numbers of Norse settlers from earlier settlements in Ireland and along the west coast of Scotland began to colonise this sparsely populated region around the Irish Sea. Recent research has provided a more balanced picture of the Norse achievement, pointing to their high artistic attainment (particularly in metalwork), the wide trading contacts extending as far as the Far East, and their skilled seamanship. Place-name analysis in Scotland has suggested that much of their colonisation was essentially a peaceful infilling of sparsely populated areas rather than the pillage and conquest of popular legend. This conclusion is also borne out in the district around Preston.

Evidence of Norse settlement is most concentrated in the western, low-lying marshy districts of the Fylde, though, Preston apart, Scandinavian place-names abound throughout Amounderness. Here large tracts of land remained to be brought into cultivation and most writers agree that this was a peaceful development in what was, well into the Middle Ages, a thinly populated region. Both Anglo-Saxon and Norse settlers came from the same region of Europe, and their languages would not have been unintelligible to each other; as F. T. Wainwright argued, Norse settlement in Lancashire was parallel rather than superimposed. The largest number of Norse place-names have survived in the parishes of Kirkham (14), Poulton-le-Fylde (7), Garstang (17) and St. Michael's on Wyre (5) – a region which might thus perhaps be better regarded as Anglo-Scandinavian rather than Anglo-Saxon.[20]

Significantly, many place-names include both Saxon and Norse elements, such as Stalmine. Preesall contains Norse and earlier British, whilst Goosnargh (*Gusansarghe* 1086: the *erg* or shieling of the Irishman, Gusan) contains Norse and Irish. Occasionally composite place-names formed of complete English and Scandinavian names occur, such as Eccleston with Larbrick, or Medlar with Wesham.[21]

The Cuerdale Hoard

The artistic skills and wide-ranging trading activities of the Norse population, and particularly their links with settlements in Ireland, have been revealed locally by two very important archaeological discoveries: the Claughton-on-Brock burial and the Cuerdale Hoard.

The discovery at Claughton was made in the early nineteenth century and recorded and illustrated by John Weld. In an earthen burial cairn was found an urn containing a cremation burial and what may have been a box containing an iron sword and spearhead, fine silver brooches, and red and white beads. One brooch had been converted from a gilt mount but the other two are fine 'tortoise brooches', perhaps made in the Norse settlements in Ireland in the period 830–950. Curiously, the burial also contained a stone battle axe of familiar Bronze Age type, so that the urn and axe may have formed part of a much earlier cairn burial into which the Norse items were later inserted.[22]

The dramatic discovery at Cuerdale provides a colourful insight into Norse society at this time:

> At six o'clock in the evening of the 15th May, 1840, a number of workmen were engaged on the river bank repairing the damage done by the winter floods, which had disturbed the alluvial soil from the bank . . . It would appear that stakes of wood were being driven into the river bank with the object of forcing away the soil when the treasure was disclosed . . . One of the men struck the leaden chest with his pick when it immediately burst open, whereupon he remarked, 'It's quare 'ow these cockle shells her gotten theere'. But it was quickly realised that the 'cockle shells' were really silver coins.[23]

Although about a dozen similar finds are known from these troubled times, the size of the Cuerdale Hoard makes it spectacularly unique – over 8,500 pieces, mostly of silver, weighing 1,265 ounces. A lead-lined box contained small bullion bars, cut up silver jewellery and money bags holding some seven thousand coins.

The latest coins (those of Louis the Blind, Emperor of the West Franks, 901–905) suggest that the hoard may have been buried at some time around 905. The absence of complete examples of jewellery incidates that this was not a metalworker's hoard or stock, but rather that it was money. Earlier writers believed it to be the pay-chest of the Scandinavian forces defeated at the Battle of Brunanburgh. It has recently been established that it may rather have been the funds of forces assembling in the Ribble Valley for a campaign in Ireland following the temporary expulsion of the Norse from Dublin in 902, and their consequent re-settlement in Lancashire. Much of the bullion was Irish in origin and the hoard contained the remains of over forty Irish brooches.

How this treasure, the proceeds from much booty and trade, came to the banks of the Ribble above Preston, and why it was never recovered, can never be known with any certainty. As a time capsule, however, it gives a vivid insight into the boundaries of the Norse world, the shifting political groupings around the Irish Sea, and the settlement processes apparent in mid-Lancashire at this time.

—— *Preston in the Domesday Book* ——

Although the Domesday Book, completed in 1086, is popularly taken as a major turning point of English history, following as it does so closely the Norman Conquest of 1066, it may also be seen as a postscript to the so-called 'Dark Ages'. Money was a central concern of the men who compiled the Domesday Book, and money meant land. William the Conqueror, not unnaturally, wished to know who had what, and what it was worth before his conquest and after. In the heart of England very detailed accounts were made but in the north details are very sketchy and the few facts that were recorded must be interpreted with great caution.[24]

The entry for Amounderness is in fact included in the folio listing the land of the King in Yorkshire, and is quite separate in the book itself from the land south of the Ribble. A concept of Lancashire as a distinct entity did not yet exist and the Ribble still formed an adminstrative boundary between the old kingdoms of Northumbria and Mercia. Whereas the lands between the Ribble and the Mersey formed part of the estate of the King of England, Amounderness, which had been granted to the diocese of York in 903, had by the 1060s been taken over by Earl Tostig of Northumbria. After the Conquest William had granted it to one of his loyal subordinates, Roger of Poitou. Of the settlements, *Aschebi* has long since disappeared, but the remainder still form the basis of the modern geography of the region so that, even though precise details are lacking, the Domesday Book seems to provide a fairly reasonable outline for the contemporary settlement pattern. The greatest emphasis in the entry is given to Preston, which thus appears to have been the most important place in the district – the capital manor for the purpose of tax collection.

In each settlement the area of taxable land is given in *carucates*, a Scandinavian land measure similar to the Saxon *hide*, equivalent to perhaps 120 acres. Yet these are purely nominal values which, like the references to money in the Domesday Book, relate not to the actual

When the settlements recorded in the Domesday entry for Amounderness are mapped in the sequence in which they occur, they appear to indicate the round, or series of rounds, of the Saxon tax collectors on whose lists the return may have been based. The system of taxation was related to the amount of agricultural land in each township, and this was measured in 'carucates' of roughly 120 acres. A number of local settlements – Fishwick, Lea and Goosnargh, for example – paid for only a single carucate, but Bispham was taxed for eight, Garstang and Preston for six.

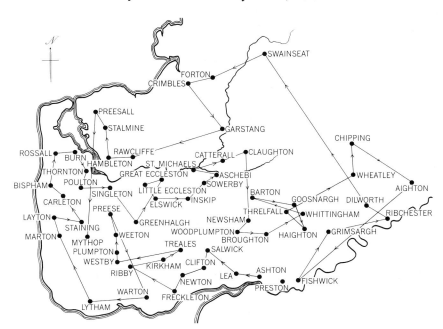

reality but to what officials thought might be there to tax. Essentially, they are abstract accounting terms. Indeed, it has been suggested that the Conqueror's surveyors did not penetrate the region but that their account was based on earlier Saxon tax returns or 'geld books'. By mapping the sequence of place-names listed in the entry for Amounderness, it is clear that the order of places is not a random list but rather a series of routes centred on Preston. Given the vagueness of the facts recorded – 'sixteen of them have a few inhabitants, but how many is not known' – it seems likely that these were not the product of trained surveyors but rather the 'rounds' of an earlier official.

The reference to the large number of unspecified settlements lying 'waste' has been the subject of much speculation, though the problem is far from clear. These may have been devastated during the turbulent days of Earl Tostig's tenure, or during William's celebrated 'Harrying of the North' in the years following his Conquest. Alternatively, 'waste' may indicate that these areas were merely uncultivated, and perhaps pasture land. It is also unclear whether the reference applies to Preston itself.

To the south of the Ribble, Walton-le-Dale was listed, along with the castle and burgesses at Penwortham, whilst the township of Leyland may also have been, like Preston, a centre for the collection of local taxes. Earl Tostig's landholding in Preston – about 700 acres – was matched at Ribby, Marton, Layton, Staining, Thornton, Singleton, Garstang and Preesall, and exceeded at Bispham. But the town's importance as the administrative centre of the Greater Fylde district is clear. Preston's early natural outlook was thus to the rich agricultural lands of the west.

CHAPTER TWO

The making of the royal borough

PRESTON was not a dynastic stronghold with a castle and walls like Lancaster or York; rather the early town plan was dominated by its market place, and it was as a market centre meeting the needs of the region that the town emerged and continues to develop a thousand years later. This has profoundly influenced all aspects of the town's history, making it quite distinct not only from the manors and rural townships of mid-Lancashire but also from many of the other towns of the North West. Preston in early medieval times was a community living by trade, which rapidly acquired its own rights and in so doing attained a measure of self-government.

The great market

Preston's growth was organic. It developed naturally as a market centre in response to local needs, and it was not imposed upon the landscape in the way that many military settlements were; neither was it one of the many known 'planned' towns of the Middle Ages. Central to this process was its location on the Ribble estuary, enabling relatively easy access to the sea and beyond, and eastwards along the Ribble Valley into Yorkshire. In addition it dominates the lowest bridging and fording points on the river, making it an important focus of the route between the north and south. It was therefore an important route centre from early times, with the additional advantage of easy access to the sea. Within the local context of mid-Lancashire its position was equally propitious, being at the intersection of quite distinct natural landscapes enabling the town's market to become the obvious centre for the exchange of various products and produce.

Preston has a large market place, a feature which was frequently

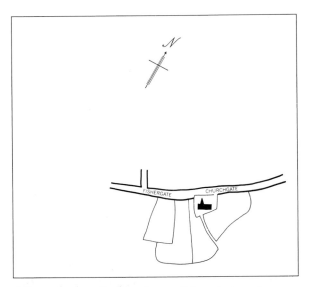

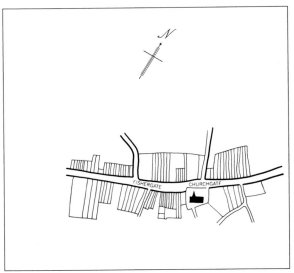

Schematic maps showing the possible evolution of Preston's town centre and market square.
1. The Parish Church and its grounds are laid out on a piece of land taken in from the irregularly-shaped fields which characterised the ancient pre-urban landscape.

2. The Church Street ridge emerges as the axis of the urban settlement. The town's principal burgage plots and fields are laid out from it. The widening of Church Street to the west of the church may indicate the original location of the town's developing market.

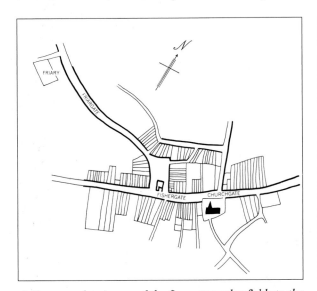

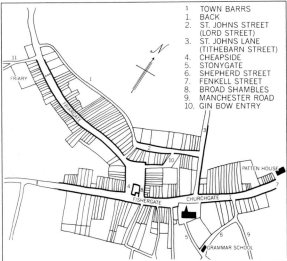

```
    TOWN BARRS
1.  BACK
2.  ST. JOHNS STREET
    (LORD STREET)
3.  ST. JOHNS LANE
    (TITHEBARN STREET)
4.  CHEAPSIDE
5.  STONYGATE
6.  SHEPHERD STREET
7.  FENKELL STREET
8.  BROAD SHAMBLES
9.  MANCHESTER ROAD
10. GIN BOW ENTRY
```

3. Burgage plots in one of the five rectangular fields to the north of Church St are swept away to create a large market square. The site of the Town Hall may date from this event, though a Manor Hall must have existed earlier. In the field to the east of the new market square, the far ends of the burgage plots are turned through 90 degrees to provide shop frontages facing the Flag Market.

4. A sketch map based on Kuerden's survey and map of Preston c.1680. The medieval town plan, completed with the development of Friargate and Bock Lane, and seen here in its final form, was to influence the development of the town centre well into the nineteenth century. Compare this plan with Lang's map on page 32 and Shakeshaft's map on page 153.

Plan of Preston Market Place c.1850. The ground plan of these buildings clearly illustrates the system of land allocation laid down in the town's Custumal.

alluded to by early writers. Analysis of the series of plans produced in 1684 by Dr Kuerden led M. R. G. Conzen to suggest three phases in the early development of the town. The earliest phase comprised settlement around the Parish Church and along the line of Church Street, coinciding with the ridge top. The widening of the street near the Parish Church may indicate that this was the original site of the market. Subsequently the east-west line of Fishergate and Church Street developed as the most important street, and the fields and burgage plots (narrow strips of land end on to the road and containing the burgesses'

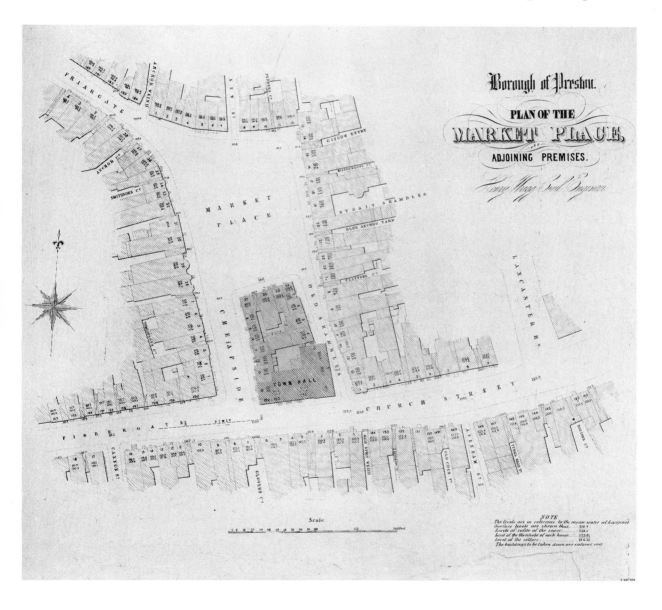

houses and gardens) were laid out based on this line rather than Friargate which thus seems to have been of secondary importance. The final phase saw the formation of the market square: one of the four large fields to the north of Fishergate adjoining the junction with Friargate was formed into a market place, and the burgage strips in the field to the east were re-aligned to face onto the new market square.[1]

The main feature of Preston's town plan which reflects its function as a market centre may thus have been in place as early as 1250, by which time the legal and economic rights on which the continued growth of the town depended, and which governed the everyday life of its inhabitants, were also firmly established.

—— *The early charters* ——

Preston received its first recorded royal charter from Henry II in 1179. For this privilege, similar to one granted to Newcastle-under-Lyme a few years earlier, the burgesses had to pay a hundred marks, and they duly advanced their first instalment of 25 marks. In return the town's status as an important regional market was implicitly recognised, the burgesses were to be allowed to trade throughout the country free of tolls and many of the petty duties then levied, and were to be free to regulate their own trade affairs through an institution called a Guild Merchant. They were also to be allowed a measure of security through their own courts, and to retain many of the fines they duly levied for themselves. In all there are known to have been fourteen royal charters between 1179 and 1828, each confirming, modifying or extending the rights granted to its predecessor, with the monarch of the day receiving a suitable payment.[2]

One of the town's early seals, 1376.

In many cases, perhaps including that of 1179, these charters merely sanctioned practices which had already long existed. In 1611 Judge Thomas Walmesley signed an affidavit that he had seen a charter granted by Henry in 1100, but subsequent writers unable to find any further trace of it have tended to the opinion that he was mistaken. Nevertheless, most agree that Preston may well have already possessed the attributes of a borough for some time.

The charters were not the dry legal pronouncements that they appear today – they conferred valuable rights. King John's Charter of 1199, confirmed by Henry III in 1227, and Edward III in 1328 and 1352, sanctioned the burgesses' right to hold fairs, enabling the town to develop as a centre of

*The Preston Guild Court
1922. Preston's Guild
Merchant, held every 20
years from 1542 to 1922,
and resuming in 1952 after
the war, provides a living
link with the town's ancient
origins as a burgesses'
market town and Royal
Borough.*

exchange over a much wider area than that served by its markets for local goods. An element of this distinction can still be seen in the town's annual pot fair, where dealers from a wide area still visit the market place on an annual basis, in contrast to the markets for local produce held three days per week. The charter of King John also confirmed the burgesses' rights in respect of the great woodlands to the north of the town, to Fulwood Forest and to what subsequently became Preston Moor. Once again this was a valuable concession, the woodlands being an important source of fuel and building materials, as well as an area for pasturing animals.

The clearest account of the townspeople's rights at this time, however, comes not from a charter at all, but from the *Custumal*.[3] This is a document drawn up to codify and clarify the many sources of the burgesses' rights as they had evolved by the late thirteenth century, perhaps in response to the fairly frequent demands that they justify their claims. Such a demand was made in 1291 and the undated *Custumal* may be associated with it. The central tenet is the burgesses' right to enforce a strict monopoly over the town's trade by restricting participation in it to members of the Guild Merchant, 'so that no-one who is not of that Guild shall make any merchandise in the said town unless with the consent of the burgesses'. Their commercial rights are codified, the freedom from many internal tolls is rehearsed and practices of buying and selling are regulated. For example it was forbidden to sell goods purchased earlier the same day, and complaints about goods purchased had to be made on the day of purchase before sunset. The prices of the main ingredients in the diet of Prestonians – ale and bread – were regulated at the assizes, and the burgesses could invoke draconian measures to stop those who sold far above the regulated price, for 'if a burgess sell for more than the assize he shall be liable to a fine of 12d, and he who purchased it to nothing: the burgess of the court aforesaid shall have duel, fire and water, to make judgement'. Consistent offenders should 'pay a larger fine or go to the cuckstool', which seventeenth-century records indicate stood in the vicinity of East View off Deepdale Road.

Many regulations are not, however, commercial; rather, they define civil rights – the rights or freedoms of the individual. The burgesses had at least a measure of defence against interference in their town's affairs, for 'no sheriff shall intermeddle within the Borough of Preston . . . concerning any plea, plaint, or dispute, or any other thing pertaining to the aforesaid town, saving the [pleas of the] King's crown'.

Preston was particularly fortunate that following the confiscation of Roger of Poitou's estates the Manor of Preston passed to the Duchy of Lancaster and ultimately to the Crown, who granted its rights to the townspeople for £15 per year.[4] This was a shrewd bargain since its income in 1241 was estimated at £40 per year, but the civil effects were particularly important since the townspeople had a firm control on their own affairs and their daily lives were not so open to the arbitary interference of the neighbouring magnates. On the adjoining estates of the Ffaringtons, Langtons and Hoghtons this measure of protection did not exist, and the rights of the Lord of the Manor were paramount. A serf from these districts could establish his freedom provided that he live 'in the town and hold land, and be in forenamed Guild and Hanse [the Guild Merchant], and pays lot and scot [taxes] with burgesses for a year and a day'. A steady drift into the town from these districts may therefore have been an important feature of its growth at this time.[5]

The *Custumal* asserts the burgesses' rights over more personal matters such as the right for one's daughter to marry without licence, and the arrangements for the milling of one's corn. For most events in people's lives the lord or the Church could exact a fee, particularly at death, but 'if a burgess of the town die a sudden death, his wife and his heirs shall quietly have all his chattels and lands, so that neither his Lord nor his justices may lay hands on the houses and chattels of the deceased . . . Also the wife of the deceased may marry whomsoever she please'.

To acquire these not inconsiderable rights one had to become a burgess: 'if anyone wish to be made a burgess he shall come into court [the town court or council] and give to the reeve 12d, and shall take his land from the bailiffs.' On this plot of land, to be at least 12 feet wide at its frontage to the street (Fishergate or Friargate) a new burgess had to build a house within forty days. The relations between burgesses are closely defined, the officers of the Council were to be respected, and the burgess had to play his part in the town's affairs. 'If a burgess wound another, and they shall be willing to agree, friends appointed between them may require for every hidden cut of a thumbs breadth 4d: for every open or visible wound 8d.' The wounded man was also to be compensated for loss of work, and his doctor's bill was to be paid for him. Married women were to be respected and not slandered, under threat of a 3s. fine (three times the large sum required to become a burgess), unless 'He by whom it was said . . . shall take himself by the nose and say that he hath spoken a lie.'

The steady development of Preston's standing as a market centre in the period *c*.1150–1350 is thus reflected in the evolution of the town's plan, and in the parcels of rights which the Burgesses had managed to acquire. The vehicle for the application of, access to, and further regulation of, these privileges became the Guild Merchant, a widespread and indeed common type of institution not unique to the town and shared by Wigan, Lancaster and Liverpool among other places.

The origins of Preston Guild

The Guild, perhaps Saxon in origin, was mentioned with the town's other rights in the charter of 1179. The earliest properly recorded Guild meeting is that of 1397 and, except for 1942, the guild has been held every twenty years since 1542. The function of the Guild meeting was originally to effect the trading and commercial clauses of the charters, that is to implement the monopoly of the town's trade enjoyed by the burgesses. Writing at the end of the nineteenth century, an era which was believed to have seen the triumph of the principles of free trade, Anthony Hewitson was scathing of this aspect of Preston's most famous tradition: 'Trade protection was then deemed the only safeguard against destruction; exclusiveness was held to be the synonym of self preservation, competition was viewed as a deadly enemy. More to the absence of commercial light than to the wilful wrongheadedness of the people must the monopolising, strongly circumscribing measures of these old times be attributed.'[6]

The meetings of the various individuals and trades to re-affirm their rights became known as the Guild Merchant, and the meetings of the Mayor's Court which presided over the proceedings originally lasted a month, this being reduced to two weeks in 1822 and one week in 1842. The Guild Court with its Mayor, officers and bailiffs was able to enact

'Orders of the Guild', in effect laws for the government of the town something akin to municipal bye-laws. Occasionally these were redrafted and codified as in 1542 and 1662, but usually they were merely re-enacted for implementation by the burgesses' permanent court, the Court Leet. Presumably the administrative business of the Guild was from an early date accompanied by much merrymaking, dancing, eating and drinking of ale. In Preston these laudable activities came to overshadow all others – and so to ensure the Guild's survival to the present day – whereas in other towns Guilds were abandoned as their functional purpose was superseded.

Preston's Guild, and those of other towns, assumed a distinct economic function directly related to the community's everyday trading life. Entry on the roll of burgesses conveyed very positive economic advantages and it was deemed most important to admit only those people who had the

The Sessions House (1903). A dramatic photograph of work underway on the tower, almost 200 feet above the street. This building replaced the old court house beside the prison.

right to them. The Guild Court kept the list of burgesses up-to-date, striking off deceased members, admitting their sons, qualified apprentices, and newcomers to the town, on payment of the correct fee. These people were known as In-Burgesses, and in addition there was also a class known as Out or Foreign Burgesses who comprised the local gentry with an interest in the town's affairs. Over the centuries the list became something of a Lancashire 'Who's Who'.

The various trades were represented, including, in 1397, chaloners, millers, saddlers, spicers, wrights and tailors. These trades were later formed into companies and in 1628; for example, a united Company of Drapers, Mercers, Grocers, Salters, Ironmongers and Haberdashers was formed. Occasionally burgesses were admitted in respect of particular services they had undertaken, or in payment for work in future. Ralph Radcliff, 'Slaiter', was admitted a burgess 'for repairing the roof of the [moot] hall duringe his lyffe', Thomas Woodrooff for bell ringing and cleaning of the seats in church 'durynge his liffe', and John Houghton 'for Bakinge of Breade and brueinge of Beare att all such Guildes . . . duringe his lyffe'.[7]

During the Tudor period the exclusive system of trading in Preston began to break down and became more difficult to enforce, so that at the Guild of 1562 a third class is listed on the Guild Rolls – the stallingers – outsiders allowed to live and trade in the town but not admitted as burgesses. Despite these trends the Court Leet records of the seventeenth century contain many references to the continued and determined attempts to enforce the Guild Merchants' monopoly of the town's trade. As late as the second half of the eighteenth century the father of the historian Edward Baines became one of the last men prosecuted for trading in the town without the freedom of the borough by the 'Corporation acting on the old, stupid lines of commercial exclusiveness, so long fashionable here'.[8]

Most burgesses, however, must have qualified for enrolment after having been indentured and serving an apprenticeship, such as that undertaken by John, son of Adam de Saxton of Walton-le-Dale,[9] who on December 22nd 1393 was indentured to:

faithfully serve John de Walton of Preston, Mercer, as apprentice for 6 years doing such requirements for his master as a master apprentice ought to do.

His master will instruct him in his art and will keep him in food, clothing, shoes and all other necessaries during the term as other merchants do, according to the custom.

The apprentice shall not take holidays without leave of his master unless he can show reasonable excuse.

His master's doors and windows he shall not leave open by his negligence. During his term he shall not marry without his master's assent.

He shall see no damage done to his master without doing his best to

amend it or letting his master know, and any money lost or wasted by
him he shall repay doubly. The master shall pay him in his sixth year
10s. as wages under penalty of double the amount.

Though onerous to the point of severity in their early stages, apprenticeships must have been the usual path to the economic benefits of burgess-
ship, and effectively a form of admittance to the trading monopoly.

—— *Priests, lepers and friars* ——

Preston's early economic development, with its charters and Guild,
is clearly a central feature of the history of the town in the Middle
Ages. What is more difficult to appreciate today is the overwhelming
importance of religion and the Church in the medieval mind and in
people's daily lives. By about 1500 the Church's wealth in Lancashire,
steadily accumulated over centuries from the gifts of the faithful,
accounted for perhaps three times the wealth of lay people.[10] In Preston
extensive lands were owned by the Parish Church, the town's leper
hospital and friary, and by the priories at Lytham and Burscough, the

abbeys at Cockersand, Whalley and Sawley, and the Hospitallers of St. John of Jerusalem.[11]

The site of the Parish Church was central to the medieval town's plan, and two of the three main streets (Church Street and Friargate) had ecclesiastical connections. The Priests-town was noted for its religious festivals and its saints' days, particularly that of its first patron saint, St. Wilfrid: 'in old times, we learn, the inhabitants of Preston, by way of celebrating the festival of St Wilfrid, put bowers around the church, ate, drank and thanked God for giving them the saint in question as an example.'[12]

Although the present Parish Church of St. John the Divine occupies the site of the ancient St. Wilfrid's, none of the original fabric survives. The building seems to have been rebuilt in the sixteenth century when the name of the church was changed. It was repaired in the seventeenth century, evidently to Dr. Kuerden's satisfaction, but by 1770 'The roof and all the pillars on the north side of the church were reported to have fallen down'. In 1811 the precarious tower had to be partly pulled down, and by 1853 severe dilapidation meant that everything except the base of the tower had to be demolished and a new church was built on the site.[13] In contrast to adjacent townships this Victorian rebuilding does not seem to have been subsequently regretted, for 'the pretensions of the old church to architectural beauty or even character were so ambiguous that it was sometimes quoted in derision as an excellent specimen of 'joiners' Gothic'.' [14]

The foundation of the Parish Church was the subject of much – apparently tiresome – speculation among Victorian scholars: 'It doesn't particularly matter when the building we call our Parish Church was first erected: and if it did, the world would have to die of literary inanition before it got the exact date. None of the larger sort of antiquaries agree absolutely on the subject, and the smaller fry go in for all sorts of figures'.[15] The church lands may have been among those along the Ribble granted to St. Wilfrid in 670, but the church is not explicitly mentioned in the Domesday Book, and the first documentary reference occurs in 1094 when it formed a part of the grant by Roger de Poitou to the abbey at Sees.

The church and its lands were a valuable property, and for much of the Middle Ages the patron of the rectorship was the King, who was able to appoint the incumbent. Many rectors simply took the 'living' and appointed assistants to do the actual work among the congregation, and in this way prominent and favoured individuals frequently reaped the rewards from several benefices. Despite a number of scandals over the behaviour of the pluralist and absent incumbents, it is clear that the church with its staff of perhaps a dozen clergymen had a genuinely central place in the life of the town, and that the reforms introduced by Henry VIII centuries later appear to have had little popular support.

In addition to the Parish Church the town also had two small monastic institutions: the leper hospital of St. Mary Magdalen; and a house of

The Parish Church of Saint John the Divine, a lithograph by W. Physick. Located high on the Church Street–Fishergate ridge, the Parish Church occupies one of the oldest sites in the town. Although the church was rebuilt on a number of occasions, most recently in the 1850s, the base of the tower retains elements of the much older structure.

Franciscan friars. The leper hospital was supposed in the nineteenth century to have stood on the site of Tulketh Hall, but it is now believed to have been close to the present St. Walburge's Church within the 'Maudlands' to which it gave its name. The friary gave its name to Friargate, but in fact it lay some distance down Marsh Lane (formerly Friars Lane) between Lower Pitt Street and Ladywell Street. Clearly both establishments lay well away from the town centre, reflecting both the tradition of the Franciscans and the obvious locational needs of a hospital for contagious diseases. Unfortunately, archaeological evidence of these sites may have been entirely removed during construction of the local railways, and especially Maudland Bank.

Monastic institutions developed comparatively late in Lancashire, a fact which is generally believed to reflect the economic backwardness of the region. The leper hospital was perhaps founded when the monks of Savigny moved from their house at Tulketh to build the abbey at Furness in 1127.[16] The earliest reference is found in Letters of Protection to the hospital from Henry II *c*.1178, and a number of early charters have survived. Around 1200, Walter de Ingol made a grant of lands in Ingol to the Brethren of Saint Mary Magdalen of Preston, 'for the health of the souls of King Henry, King Richard and their ancestors, and for the souls of Walter Hervey, his wife and ancestors, and for the souls of his father, mother, ancestors, and all the faithful departed'.[17]

There was a clear need for such a hospital, for lepers were generally treated as outcasts. The hospital had a warden, a chapel with a chaplain, and a nursing staff of ecclesiastical brothers and sisters. During two months at the height of the Black Death in 1349, £32 was reported to have been received in offerings in the chapel – a huge sum of money then – and during the fourteenth century it seems to have been an important place of local pilgrimage.[18]

With the decline in the extent of leprosy the hospital's importance waned: 'Neither the chapel nor the hospital to which it was attached was probably of much size or splendour. From about 1520 to the chapel's dissolution the building seems to have been more or less ruinous'.[19] At its dissolution in 1548 the building was open at both ends, and in 'grete ruen and dekey'. The hospital's land, like that of nearby Penwortham Priory, was ultimately acquired by members of the influential Fleetwood family.[20]

The Franciscans worked among the poor of the town, and lived by begging. The friary seems to have been a larger institution than the hospital, but comparatively little is known about it. The earliest reference is found in a grant by Henry III allowing the monks to take timber from Fulwood for building in October 1260, though Edmund Earl of Lancaster usually takes the credit for its foundation in 1260. Details of several bequests to the friary for masses to be said have survived, including those made by Sir Richard Sherburne of Stonyhurst (1437), and Sir William Ffarington of Farington and Leyland (1501). William Clifton left the friars 'a cowe and a calfe', and 'a bullocke with a cut tayle', to say masses

Statue of Saint Wilfrid. Preston's foundation may date from the grant of lands in the district to St. Wilfrid's church at York in the seventh century. Up to the sixteenth century his Saint's day was enthusiastically celebrated in Preston, and the Parish Church was dedicated to him.

and to pray for his soul.[21]

Estimates of the size of the monastery have been particularly confused. Dr. Kuerden described it *c*.1680: 'A little more remote from the town stands the ruins of an antient Pryory, formerly built for the relief of begging fryers, or of the minor order cald Gray Fryers, but what is best thereof now standing is imployed for a House of Correction for the country's use.'[22] Whittle's account of 1835 greatly exaggerated the importance of the institution which 'when in its splendour and glory, would have accommodated the proudest monarch: was built in a style of the richest gothic magnificence, enclosing within its walls apartments for upwards of 500 monks. The demolition, in 1539, was so complete, that little remains, excepting some outward walls, painted window mouldings, and gothic arched doorways . . . The extent, number, and intricacy of the subterraneous vaults, were such as to afford retreat for lawless banditti. There were also orangeries and greenhouses, surrounded by a number of separate parterres, or islands, decorated with statuary and columns brought from afar. But all is now destroyed, and the stranger only learns from the sorrowful tale, that our ancestors had taste and discernment in their day'.[23] Baines's description seems the most realistic assessment of the scale of the buildings: 'In its original state the friary was a small square collegiate building with a chapel attached to its quadrangular cloister'.[24]

The friary was dissolved in 1539, but, significantly for the subsequent religious history of the town, a nearby holy well – the Lady Well – continued to be revered by the devout to the nineteenth century, three hundred years later. [25]

—— *Early prosperity and progress* ——

P reston's early charters were granted in a period of rising prosperity: in the period from the Domesday survey to *c*.1300 the population of England doubled, economic growth surged ahead, and financial and commercial activity increased. In the agricultural sector which employed a huge majority of the population, arable farming was intensified and the townfields and pastures began to encroach on the great primeval forests. That Preston was at the forefront of these developments in the county can be demonstrated by its early grants of charters and fairs, and its early and extensive ecclesiastical foundations: [26]

Borough Charters

Preston	1179
Lancaster	1193
Ulverston	1200

Liverpool 1207
Wigan 1246

Fairs

Preston 1189
Kersal 1191
Lancaster 1193
Clitheroe 1205
Liverpool. 1207

The range of the town's trade at this time can be demonstrated by the details of the various tollage fees which the burgesses were allowed to charge on goods entering the town. When in 1314 they were granted the right to raise tolls of a farthing to twopence for five years to pay for the paving of the streets, the range of goods included: food: (a horse-load of corn, ¼d; 1000 onions, ¼d; half a dozen cheeses, ½d; a horse-load of butter, ½d; a cart load of salt, 1d; a horse-load of sea fish, ½d; a hogshead of wine, 2d); animals: (horses, cows, oxen, ½d; hogs, ¼d; 2 small pigs sold before Easter, ½d); animal hides: (10 skins of stags, hinds or fallow deer, 1d; skins of horses, rabbits, cats, wolves, squirrels, 1d; a cart load of tanned leather, ¼d); building materials: (cart load of timber, ½d, 1,000 roofing shingles, ¼d; 1,000 nails for house building, 1d); and textiles: (100lbs of flax, 1d; a quarter of canvas, 1d; of Irish cloth, 1d; cloth of silk

Whit Monday 1896. A man selling comic balloons and a girl selling oranges, on the forecourt of Preston Railway Station, await the crowds of people attending the Whit processions.

Bert Hughes' Whitsuntide fair boxing-booth c.1935. In medieval times, fairs were an important element of the town's market-based economy. The Whitsuntide fairground and the pot fair continue the tradition to the present day.

with gold thread etc., 1d; a bale of silk, 2d; bundles of cloth, 3d per cart load; 1,000 lbs of alum, 1d).

All this was in addition to firewood, iron, oil and other merchandise 'coming to the town'. A similar award was made in 1400 for the collection of tolls on the Ribble Bridge to make good repairs to its structure which had been damaged by frost and ice and to replace it with a stone bridge. When nothing had been done the grant was renewed in 1407. In addition to the staples listed in 1314, these tolls included Irish Galway cloth and worsted, and coal.[27]

The various national taxes raised periodically allow a comparison to be made between the townships within Preston parish and between Preston and the other Lancashire towns. Among the local towns Preston contributed ten times as much to the King's funds as Liverpool in 1219. In 1332 Preston parish paid £9 4s. 7¼d. of £53 18s. 2¼d. raised in the county, and the town itself accounted for just a little over a quarter. Notwithstanding their local importance, the Lancashire towns were not successful in any national sense; in an assessment of 1334 none of the towns was valued at over £40 a year. By contrast the nearest comparable town to the south – Derby – was worth £300, but itself only ranked 36th in England.[28]

The early fourteenth century was a period of great instability in the North West, and of particular significance was the series of Scottish raids, culminating in the raid led by Robert the Bruce in 1322. The town was very near to the front-line of activity in these years and suffered accordingly. Royal proclamations issued from Preston in 1306 suggest that Edward I visited the town, and several members of local families took a very active part in them. In 1303 a number of Preston people were pardoned serious crimes for 'services in Scotland': Aveyse de Preston had murdered his wife, Emma, whilst Robert Rudde had been arrested for robbery.[29] As a result of the Scots raids the taxation rating of the parish was reduced from £66 13s. 4d. in 1292 to £23 6s. 8d. in 1317. As late as 1347 a survey states 'they [the local clergy] also say that on account of the ravage there made by the Scots, and on account of the unendurable burdens which increase day by day, there are lands in the same parish lying waste and uncultivated'.[30]

Following closely on these events was the great plague which raged throughout England between September 1349 and January 1350 – the Bubonic plague or Black Death. Estimates of the number of deaths vary greatly, but probably exceeded the third of the population which died in 1631. Ecclesiastical returns indicate that 'Between 8th. September, 1349, and 11th. January 1350, the churches of Lytham, Poulton, Lancaster, Kirkham and Garstang, half the beneficies of the deanery, were all vacated by death, the last two twice. In addition to these the chapel of St. Mary Magdalen at Preston was vacant for 8 weeks'. In a subsequent dispute over moneys due from these vacant benefices, it was claimed that over thirteen thousand people died in Amounderness, with three thousand deaths in Preston, Lancaster and Kirkham, and sixty in Chipping.[31] Clearly the effect was devastating whatever the precise numbers involved, and further outbreaks occured in 1361 and 1369.

The plague had important effects on English society, and the resulting labour shortage did much to hasten the development of a money-based wage-earning economy and thus speed the demise of serfdom. These important developments seem to have been apparent at Preston, for 'trouble with the labourers' followed the plague here. This was thus perhaps the most troubled and traumatic period in Preston's history.[32]

These events clearly mark changing economic conditions as the period of steady growth in early medieval times came to an end, the proportion of arable land fell, and pasture expanded, so that by 1500 two-thirds of the Lancashire markets had failed. During much of the fifteenth century the town appears to have stagnated, and perhaps even declined. The Preston Guild Roll of 1459 shows that the number of 'in-burgesses' had fallen from 188 to 72 since the previous Guild in 1415: as W. A. Abram concluded, 'As an urban community, Preston had not been growing in these years, but had rather decayed'.[33] Yet during the following century the town revived, and by the Guild of 1542 was once more growing steadily.

Throughout the Middle Ages, therefore, Preston was able to maintain the position among the Lancashire towns which it had established in the twelfth century. It received its town seal in 1349, bothered to send members to Parliament more regularly than any other local town apart from Lancaster, and when the 'corrupt and pestiferous air infected with divers infirmities and deadly deseases' of the latter proved too much, was the centre for important law courts.

CHAPTER THREE

The medieval landscape

THE modern town of Preston has extended far beyond its ancient bounds, over the range of quite distinct environments which contributed to the success of the early settlement – the town fields, the moor, Preston Marsh and the Forest of Fulwood. Between Penwortham and Preston the Ribble cuts through the Lancashire Plain, so that the centre of the town occupies a high cliff or bank overlooking the river, in marked contrast to the lower lands a short distance to the west and north. At its most pronounced this feature forms a gentle if narrow ridge surmounted by the Parish Church and the line of Church Street and Fishergate. It can most clearly be seen at the top of Lune Street and where Cheapside joins Fishergate on the ancient site of the Moot and Town Hall. To the north Friargate can be seen falling away to the former Preston Moor; Glovers Court falls steeply to the south and Fishergate falls westward to the river crossing near Broadgate. It was along this ridge that the church and few timber buildings of the early town clustered.

The town fields extended less than a mile either side of Church Street, and were bounded by what are today culverted and invisible subterranean streams. To the south Swill Brook formed the boundary between Preston and Fishwick; flowing parallel with New Hall Lane it crossed London Road in the vicinity of Albyn Street to enter the Ribble a few yards upstream of the old tramroad bridge, where its culvert still emerges. To the north Moor Brook (or Preston Brook or Deepdale Brook) flowed westward from the vicinity of Lowthorpe Road in Deepdale a short distance to the south of St. George's Road and Aqueduct Street, to enter the Ribble on the boundary of Preston and Ashton. The actual line of the stream is preserved by Moorbrook Street near the junction of Garstang Road and Moor Lane.

These were to remain the essential features of the town's geography for upwards of 700 years, right up to the Industrial Revolution. As late as the seventeenth century the town's 'barrs' or gates defined a very small and compact settlement extending for less than 500 yards from the Market Place. The Church Street Barr was located near the end of Manchester Road and the Fishergate Barr stood at the top of Mount Street, so that the

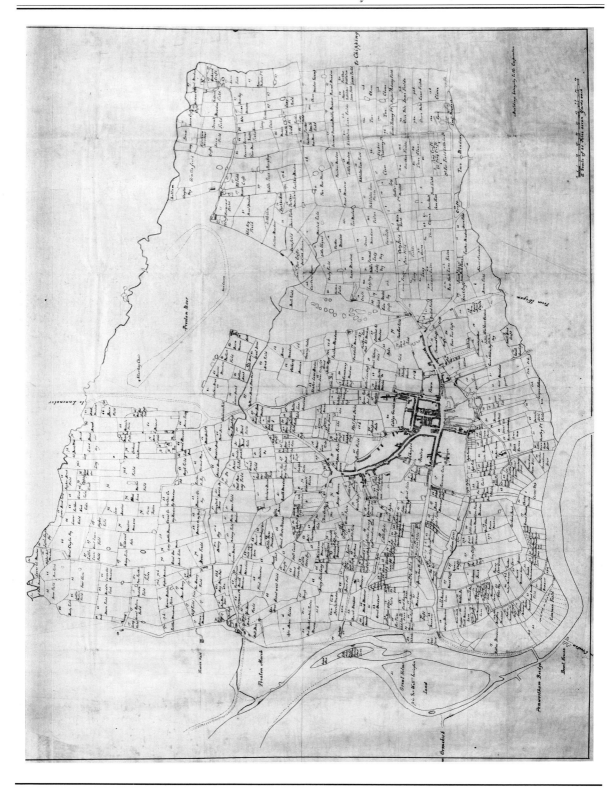

Stoneygate c.1890. Looking down Stoneygate to the junction with Lennox St., a fairly typical view of the crowded housing which had overwhelmed the medieval street plan during the town's rapid growth in the early nineteenth century. Stoneygate was an important route into the town to the south-east of the Parish Church, and up to 1841 was the site of the town's grammar school. In all, the town had five 'gates' – Stoneygate, Fishergate, Friargate, Broadgate and Churchgate.

Lang's map of Preston, 1774. Part of a very detailed survey of the town three years before the establishment of its first cotton mill, the map clearly reveals the medieval town plan, the fringe of townfield strips and the more distant townfields, moor and marsh. The overall impression is of the small size of the township and borough, before the inclusion of Fishwick, Ashton, Ribbleton and Fulwood.

distance between the 'town ends' was considerably under half a mile and only a matter of a few minutes' walk. The barr on Friargate lay just beyond the crown of the hill to the north of St. Mary's Church.

Along the town centre streets, extending on either side into the surrounding fields, lay the burgage plots. These were narrow strips of land fronting onto the streets, and contained the burgess's house and often his shop, with a garden at the rear. The latter was very important because most burgesses kept farm animals (cows, horses, pigs, or geese) for which they had the right of pasture on the town's meadows and common lands. The strips might contain a barn or other outbuildings to house them, or alternatively vegetable or cereal crops might be grown on the gardens. By the eighteenth century many had been developed as orchards, and some as ornamental gardens. The sub-division of the narrow timber houses, and the tendency to squeeze in as many plots as possible along a given length of street allowed fire and disease to spread rapidly and, in a small community where everyone knew everyone else, it ensured that they also knew each other's business. The sounds and smells of the farmyard were pervasive, and occasionally pigs grazed in the churchyard. The burgess, whether a craftsman or trader, shared the same farming interests as his neighbours in the outlying country districts.

The deeds and papers of the great Hoghton estate provide many details about the burgesses and their properties. In 1280 Robert, son of Stephen of Penwortham, granted his brother, Adam the goldsmith, half a burgage and an acre of meadow for an annual rent of 'a pair of white gloves to the

The top of Glovers Court c.1910. One of the many narrow weinds to the south of Church St., Glovers Court was considerably widened in 1915. The portico of the old Town Hall on Cheapside can be glimpsed through the entrance.

Archaeological finds from medieval Preston c.1300– 1400 AD. A large water (or beer) cistern was recovered from the site of the Lancashire Evening Post offices in Castle Yard, whilst the water pitcher was found almost twenty feet down in deposits excavated near India Mill in New Hall Lane.

granter and 12d to the King according to the custom of the vill of Preston'.[1] The plots are frequently defined as lying between those of specified neighbours. In a deed of similar date, 'Richard son of Jordan de Preston granted to Sir Adam de Hoghton a burgage between the houses owned by the Abbey of Cockersand and Jordan son of Sywar, for five marks and an annual rent of a peppercorn'.[2]

Occasionally individual buildings are mentioned: '. . . two burgages in Preston . . . with a bakehouse in the garden' (*c.*1280); 'A barn in the Fischergate lying between the house of William . . . and the barn of Adam' for the annual rent of an arrow (1293); and a tavern in Preston 'lying between the forge of John the Marshall and the Moot Hall,' for 8d a year rent to the corporation of Preston (1397).[3] Some leases also specify the duties of the tenants. In 1378 William de Gavy leased a burgage for an annual rent of 13s. 4d. on condition that he built a barn on the burgage, a kitchen on the plot, and a 'wardrup' in the chamber of the hall, 'and will keep up those houses and deliver them at the end of the lease by view of the neighbours under penalty of £20 silver'.[4] In 1395 John de Knoll, a tailor, and his wife Maud were granted a burgage with lands 'in the Moor field by the friar's house', and a plot in St.

The Forest of Lancaster c.1150 (after Cunliffe-Shaw 1956). These legal divisions originally reflected land-use differences, including the royal hunting forests and the protective woodland belt for game around them. During later medieval times, however, the woodlands came under increasing pressure from the timber needs of the growing urban centres. The Forest of Fulwood, with its mighty oaks, was eventually cleared to provide fuel and building timber for Preston and agricultural land for the local people.

John's Weind on which it was stipulated they were to build a timber house.[5]

The congestion of houses must have created many practical difficulties. In 1331 John de Gayforth, a chaplain, granted a strip of land eighteen inches wide to his next-door neighbour to enable him to rebuild his house. But the neighbour, John de Ascheton, was expected to 'keep him from damage done by water' and to make a gully between their houses 'so that the water may have free exit into the highway'.[6]

By the sixteenth century many local gentry families owned burgage plots in Preston, and in the 1620s Robert Blundell of Ince Blundell was particularly active acquiring property.[7] Premises with well sited shops were much sought after and examples owned by Thomas Hoghton seem to have been particularly valuable. His new three bay building 'near the Buttercrosse in Preston' in 1562, shops under and lofts above were let to John Cowell a nailmaker, and James Dyke 'Wollen Webstre and Shereman' (cloth-cutter) for 6s. 8d. per year. James Page of Casshall, county York, leased another newly built burgage in the 'Freregate' for 5 shillings.[8] Five years later James Dyke was able to buy his house outright for £20; 'A dwelling house, buttery, two chambers beneath the house, two shops with lofts, a kechyn, a stable, a little outhouse with the handy mill within the same, two swynecotes at the back of the dwelling house and the court at the back.' Even a prosperous cloth merchant with a shrewd eye for a bargain had an interest in farming, with his pigs and his right to pasture on the townlands.[9]

The town's lands

In the townships around Preston the arable townlands, divided into a number of open fields, lay close by the centre of their settlements. These were frequently the most fertile and oldest cultivated lands in the district, as field names such as 'old field' may indicate. These fields were in turn divided into narrow strips well suited to the oxen plough technology of the day, known as 'furrowlongs' or 'furlongs' 22 yards long. Although the strips were unfenced they were clearly delineated from each

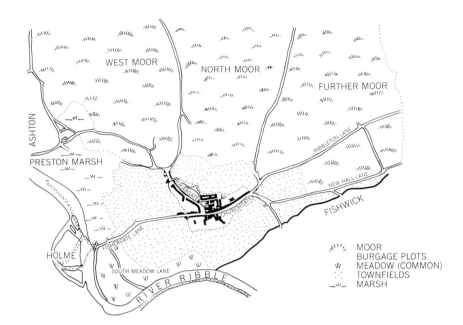

Land-use divisions in pre-industrial Preston.

other; their boundaries would be well known to the villagers and like the burgage strips they could be passed on from one owner to another by inheritance, gift or sale. R. Cunliffe Shaw suggested that the Lancashire townfields might be better regarded as groupings of single strips, rather than as fields divided into strips.

These lands were also cultivated in a quite different way from those in the three-field system common elsewhere in England. Crops, especially oats but with barley, beans and peas, were sown in spring, harvested in summer, and fields lay fallow through the winter. Each field therefore had six months in crop followed by six months fallow. Accordingly these were referred to as 'half-year lands' and could be rented on a six-monthly basis. Fields or strips where animals were to be kept had to be fenced or 'ringed' to keep them from straying onto neighbours' crops: the Court Leet of Preston in February 1658, for example, ordered 'Ye Pinders to give Notice to all ye Inhabitants of this towne that they make their gardens, hedges and ringe yards before the 5th of March or pay 06s. 08d'.[10] Overall this was so successful an adaptation to local conditions that many townfields remained in continuous cultivation for upwards of a thousand years.

Beyond the arable townfields lay the pastures which were often common lands on which the inhabitants had the right to graze their animals. In Preston these comprised Preston Moor, the Marsh, and a number of riverside meadows. Animals could also be kept and grazed on the townfield strips once crops had been cut. Controlling the townspeople's herds on the common pastures was a major problem and accordingly 'hedgebreaking' – deliberately damaging hedges or fences – was considered a crime serious enough to be punished 'either by stockes or ye Rouges Poste'. In 1656 George Mery, 'A Breaker of Hedges', was perhaps lucky to be fined 3s. 4d. 'and to bee made a publique example to the terifinge of all others'. [11]

In an important market centre such as Preston the importance of the town's lands as a principal source of cereals and other foodstuffs must have been challenged from quite an early date by crops brought in from the surrounding country. However, the early charters reveal that a highly organised system for operating and administering them had developed, overlooked by the town council and controlled by its Court Leet and paid officials, a system which was to survive to the end of the eighteenth century.

——— *Preston townfields* ———

Preston's arable townfields formed a broad belt around the centrally placed burgage strips. These were the ancient farmlands of the town and the area of the earliest woodland clearance, within the fringe of the forest which throughout the medieval period and beyond extended over wide areas of Lancashire. From surviving documents and early maps it is possible to provide an estimate of the extent of these fields in early medieval times.

To the south of Fishergate the arable townfield seems to have been defined by the Swill Brook (the boundary with Fishwick) and the escarpment along the top of Avenham Park (Ribblesdale Place – East Cliff – West Cliff). The low-lying riverside meadows to the south and west, which today comprise much of Avenham Park and Broadgate, may have formed common meadows. This townfield was drained by a brook, the Avenham Syke, which formed a natural boundary to the burgage plots in the vicinity of the Parish Church, and the course of which can still be detected cutting diagonally across Winckley Square from Cross Street. To the north of the Syke the fields fronted on to Fishergate, and to the south bounded by the Avenham escarpment and Manchester Road, lay the great Avenham townfield. The ownership of individual strips within this field is recorded from an early date and many of them almost certainly lay in the vicinity of Avenham Lane.

To the west of the town barr at the top of Mount Street, the pattern of fields along Fishergate comprised narrow blocks and strips laid out narrow-end-on to the road between the Avenham Syke in the south and the Furnham or Suckling Syke to the north. To the north of the latter, extending as far as the end of Friargate, a more regular field system is perhaps indicative of later enclosure. Marsh Lane, on the line of ancient tracks, crosses this belt which extends westwards from the barr at the end of Friargate to Preston Marsh, which was bounded loosely by Watery Lane, Strand Road and the dockland estate. From the north end of Friargate, the line of Walker Street eastwards to Ringway and Stanley Street broadly accords with the limits of the townfield, but as along Marsh Lane the medieval field pattern is difficult to identify. To the east of the junction of Stanley Street and Church Street, a series of narrow field blocks between and parallel to Ribbleton Lane and New Hall Lane, and extending as far as Horrockses' Centenary Mill, may be indicative of the early enclosure of the edges of Ribbleton Moor.

To the north of the town's fields lay Preston Moor, a great expanse of open heathland resulting from the clearance and subsequent grazing of Fulwood forest. Up to the nineteenth century the moor lay in a great arc to the north of the line of Stanley Street, Ringway, Walker Street and Fylde Road, as far as Ashton. This moorland thus formed the largest area of the townlands, and comprised three units, 'West Moor' (between

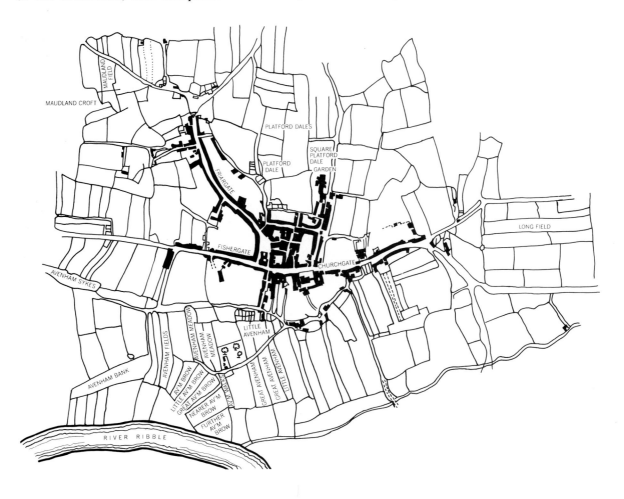

Ashton and Garstang Road), 'North Moor' (between Garstang Road and Deepdale Road), and 'Further Moor' (between Deepdale Road and New Hall Lane). Smaller districts referred to in deeds include 'Friargate Moor' (at the north end of Friargate along Moor Lane), 'Churchgate Moor' (the west side of the Deepdale triangle to the south of the former Preston Royal Infirmary), and 'Peel Moor' (to the east of Deepdale Road in the vicinity of the 'Canary Islands').

Much of Preston Moor thus lay between Moor Brook in the south and Eaves Brook in the north which formed the boundary with Fulwood. Originally forest that had been progressively cleared from Saxon times, the moor was by now a grassy common on which the burgesses had the right to graze their animals and in the mid-nineteenth century the central portion, between Garstang Road and Deepdale Road, was reclaimed to form Moor Park. Around 1200, however, woodland cover was probably extant well to the south of Preston Brook (roughly on the line of St. Georges Road), lying much closer to the edge of the townfields. To the north of Eaves Brook (the line of Blackpool Road) lay the Forest of Fulwood, part of the Royal Forest of Lancaster.

The townfields with their distinctive pattern of strips thus formed the arable component of a farming system which incorporated riverside pasture and seasonal grazing on the marsh and moor, within a forest environment whose edge, even in early medieval times probably still lay less than a mile to the north of the Town Hall.

Avenham and the open fields

T his system of land tenure of ancient origin continued well into the seventeenth century, when many of the medieval strips clearly still existed. A lease of 1568 between Lawrence Wall of Preston, 'writer', and Thomas Suddell, 'tailior', describes 'one burgage, garden, and the east side of a croft in the Fysher gate . . . and one butt or selion upon Avenham, one rod of ground'.[12] By this date, however, a greater proportion of the townlands may have been given over to pasture; a deed of 1586 describes 'One further parcel of meadow in the common meadow called Arram Great Acre'.[13] As late as 1793 a document in the Lord Derby collection refers to 'a close of land called the Bury field situate in Great Avenham'.[14] A portion of these fields may have remained in common ownership, or rather the property of the town council, for in 1610 William Preston, gentleman, was to have a lease of 'the townes landes called Arram Bancke and Aram Syke for the usual term of 39 years'.[15]

On the north side of Fishergate early fields can be identified at Platford Dales and the Whittaker (to the north of the Guild Hall between Lancaster Road and Tithebarn Street). In the early fourteenth century Richard de Ribbleton acquired land in Platford-dale,[16] whilst the

Evidence of the open-fields in the Preston Townlands c.1250–1350. Surviving family, ecclesiastical and land deeds from medieval times allow the identification of some of the principal open fields in the townfields. Strips are also mentioned in the Aldefield, Woodholme, Langfield *and* Dustysarghfield. *The town's water-mill, the* Merse-Milne, *is mentioned in 1311 and the windmill on the* Wynmilne Hull *in 1330.*

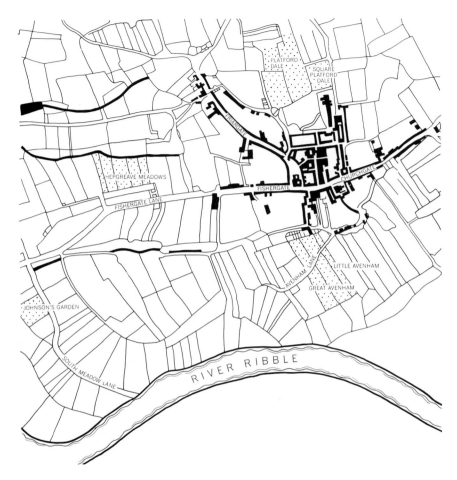

A burgess's land holdings (after Hewitson 1906). The burgesses owned parcels of land and individual field-strips widely spread through the townfields. In April 1615, for example, George Addison, a haberdasher, purchased such an estate for £160. In addition to a 'Burgage in the fishergate streete, in Preston near a cross of stone called the Butter Cross', he acquired small holdings and strips in the townfields as shown. Many of these open fields thus continued to be formed in the ancient strip holdings, including 'a butt in the Avenham extending in land throughout the field'.

Cockersand Abbey deeds refer to 'one perch of land upon Whitaker'.[17] The latter also contain several references to lands on 'Woodholme' which Farrer (perhaps following Hewitson) suggests lay to the west of Strand Road 'in the marsh', but on what evidence is unclear.[18] A detailed thirteenth-century Cockersand charter describes the landholdings, confirming that, like Avenham, this field or group of fields was subdivided into a large number of strips and units.[19]

From early times the town's fields were pushing out onto the 'moor', particularly in the Ribbleton Lane–New Hall Lane area. As early as 1290 a De Hoghton deed describes 'an acre extending along the high way to Ribbleton on the north and the way to Brocholis on the south in a new field to the east of Preston and in its territory', for an annual rent of a barbed arrow.[20] The 'New Moor' (i.e. land recently enclosed and allotted) is referred to in 1295, and the 'New Moor in Ribbilton' in 1300,[21] while in 1420 lands are described 'next the highway from Preston to Ribalton', and 'in a field called Langfield next Fysshewik More'.[22] These references demonstrate the expansion of the town's arable onto the former moorland to the east of the town, and indicate that these new lands were owned and cultivated in the traditional manner.

The town plan of Preston was thus a product of the burgage system of land allotment. The burgesses' holdings included the burgage plot with its house, shop and garden, with strips of farmland spread far and wide across the townfields, and the right of common use of pasture on the moor and marsh, and it is clear that the system continued to operate relatively unchanged well into the eighteenth century.

Many of the distinctive political, social and geographical features of the town had emerged by c.1200, and were to survive in essence relatively intact right up to the Industrial Revolution; as the town grew during this period deficiencies in the agricultural system could to some extent be compensated for by taking in new land to the north.

The Forest of Fulwood

The town and its fields were not, however, the most conspicuous feature of the early medieval landscape. This was dominated by the southern fringe of the great forest of Lancaster – a fact that must have been readily apparent to travellers from the north and east as they left the forest tracks and entered the ends of Friargate and Church Street.[23]

Forests were vigorously preserved by the Norman kings and their successors for hunting, but in the vicinity of the towns they were increasingly plundered for timber and fuel and for subsequent use as pastureland. On his visit to Lancashire in 1534 Leland bemoaned, 'Al Amoundernesse for the moste parte in time past hath been ful of wood and many of the moores replenished with hy fyrre trees. But now such part of Amoundernesse as is toward the se is sore destitute of woodde.'[24]

A distinct system of law and administration operated in the forests, with the purpose of preserving game, especially deer, and the undergrowth on which they depended for food and shelter. In the forest itself, farming activities had to take second place to the interests of game, while within a broad belt surrounding the forest it was illegal to capture the deer that strayed and damaged crops.

During the twelfth and thirteenth centuries the forest was firmly and efficiently administered by a sizeable staff. Surviving court records list the names of men accused of illegally killing deer or hunting just beyond the forest limits, suspiciously carrying long-bows or keeping 'strange greyhounds' near the forest. Lesser game was also protected; the takers of partridges, hares and herons were recorded along with the takers of 'wax, honey and bees', and thefts of 'great oaks' for house timbers and wattles for walling were prosecuted. Nationally, forest laws and rights were to remain an important political issue for over three hundred years. Access

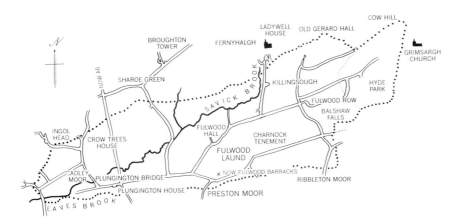

The boundaries of the Royal Forest of Fulwood (after Cunliffe-Shaw, 1956).

to the resources of the forest was as closely defined by traditional rights and usages as were all the other aspects of town life at this time, but the local gentry seem to have been quite willing to share in the illicit bounty the forest could provide, as several legal suits indicate, including the case of three gentlemen who 'entered the King's forest of Folwod and . . . hunted deer, harts, hinds, bucks and does with horns, greyhounds and running dogs, and took there three harts and carried them away'.[25]

Of much greater significance for the long term reduction of the forests was the steady pressure in favour of their wider exploitation and agricultural use. In Preston the burgesses insisted on preserving their ancient rights to the resources of the forest, ultimately leading to the wholesale clearance of the Forest of Fulwood.

The vague detail of the deeds on which the burgesses' claims were based resulted in much argument on the ground between foresters and burgesses, and the latter were summoned before the Justices to defend their rights at the great forest courts of 1286 and 1334. Producing the actual charters, they claimed that the right to timber 'to build their town' meant access to as much wood as they liked whenever they wanted it for buildings and repairs, to blackthorn for fencing and to wood for fuel, whilst 'pasture' meant the right to pasture their animals in the forest. As Cunliffe-Shaw concluded: 'When one realises that the houses were framed in oak and the bridge across the Ribble was also a timber structure and that wood was the principal fuel, the wastage of the forest must have been rapid in the twelfth and thirteenth centuries when the town was becoming increasingly prosperous'.[26]

Prior to the growth of the town in the twelfth and thirteenth centuries the southern limits of the forest probably lay close to the line of St. George's Road, clearly visible from the town centre. Although apparently pushed back close to the line of Watling Street Road in the thirteenth century, the forest still extended over two thousand acres 250 years later.

A survey of 1228 clearly described the boundaries of 'Fulewude', '[wherein] the men of Preston ought to have timber for their buildings, and to burn, and pasture for their beasts'.[27] For much of this period the forest administration took great care of the woodland, and resisted the claims and incursions of the Prestonians. The 'great oaks', centuries old, were granted sparingly by royal edict. In 1260 Henry III granted five oaks from the Sydewood for the Friary in Preston, and in 1373 Sir Adam de Hoghton was commanded to deliver 'four oaks with their bark and branches from the forest of Fulwood' to construct the fence around the leper hospital of St. Mary Magdalene in Preston. By contrast to these minor inroads, repairs at Lancaster Castle in 1377 required 260 oaks from the Forest of Quernmore.[28]

Early settlement within Fulwood must be seen firmly in the context of a forest environment, and the early forest court rolls contain many references to 'assarts' or clearances for farming. During the fourteenth century pressure on agricultural resources resulted in the extension of clearances, with many prosecutions for illegal ones, so that by 1346 there were at least nine farms in the forest, mostly to the east of the line of Fulwood Row and Gamull Lane.[29]

In the following centuries the forest was gradually replaced by open common and small farms with their enclosed fields, a process opposed by the Borough of Preston whose burgesses maintained the right to pasture their animals in the forest. Clearance of woodland in the sixteenth century was frequently undertaken by people who were inhabitants of neither Preston nor Fulwood, whilst large numbers of squatters were harried by Preston Corporation: 'John Shakeshaft enclosed an acre of common within the last four years and half a rodland within 12 years on which he built a barn. Robert Harrison deceased enclosed two acres about 20 years before. Grace Shakeshaft enclosed half an acre on which she built a turve house within the last six years.'[30]

The deforested 'wastes' or 'moor' of Fulwood were steadily enclosed, and the much reduced wooded portion seems to have been concentrated around Sharoe. In 1623 enclosure fences marking out fields for farming were removed by 'a great multitude' of nocturnal rioters from Broughton and Fulwood, fearful of losing their rights to common pastures. [31]

The various disputes over land rights had a profound effect on the condition of the forest. In 1639 it was reported that the forest 'Hath heretofor been replenished and stored with deer and other beasts of forest, chase and warren, which have been long since utterly destroyed by the inhabitants there about . . . and also that the said common or waste grounds have heretofor been replenished with great store of timber trees, woods and underwoods, which were not only a great refuge and preservation of the said deer, but yielding also good annual profit to his majesty . . . All these timberwoods and underwoods have likewise been destroyed by the inhabitants thereabouts.' [32]

By this date the great forest of Fulwood had virtually disappeared and the resulting common-land had been reduced to just over four hundred acres by land enclosure and cultivation. A commission of enquiry held in

1639 awarded 150 acres of this to Preston, forty to Broughton and ten to Ribbleton in respect of ancient rights, and the rest was reserved by the Crown. This settlement was once again resisted by the local tenants who were to lose their rights to common land on which to graze the family cows or pigs which provided a valuable source of food. The final 'wasteland' remnants of the great forest were divided up and enclosed in 1817. [33]

CHAPTER FOUR

Preston under the Tudors

The covered market, seen from Lancaster Road c.1920. Preston's markets continue to attract traders from a wide district of mid-Lancashire, as they have done for perhaps a thousand years.

LANCASHIRE at the start of the sixteenth century lingered in the shadow of its medieval past. It was a poor and troubled border region, remote from the new learning of the European renaissance, its trade dominated by the ancient and inward-looking towns of Preston, Wigan and Lancaster.

Yet it is under the Tudor monarchs that the emergence of the Lancashire textile industry can be traced with the growth of the textile centres of Bolton and Manchester, which came to challenge the pre-eminence of the medieval market centres. A statute of 1544 for the assistance of the 'decayed towns' of the kingdom where 'There hath been in times past many beautiful houses in those places which are now falling into ruin' cited 'Lancaster, Preston and Liverpool, and Wigan in Lancashire,' though even here the processes of textiles-led economic growth had become apparent by the end of the century.[1] Economic progress ran hand in hand with fundamental social change brought about by the Reformation and the breaking up of the great ecclesiastical estates, and the emergence of Preston as the centre of the largest Catholic enclave in England.

The textile industry which developed especially in the south-east of the county also influenced Preston. The increasing number of burgesses listed in the sixteenth-century Guild Rolls attests to the continuing and rising importance of the Preston Guild Merchant, and the wool, flax and linen trades were well established in the town. In 1565 William Hodgkinson, a chapman or linen trader, was accused by a London merchant tailor of refusing to pay for one hundred bales of flax he was alleged to have contracted for. Six years later the town's mayor informed a county official that the most important 'clothes commonly maid nere about Preston and which be comonlie sold in the said towne are narrow white kearses [coarse woollen cloth]'.[2]

Contemporary writers, risking life and limb on the county's rough tracks to visit the town, have left only brief records of their stay. The

Earl of Sussex wrote in 1537 that there was 'not a scarcer county both for horse meat and man's meat in England'.[3] Camden, the noted antiquarian, was much taken with Ribchester, described Preston as 'A large, and for these parts, handsome and populous towne, so called from religious persons, as much as to say Priest's-town'.

He was favourably impressed with the district's agriculture:

> The goodly and fresh complexion of the natives does sufficiently evince the goodness of this county: nay and the cattle too, if you will; for in the oxes, which have huge horns, and proportionate bodies, you will find nothing wanting . . . this soil bears oats pretty well, but it is not so good for barley: it makes excellent pasture especially towards the sea.

Travellers across the Morecambe Bay sands, the main route north, should beware, he warned, for 'Here are also some Quicksands so hazardous to travellers who think to shorten their journey when the Tide is out, that they are in danger of being shipwracked and sunk in a land journey'.[4]

Edmund Hopwood in 1591 described Preston as 'A very great markette towne as any within Lancashire',[5] and Leland, antiquary to Henry VIII, provided a slightly confused outline of the geography of the district. Travelling from Chorley and deciding not to visit Leyland:

> Within a mile of Preston I came over Darwent River . . . and a mile above beyond the Place where I passed over Darwent Mr. Langton dwellith, at Walton-on-Darwent I passed over the great stone bridge of Rybill, having 5 great arches. From Ribyl to Preston half a mile. Preston hath but one Paro Chirch. The Market place of the Town is fair. Ribil goith round aboute a greate Peace of the Grounde aboute Toune, yet it touchith not the Toune selfe by space of almost half a Mile. Penwordine semid to me more than half a mile from Preston.

He thus clearly appreciated the location of the early town site, in a bow of the river but some distance from it, and in the space of less than thirty words spelt Ribble in three different ways![6]

The farmyard at Higher Brockholes Farm 1911, a fine local example of sixteenth- and seventeenth-century timber and plaster work on a stone base.

Horse gin, Bowland c.1910. Much of the technology which was to power the early stages of the industrial revolution had been developed by Tudor times – the horse gin, windmill and watermill.

In Preston, neither the Crown nor the rising class of merchant families with their medieval burgesses' rights were effective in keeping control. A serious dispute broke out in 1527 during the election of the town's mayor. Sir Richard Hoghton, a man noted for his 'high voice and angry countenance', summoned the burgesses to a nocturnal meeting in an alehouse and told them who they had to elect, and at the election they wisely did as they had been instructed. When the former Mayor, James Walton, asked Sir Richard 'in the Kings name' not to interfere, he was told 'Scornefully and yn dyrysion', 'Commandest thou me in the Kinges name! gett the hom to thy soper'. Walton and over fifty burgesses accordingly fled.[7] Legal actions begun by Sir Henry Farington (himself no stranger to the use of 'strong arm' tactics) and the burgesses resulted in Hoghton being bound over to keep the peace in £200, the ejection of his candidate, and the drawing up of new rules for the election of the mayor.

A similar dispute arose in 1534 when Sir Richard, apparently outraged at the 16d. per day expenses of Preston's MP, James Walton, sought

The future Edward VII's visit in 1885, when crowds thronged the Cheapside portico of the Town Hall. The Prince of Wales lunched in the Town Hall during his visit to lay the foundation stone of the Preston Dock. The property in the centre of the photograph was later demolished to make way for redevelopment which included the building of the new post office.

further to influence both the mayor's appointment and the town's choice of member. By way of reply Walton accused Hoghton of keeping his step-daughter in adultery, and of trying to marry off 'his two bastard daughters' to prominent burgesses. At his visit in 1533 Thomas Benalt, the King's Herald, reported that 'The said Sir Richard hath put away his lady and wife and keepeth a concubine in his house by whom he hath divers children'. Hoping for a gratuity he was disappointed, 'He gave me nothing nor made me no good cheer, but gave me proud words'.[8] Sir Richard Hoghton clearly regarded the important offices in the town as his prerogative, and the Hoghton family dominated affairs in Preston.

The scale of local and family feuds could frequently develop to alarming proportions. In 1589 a dispute between Thomas Hoghton and Thomas Langton, baron of Walton, over grazing rights, resulted in something between a riot and a pitched battle at Lea, during which Hoghton was killed. The affair ominously began to develop a wider significance as both sides mustered their supporters. The Earl of Derby recommended that legal proceedings be dropped since the district's chief landlords 'Are so great in Kindred and affinity and so stored with friends as, if they should be burnt in the hand, I fear it will fall out to be a ceaseless and most dangerous quarrel betwixt the gentlemen that any country of her majesty's have this many years contained'.[9]

The dispute was settled some years later and Langton surrendered the heavily mortgaged manor of Walton to the Hoghtons.

The capital of Catholic Lancashire

The Reformation profoundly shaped the subsequent social develop-ment of Lancashire and, indeed, was one of the great formative periods in the history of the town. The county effectively split into two halves, a Catholic north and west and a Protestant south and east, divided on a broad line between Warrington and Burnley. Preston, at the centre of the Catholic district comprising the Fylde, West Lancashire and the lower Ribble Valley, thus became for a generation the *de facto* capital of Catholic Lancashire.

The Reformation had little popular support in Lancashire, and aroused much opposition. In contrast to the more disillusioned south where reform of the medieval Church with its corruption and outstanding abuses was seen as long overdue, the ecclesiastical foundations in the north still commanded much loyalty. Here the Church undertook valuable work among the poor, and the priories and abbeys were not in general tainted by bad landlordism.

The highly conservative local gentry, though usually quite prepared to expand their estates at the expense of the very establishments which they and their forefathers had endowed, saw little reason to alter their beliefs and religious practices. The inability of a distant government to coerce them, and the limited resources of the newly established church under the hard-pressed Bishop of Chester, account in large measure for the survival of Catholicism as a popular religion in this part of the North West.

Many of the abuses manifested by the unreformed Church were clearly apparent at Preston. Nevertheless, local people seem to have been in broad agreement with the Croston priest who was reputed to have called out at the proclamation deposing Catherine of Aragon in 1533, that 'Queen Catherine was queen, and that Nan Boleyn should be no queen, nor the King no King but in his bearing', adding, 'who the devil made Nan Boleyn, that whore, queen, for I will never take her for queen'.[10] Yet the rising of the northern counties, the so-called 'Pilgrimage of Grace', seems to have met with little response in Lancashire apart from the district around Whalley where activity was intense. Indeed, Preston was an important base for the Earl of Derby's counter measures against the rising, of which he subsequently boasted, 'I do verely beleve to have cumen thrugh this shir if they had not byn affrayd of me and other your true subgette soo assembled as is aforesaid at Preston'.[11] In the subsequent disposal of monastic property, the Fleetwoods acquired the Penwortham Priory estate and the Leper Hospital, John Braddyl and Richard Assheton purchased Whalley Abbey, whilst the Friary with that at Lancaster and Cartmel Priory went to Thomas Holcroft. Henry VIII was equally prepared to persecute Protestants, however, and Robert Singleton, who as a boy had been Vicar of Preston in 1516, was executed as a 'heretic' for 'treason' in 1543, becoming Lancashire's first Protestant martyr.[12]

Perhaps the most significant feature of the Reformation in the Preston area is that it had so little immediate effect. Away from the south east of the county with its close trading links with Protestant areas (Preston's links in the linen trade lay with Catholic Ireland), the early Protestant missionaries made little progress. As early as 1541 Bishop Bird of Chester reported that his diocese was far behind those of the south, and that 'Papist idolatory' was likely to continue.[13] Little of substance seems to have changed at Preston, for an inventory of all 'jewellery, vestments, ornaments, plate, bells, and all other gudds' made in 1552 lists 'one holywater pot of brasse, two sensaurs of brasse, one pyxe of brasse, four sackering bells, two handbells' and 'one painted clothe wyche was about the sepulcre'.[14]

Under the Catholic Queen Mary (1553–8) efforts were made to restore the church of the 1520s, and the apparent speed of many of these 'restorations' tends to confirm that many of the earlier 'reforms' had never been fully carried out. Efforts were made to restore the Chantry at Longton; Preston Parish Church was again used for ordinations, whilst one of the masters at Preston Grammar School suspected of being a Protestant was replaced. Under Queen Elizabeth the prevailing doctrine

changed once again, although the Protestant Settlement of 1559 was liberal in essence. In the early years much seems to have gone on as before. Few local people were actually prosecuted for recusancy (refusal to attend Anglican church services) and priests seem to have been relatively free to come and go in the district. Conversely, local Catholics failed to support the 'Rising of the North' in 1569 in support of Mary Queen of Scots, and seem to have been loyal in their support of Elizabeth's government despatching forces to the many military levies for service (particularly in Ireland) during the period. Nicholas Bannester, Evan Bannester and Edward Howard, all officially 'Wanted priests lurking in Lancashire', were able to serve twenty-year stints in the district.[15]

In 1570 the Bishop of Chester deplored this situation: 'In Lancashire the people fall from religion, revolt to popery and refuse to come to church.'[16] An ecclesiastical commission appointed to investigate this Lancashire phenomenon concluded that the key element was the local gentry who remained highly conservative in religion. As the government established increasingly harsh penalties for non-attendance at church and the harbouring of priests, the local magistrates simply failed to implement them. Significantly a recent study of the period has not detected extensive evidence of sectarianism. Many may simply have believed, like Sir Richard Shireburne, that a man's religious beliefs were his own business, so long as he was loyal to the Crown.[17] In short the local gentry were asserting their ancient independence, leading Ferdinando, future Earl of Derby, to describe their county as 'This so unbridled and bad an handful of England'.[18]

It might have been easier for the authorities to impose their will in towns like Preston than in the isolated communities, yet little appears to have been achieved before 1600. In Preston 'Nothing seems to be known of the first Elizabethan vicars, but from the character of the district the conformity with the religious legislation of the time was little more than nominal'.[19] Trouble only arose when a strongly Protestant vicar was appointed in 1572: Nicholas Daniel was soon at odds with his Catholic curate William Wall and his conservative congregation. Having taken the names of those of his parishioners refusing to take communion in the prescribed way and having failed to have them prosecuted to his satisfaction, he wrote to the Bishop of Chester: 'Many grefes are in my mynde, my good Lorde, but I am lothe to troble yr . . . table wh we mynistr on ys an old alter, whereon' stones and idolls seats standing, and I have moved to abolish such abuses, but I cannot be hard [heard]'.[20] He accused the curate of 'many other abuses long to reherse . . . horedom, dicing, carding drinking from morning to night . . . and even this daie hath an hoore great with chyld within 8 myle of Preston'.

In reply to these charges, and supported by the parish clerk:

William Wall curate of Preston confesseth that he hath comytted adultery with one who called herself Elizabeth but her surname he

Preston has always had a large Catholic population. Many in the town rejected the Reformation settlement, preferring to remain loyal to the old religion. The Catholic population was then supplemented particularly in the nineteenth century by significant numbers of Irish immigrants.

Top left, we see the façade of St. Mary's Church, which nestles behind the shop frontages of Friargate.

Top right is the elaborate façade of St. Wilfrid's on Chapel Street, which unfortunately is hidden from proper view by buildings on Fishergate.

Bottom left is St. Joseph's on Skeffington Road, whilst at bottom right we see one of Preston's architectural gems, St. Walburge's, whose spire rises above the Preston skyline.

knoweth not . . . He confessed that he had used cardinge and dicinge for drink, but hath cast ytt this III yeres altogether . . . Denied that he administered the holy communion in any Ale House except but it were to sick folks.[21]

Vicar Daniel resigned in 1580 to be succeeded by the 'evil curate's' father, Thomas Wall, Vicar 1580–92, 'An old grave man of simple persuasion in divinity and one that in his youth hath used sundry callings and now at last settled himself in the ministry'.[22] With the tolling of the church bells for the dead, the refusal to sing 'Geneva Psalms', or to receive the host at communion in the hand, the Reformation had clearly made little progress in Preston in almost fifty years.

In the 1580s the serious international situation, and especially fears of an imminent Spanish invasion, and the arrival of Catholic missionaries and agents from Cardinal Allen's college at Douai and the Jesuit College of Rome, led the authorities to take affairs in the Catholic enclave in Lancashire much more seriously, it 'being the very sink of popery, where more unlawful acts have been committed and more unlawful persons holden secret that in any other part of the realm'.[23] In 1582 and 1583 respectively the Bishop of Chester was warned by the Lord President of the Council of the North, 'Good my Lord, be careful of Preston and other places in your file [Fylde] country,' and, 'In your like countries there is plenty Jesuits and massing priests. I wish I might hear that some preachers are planted there to cross them. I hope that before this you have planted one in Preston'.[24]

Fines for non-attendance at church were raised to £20 per month, and in 1585 the death penalty was introduced for convicted seminary priests. Great efforts were made to capture Edmund Campion on his visit to Lancashire as a guest of the Southworths and Hoghtons in 1581, yet despite the repeated drives against Catholics in the 1580s and '90s, few were actually convicted. In 1592, for example, eight hundred people were prosecuted for recusancy, two hundred were indicted, but only twelve actually paid their fines.[25] Similarly, Puritan protests against the religious content of the 1582 Guild Merchant, 'To this effect, that the Guild should begin with procession and a Mass of the Holy Ghost – now not tolerable – and divers other superstitious rites and ceremonies now abrogated', went unheeded.[26]

Many of the contemporary lists of the non-attenders at church (the Recusancy Rolls) have survived. The roll of 1593/4 lists:

Wm Garstang, owed [in fines] £80; Sir John Southworth owes ⅔ of £180, that is £120, for that he did not frequent any church, chapel or usual place of common prayer, but withdrew himself for the space of 9 full months.

By contrast the list of 1595 includes a large proportion of poor people:

Robte Worthington of Preston late a draper, a vagrant person and wandereth about Preston.

Elizabeth Blundell, Margaret Cowpe of Preston, wydowes, householders, indicted, poore.
William Hadocke of Colton, gent.[27]

Local Catholics, a large proportion of the population, suffered
relatively little harassment in Leyland Hundred and Amounderness.
Even convicted prisoners rarely felt the full force of the law; in 1598 those
held at Lancaster were to be free 'To hunt, hawk, and go to horse races at
their pleasure'.[28] A modicum of conformity to the newly established
Church would often satisfy the authorities. William Singleton of
Brockholes, being ill in prison, was brought before the Earl of Derby and
allowed to go home. When well enough he was to attend church 'and shall
receive the Blessed Sacrament of the Communion in the Parish Church of
Preston in the face of the congregation, on some Sunday or Holy-day before
the said 27 day of May'. Perhaps more importantly, he was not to encourage
others in his views:

> Nor shall he hear Mass or be present at any old Romish service
> prohibitted, nor lodge, receive, entertain or relieve with meat, drink,
> clothes or money, any ye priests, especially Vaux, Allen, Hargreaves,
> Murrin, etc. that have refused the ministry or forsaken their cures, or
> are vehemently suspected to be of unsound religion.[29]

After 1585 very real fears of a Spanish invasion led to increased
military preparedness. In October 1587 the trained bands were mustered
by the local gentry, in all 1170 trained men, with the horsemen stationed
at Wigan and Preston for rapid deployment in the event of landing on the
Lancashire shore. In the summer of 1588 the county answered the queen's
call to defend, 'country, liberty, wife, children, lands, life and that which is
especially to be regarded, for the preservation of the true sincere religion
of Christ'. [30]

During these tense years a very close watch was kept on the local
gentry. In 1592 the spy 'Dingley' was actively reporting on the
Southworths, the Hoghtons and Baron Langton of Walton-le-Dale, 'Who
would be more determined than any to take Dingley's life if he only knew
what our informer had said'. The spy also reported on the attitude of the
local 'Anglican' clergy, many of whom were sympathetic to the Catholics'
right to worship as they pleased: 'of ecclesiastical persons, I deem these
greatly to favour papists – the parson of Sephton, the parson of Halsted,
the Vicar of Croston and the Vicar of Preston'.[31]

A report of 1590 reveals the remarkable continuity of religious practice,
and the half-heartedness of the efforts by the local magistrates to
suppress it. There were:

> Popishe ffastes and ffestivales (now abrogated in the Churche of
> England) duely observed in all these partes, and that with greater
> devotion than the sabbath against which daies crosses in streetes and
> high waies ar[e] in many places often devoutly garnished, and wax
> candelles duely prepared.

This was attributed to the attitude of the local gentry: 'there are in all partes divers notorioose recussantes not yet reformde: whose presumption (they being of the better sorte) drawethe the inferior sorte into no small bowldnesse'.[32]

As the likelihood of invasion receded and the bonfire men on Rivington Pike and Bowland were stood down, local Catholics became much more open in their religious practice in anticipation of changes in their favour under the Stuart James I. In August 1600 the arrest of local Catholics in Garstang resulted in the attack 'by a score of armed men, some of whome fired muskets' on a Puritan preacher and the Vicar of Garstang in his vicarage. Of 73 people questioned all denied any knowledge of the affair and, typically, no-one was punished. The following month the 'noted trouble-maker' and priest Thurston Hunt (alias 'Robert Greenlowe'), attempted the violent rescue of a fellow priest Robert Middleton, again near Garstang. The same year attempts were made to rescue recusants at Chipping.[33] It has been suggested that a Catholic chapel was re-established in Preston town in 1605, but on what evidence this assertion is made is unclear.

Hopes of a Catholic revival were dashed in 1605 by the 'Gunpowder Plot'. John Sumner of Peacock Hall, Leyland, was in London at this time, and described the 'Wicked Practices' in a letter to his master William Ffarington of Worden. He concluded, 'Great Bonfires were made throughout all the streets and ringing of bells throughout all London for upon Tuesday the 5th of November at night for joy the same devilish practice was revealed'.[34] In Preston that year 68 recusants were prosecuted, with a further nineteen in the wider parish. These included William Ridley who was 'supposed to have many masses said in his house since the death of the queen, whereunto many have resorted,' and 'William Urmston, gentleman, a great seducing Papist, who seduceth the people very much, and sometimes a crafty subtle lawyer'. [35]

The early years of the seventeenth century mark an important watershed. The compromise of the Church of England proved acceptable to most Englishmen at least up to the Civil War, whilst in mid-Lancashire Catholic practices were henceforth to survive relatively unmolested, largely accounted for by the geographical remoteness and insularity of the district, and the attitude of the leading local families.

Protestantism did make some headway, however. As early as the 1580s William Chadderton, Bishop of Chester, organised group meetings for the Protestant clergy in Preston, to undertake study under Puritan guidance of selected passages from the scriptures.[36] Although not successful in the old towns in the sixteenth century and making little progress in the seventeenth, Puritanism did become firmly established in the south east of the county, encouraged by Elizabeth's government as a counter to the emerging 'papist' enclave around Preston.

Under James I and Charles I Nonconformity and Presbyterianism developed to such an extent that by the end of the Civil War they had control of much of the religious worship in the established Church in

Lancashire. Pro-royalist high church clergy were accordingly ejected, such as Vicar Rothwell of Leyland, but on the restoration of Charles II and in particular the re-introduction of the Anglican Prayer Book many Puritan clergy were in turn ejected from their livings.

Although throughout much of the sixteenth century the clergy at Preston Parish Church had clear Catholic leanings, religious orthodoxy made progress during the ministries of William Sawrey (1592–1603) and John Paler (1604–21), 'a distinguished labourer in God's vineyard, departed in the Lord, piously and peacefully . . . whose memory was held in blessing.'[37] In 1602 an order of the Preston Guild forbade trading on the sabbath, and in 1616 the town council ordered housekeepers to keep their street doors shut during service time on Sundays and festivals, and to prevent their children playing in the streets or sitting in the doorways on the sabbath. Alehouses were ordered to close at 9p.m.[38]

To some extent the decline of Catholicism and progress of Anglicanism in the town (as distinct from the surrounding country) can be accounted for by the changed attitude of the Hoghtons. On the death of the 'fugitive' Thomas Hoghton in 1583 Elizabeth's court took great pains to ensure that the eventual heir, the infant Richard Hoghton, should be brought up in a strict Protestant tradition. This change in the outlook of Preston's leading family must have had a profound effect on religious observance in the town. In 1600 the Bishop of Chester was able to write favourably of the progress of the Protestant cause in Preston, and to single out Richard Hoghton's efforts on its behalf for special praise:

> The High Sheriff of Lancashire in this year of his office, and Sir Richard Haughton both heretofore and now of late, have done great service in apprehending of sundry priests, pestilent persuaders to rebellion, and are the ablest and fittest persons in regard of their state and their near dwelling to the most corrupt places of Lancashire, to hunt out these seditious priests and suppress the insolences of the people, and being encouraged therein, will be willing doubtless in such services to do their best.[39]

James Martin, instituted Vicar of Preston in 1621, was ejected from his living in 1623. His final appeal against his ejection is one of the town's most remarkable documents. In it he claims to be the victim 'of a strong combination of the puritans against me (merely for my conformity to his majesty's canons and opposition to their wild fancies)'. It may be no exaggeration to suggest that these events may literally have driven him out of his mind, for, bereft of his income, he claimed that his 'poor wife', a daughter of Sir John Southworth, 'and a son (having nowhere else to live) were starved to death in the streets'.[40]

Isaac Ambrose, vicar 1640–58, was to be a victim of the high church party at the restoration of Charles II. He left Preston to become vicar of Garstang, complaining of its 'Jarres, envies, pride, discords, and policies of men in streets and townes', hoping to be able to 'walk the silent fields and woods and hear more frequently the various tunes of melodious birds and keep consort with them, who without jarres are ever in their kind praising God'. A close friend of the Hoghtons, he was subsequently ejected from his living because of his nonconformity, dying at his house in Church Weind, Preston (St. John's Street) in 1664, 'Honoured by God and Good men'.[41]

Although most of the seventeenth-century vicars of Preston were apparently at odds with their congregation at one time or another, the ministry of Seth Bushell (1663–82) seems to have been historically a very significant one for:

> a loyal, pious, and charitable man . . . of moderate disposition [he] much discouraged persecution for religion or prosecution of any of his parishioners for what was customary due, and very courteous to dissenters of all denominations, so that none of his parishioners were troubled by him.[42]

Yet in the hamlets and communities beyond the town Catholicism survived relatively unmolested, and eighteenth-century surveys list Catholic familes in all the surrounding districts. Just outside the town Fishwick Hall became an important centre for holding mass, and holy wells at Fernyhalgh and Red Scar continued to be frequented. The visit by Bishop Leyburne in 1687 revealed the extent of what was clearly a far from beleaguered group. In September of that year he confirmed almost nine thousand people in Lancashire, most of them in and around Preston. A survey of 1717 listed 643 papists in the town, whilst 1767, 762 Protestant, 145 papist and 21 dissenting families were recorded.

Thus the course of the religious changes in the sixteenth and seventeenth centuries was to leave a profound imprint on the subsequent social history of Preston and district, which in many respects makes it quite distinct from that of other northern towns and whose influence can still be felt at the end of the twentieth century. Yet it would be quite incorrect to infer from a study of the period that the Prestonians of the day were theologically well-read. In fact the majority of people probably had little clear idea of the doctrines involved, and visitors to the county were frequently aghast at the apparent godlessness and ignorance of the people. Superstition was rife, and witchcraft (best exemplified locally by the case of the Samlesbury Witches) was perceived as a very real threat, while 'magic' still played a role in popular religion. Frequently the standard of the clergy seems to have been little better; the case of Preston's William Wall has been considered, but more notorious was George Dobson, Vicar of Whalley who in 1575 was accused of being:

> A common drunkard and such an ale-knight as the like is not in our parish, and in the night when most men be in bed at their rest then is he in the ale-house with a company like to himself, but not one of them can match him in ale-house tricks, for he will, when he cannot discern black from blue, dance with a full cup on his head, far passing all the rest.

Preston Grammar School c.1850, a lithograph by Day and Son. Standing near the corner of Cross St. and Winckley Square, this fine building was demolished in 1957. A schoolmaster at Preston is mentioned in documents as early as 1358, and the existence of a 'grammar' school by 1400. The school moved from Stoneygate to this building in the early 1840s.

George Hesketh at Halsall was notorious for his lechery – 'This is he that corrupteth all the women in the county'![43]

It is all the more remarkable, therefore, that Preston and its surrounding district was to provide the county's first Protestant martyr, and the largest proportion of Catholic martyrs.

Red Scar, Grimsargh c.1900. Though much of the black and white timber work was imitation, at least a part of the house dated from Tudor times. A nearby holy medicinal well, 'Boilton Spa', was removed c.1850. The Red Scar estate overlooked the great sweep of the River Ribble, a view described by Charles Hardwick as 'an Eden Spot'. The estate was purchased for the site of Courtaulds' huge factory in 1929.

Stoneygate 1796, an engraving by Walker. Stoneygate was one of the principal entrances into the town. This perspective illustrates the prominent position of the Parish Church, on the Church Street ridge. From the top of the tower, 'The Merse Officer' had a clear view of the fighting in 1715.

CHAPTER FIVE

Dr. Kuerden's Preston

P RESTON is particularly fortunate in having a wide range of surviving documents from the seventeenth century, from which a clear picture of everyday life in the town emerges. One of the most important of these sources is the parish registers, which date from October 1611, with the exception of just two pages dated 1603. Most registers contain periods where they have clearly been neglected, and the Preston registers only appear to become an accurate general record after about 1670, although occasional runs of earlier years appear to be complete.[1] In addition to providing the most important source for family historians and genealogists the records give an impression of the size of the population (which in the parish may have comprised 3–4000 people) and reveal the changing pattern of baptisms and burials, especially the incidence of famine and disease.

In December 1651 Vicar Ambrose was accused by the parish officers of not keeping the registers properly:

> Now forasmuch as there hath beene of late, a great neglecte of Registringe such said persons, which may happen to prove very prejudiciall to some therein that be concerned, And that Mr. Ambrose the present Minister of this parish hath been the cause of this late omission and neglecte; and seemes still to be unwillinge to keepe the said Register, and to do his duty therein as hee aught by lawe: therefore . . . wee order and desire that Thomas Maudesley, ye parish cleark doe keepe the said booke.[2]

Yet the low totals for these years may also reveal the aftermath of the great plague of 1631, an event which the registers record in very great detail.

The disaster which overwhelmed Preston in 1631 rivalled the Black Death of 1349 in its intensity. Having escaped the severe outbreaks of plague which affected Wigan in 1603, and at Manchester in 1605 (when over two thousand people died), Preston was less fortunate a generation later. The plague first appeared in Preston in October/November 1630, and the register for the latter month is headed: 'Heare begineth the Visitation of Allmighty God, the Plague'. The first two burials are listed as

The old 1781 Town Hall and adjacent buildings seen from Cheapside 1860. This block of land, between Church Street and the Flag Market, was cleared in the early 1860s to make way for Sir Gilbert Scott's Town Hall, which extended over the whole site and was opened in 1867. Earlier buildings must thus have been quite small. The old timber-framed buildings, so prominent a feature of the early nineteenth century prints of the town, had already been cleared from the rear of the old Town Hall, and for some years the council had deliberated over what to do next with the site.

'The wife of Thomas Wilkinson, 8 November, James Sudell Lining [linen] Webster'. Parcels of cloth were particularly feared as agencies of the spread of disease, and this may have been the source of the outbreak in Preston. The disease, which it is thought may have been akin to anthrax, spread rapidly within families, a tendency particularly apparent from the contemporary Bishop's Transcripts at Penwortham. Catastrophic in total, the outbreak was tragic in detail:

George et Thomas		15 December 1630
Henry et Mary	children of	16 December 1630
John et Margret	Rob. Tumlinson	17 December 1630
Jennet Wife of Robt Tumbleinson		22 December 1630

In neighbouring Walton-le-Dale and Broughton the outbreak seems to have been so severe that no record of burials or other church ceremonies was maintained at all.

Great efforts were made by the county administration to contain the outbreak. Public assemblies were banned, and the parish officers were ordered to keep a watch for people escaping from Preston, and threatened with fines of £20 if caught neglecting their duty. Even five years later the officers in the Forest of Pendle were ordered by the Preston magistrates to watch the house of Nicholas Hargreaves, whose daughter, recently arrived from London, had 'brought with her certen clothes packed upp in a bundell or truncke, much dreaded to be infectious'.[3]

In Preston a 'Pest House' was established for the sick, but where entire families were afflicted their houses were simply boarded up with them inside. The town was put into quarantine, causing great distress as the winter drew on. All trade and markets had been stopped and, with no income, the townspeople were dependent on a relief fund established by the council and on donations from other towns. A great fuel shortage developed as Prestonians were not allowed out of the town to gather fuel, and no-one else would risk taking it in.

A series of letters written by Alexander Rigby to his brother provide an eye-witness account of events. In 1630 he described the disease 'Which our tradesmen will not call the plague,' as very infectious. By the end of July the following summer the outbreak reached its peak:

The sicknes in these partes increaseth much and disperseth: it is now in Fulwood, Cadeley, and Broughton, and in Kirkham, so that the inhabitants and bordering neighbours leave their houses and seeke and resort to forein places.[4]

The onset and monthly progress of the plague, and its sheer scale in numbers of deaths, can clearly be seen from the gross numbers of deaths recorded in the parish register (see tables opposite). At the end of April it was reported that 1390 people were receiving charitable relief, and the outbreak reached its peak in July and August, when 331 and 280 burials respectively were recorded. In the latter month William Preston, the Mayor, prepared a detailed survey of the town's 887 remaining

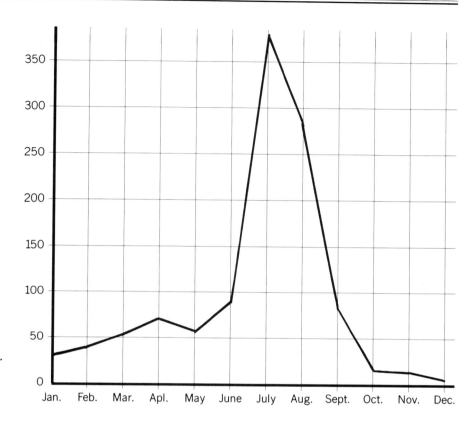

Graph showing the number of burials per month recorded at Preston during 1631.

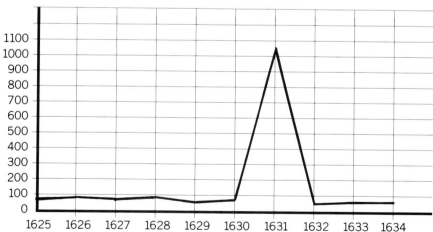

Burials recorded at Preston, 1625–35.

inhabitants. By this time one thousand people had died, and an unknown number must have fled. Stricken by sickness and death, isolated, the markets deserted, houses in Fishergate and Friargate boarded up and the town largely empty, Preston must have been a terrible spectacle that summer.[5]

PERFECT SURVEY SENT US BY THE MAIOR. August 16th 1631

The number of Persons:

In the Fishergate and Markett place which hath releife
[assistance from the relief fund] 78

Which have no releifes 25

In the Churchgate relieved 245

Which have no releife 27

In the Fryergate relieved 180

Which have no releife 79

In the Pesthouses and houses shutt upp 253

Summa Totalis of them which have releife 756

Of them with no releife 131

    total 887

    WILLIAM PRESTON, MAYOR

William Preston's survey formed the basis of an appeal to the Lancashire magistrates led by Sir Gilbert Hoghton. The townspeople could not:

longe subsiste by their private stores, but will shortly become needers also. Their winters fuell is whollie unprovided, and all those that live theire needes still increase. What in the beginninge would have served well, will now doe them little good, all their owne helpes being gone . . . Yet theire miseries are enough by the plage yet were pittie famine should also destroy them. Soe wee leave them to Godes mercie, and, for theire reliefe, to your better judgement.[6]

Half of the fatalities occurred during the hottest months of 1631, July and August, thereafter the disease declined rapidly. By the following January no-one had died of it for seven weeks, and the outbreak was deemed to be over: 'There hath been very greate care and paines taken to clense, purify and dresse the same towne: This cort doth think itt fitt that the faires and markettes bee hereafter sett open and kept within the same Towne of Preston'. Beyond the town subsequent outbreaks occurred in Chorley, Croston and Garstang. In Kirkham 30s. was paid for 'Perfuming the Church,' and 5s. for removing the rush flooring 'in the sickness time'.[7]

The town's trade had been badly affected. The Company of Drapers, Mercers and Grocers petitioned Charles I for help. These '80 poore persons . . . having been visited with the plague and pestilence' and 'banned from the exercise of their trades,' had become 'very much impoverished and weakened in their estates'. Worse still, other people, newcomers, had taken up their trades, so that they had 'lost a great part of their former trading and their markets are become small'.[8]

The survivors gathered in the parish church to thank God for their deliverance, and to hear 'The Preservation of the Godly in the Greatest Perils: In a Sermon preached at Preston when the great Plague ceased in that towne: 1631'. Taking as his theme 'Wee had beene as sodome and beene made like unto Gomorrha', Christopher Hudson, 'Preacher of Gods Word at Preston', urged his congregation to help the poor and avoid the sins of gluttony, 'fulness of bread', 'Idleness' and 'Contempt of ye Poore and needy'. He prayed that the town, 'which God hath redeemed from ye pestilence, and brought . . . from ye gates of death,' would serve God and fear His wrath. 'Because of all plagues it is ye greatest, we have dayly cause to pray, Good Lord deliver us. Amen'.[9]

An estimate of the contemporary population of the town can also be attempted from the statistics revealed by the two great national surveys of the period, the Protestation Return of 1642 and the Hearth Tax enumeration of 1663.[10]

On the eve of the Civil War Parliament ordered that all adult males should take an oath to maintain the Anglican settlement and the power of Parliament. Accordingly lists were compiled of the men in each parish, from which a nominal figure of over 3000 for the total population of Preston parish can be established.

The wording of the 'Protestation', however, made it offensive to many Catholics:

> I do in the presence of Almightie God, promise and protest, to maintaine and defend as far as lawfully I may, with my life, power and state, ye true reformed Protestant Religion expressed in ye Church of England, against all paperie and papish Innovations . . . and also ye power and privileges of Parliament.[11]

In the parish outside the town over half refused to take it, but only 23 men in Preston itself. Catholic sympathies clearly remained strong in the district around Preston. From these figures it would seem that the town may have had a population of about fifteen hundred with a further 1650 people in the parish beyond. These figures make no allowance for Fulwood which was not in Preston parish, whilst detailed studies of this method indicate that the Protestation Return is only a very rough guide to actual population numbers.

Twenty years later the Hearth Tax was introduced to raise additional revenue. Dwellings were to be charged 2 shillings for each hearth they contained, and householders were to send lists of their hearths to the collecting officer. Although the poor and those with low incomes were specifically exempted, the 'Chimney Tax' was intensely resented; chimneys were bricked up and evasion was extensive. Ultimately the tax had to be abandoned.

The return lists 577 households with 1213 hearths in the parish, of which 261 houses were located in the town and 316 in the country district. From these admittedly incomplete records, the total population of the town can be estimated at around 1,300. One feature of Preston which may indicate that this is an underestimate, however, is the very large proportion of larger houses with more than the single hearth that was so common in the outlying districts. Overall, 71% of Preston's houses had two or more hearths, compared to just 22% in the case of Fulwood, 30% in

Fishwick and 21% in Broughton. Clearly, and not surprisingly, the burgesses' town houses were much more substantial than the cottages to be found in the more agricultural parts of the parish. Preston also had far more very large houses – such as those of Alexander Rigby with no fewer than fifteen hearths, or Will Hodgkinson with eleven – and a very high proportion of moderately large dwellings.

Prior to the eighteenth century wills were often very intimate documents containing a great deal of personal information, and generally consisting of three elements: a religious introduction; the 'will' and division of the deceased's goods; and an attached inventory of the goods themselves. These inventories provide a clear insight into the everyday life of the period. John Paler, the much respected Vicar of Preston 1604–21, died on 15th April 1621, and the inventory of his possessions shows that such a man could be wealthy as well as well-educated, and have business interests beyond his vocation. The 'Bookes in his studdy' were valued at £14 10s. 0d. and, typically for the period, and notwithstanding his position, the inventory lists a number of commodities concerned with the textile trade. Less typical for the 'Distinguished Labourer in God's vineyard' were his 'Muskett bandolere and the rest . . . one pistoll' and his sword.[12]

The long inventory of James Lemon provides a detailed picture of the way of life of a wealthy Preston burgess, indicating a man of his standing to be the owner of a sizable house with a shop beneath devoted to the linen trade, as well as being a substantial farmer.

From the sixteenth century onwards local diaries and the journals of visitors to the town provide vivid descriptions of everyday life. The 1680s in Preston are particularly well endowed, with Dr. Kuerden's account and maps, and the diaries of Thomas Bellingham (1688–90: a captain in the army, stationed at Preston and in lodgings in Friargate), Lawrence Rawstorne (1683–6: High Sheriff of Lancashire 1682, he rented a house from the widow of the Rev. Seth Bushell) and Edward Fleetwood (1687–9, MP for Preston).

Captain Bellingham's diary, covering the tense years of the 'Glorious Revolution', the war in Ireland, and fears of invasion, contains much detail of local troop movements and drilling. Yet it also reveals something of the lifestyle of a gentleman in the town at this time, when Preston was a seasonal resort for the local gentry:

> Ye 23th (August 1688) – A very wet day. We heard of Mr. Billington's foot being Gangrea'd by cutting a nayle of a toe. I was with Dr. Lee and some Apothecaryes till it was late, Att Coopes etc. In ye morning I walk'd to Walton and saw Mr. Houghton, and came home by ye boathous . . .

> Ye 26th (September 1688) – Some Raine. Here was a bull baiting. Ye bull broake loose and fell down Mr. Langton's cellar stayres, and broake open the doore, and had like to have killed two children and ye drawer of ye anchor.[13]

Lawrence Rawstorne frequented the town's taverns and coffee house, often in the company of his 'cozens' Fleetwood and Ffarington:

12th May 1687. At Preston, at Coffee House and Swansey's 'ith weend and Widow Hugells with Mr. Greenhalgh, Lord Stafford's Chaplain: played bowls.

On November 5th, 1688 he was carousing with Captain Bellingham.[14]
An earlier diary, that of Nicholas Assheton of Downham (1617–18), provides an account of the visit to the district of King James I in 1617:

August 14th: Us three to Preston: There preparation was made for Sir Gilbert Houghton and other knights. Wee were desyred to be merrie, and at nyght we were soe. Steeven Hammerton and wyffe, Mrs. Doll Lyster supped wyth us at our lodging. All Preston full.

August 15th: The King came to Preston: there at the crosse, Mr. Breares the lawyer made a speech and the corporation presented him with a bowle: and then the King went to a banquet in the townhall, and soe away to Houghton: there a speech made. Hunted and killed a stagg. Wee attended on the lords table.[15]

Local folklore contains many stories of this visit to Hoghton Tower and the considerable expense that Sir Gilbert Houghton incurred entertaining the King and his company. The late George Miller, in what is perhaps the finest of the district's local histories, has revealed his underlying and pecuniary motive: he wished the King to assist him to finance the exploitation of the Pleasington alum mines.[16] Amid the junketings on the 16th, 'About 4 o'clock the King went down to the Allome mynes, and was there an hower, and viewed them *preciselie*'. Sir Gilbert received his loan and the festivities continued.

In her 'Great Journey' of 1689 the noted traveller Celia Fiennes made her way northwards from Wigan noting the many meres and marshy places, and the high-arched stone bridges required to accommodate the torrents flowing off the western Pennines:

Preston is reckon'd but 12 miles from Wiggan but they exceed in length by farre those that I thought long the day before from Liverpoole.
 Preston stands on a hill is a very good market town, Satterday is their market which day I was there and saw it was provided with all sorts of things leather corn coales butter cheese and fruite and garden things; there is a very spacious Market place and pretty Church and severall good house; at the entrance of the town was a very good house which was a Lawyers, all stone work 5 windows in the front and high built; the generallity of the buildings especially in 2 or 3 of the great streetes were very handsome, better than is most country towns, and the street spacious and well pitch'd.[17]

The most informative account of Preston in the seventeenth century is that prepared in the early 1680s by the town's great doctor, Richard

Along the Ribble at Preston c.1890. Although access was difficult, the river gave Preston an opening to the wider world. A small colonial trade developed during the eighteenth century and at least one small ship – the Blossom *– was engaged in the slave trade. However, shallow water and sandbanks made the passage difficult – requiring, in Dr. Kuerden's words, the services of 'A knoweing and well skill'd pylot'.*

The Top Walks and Bushell Place c.1860, a lithograph by R. Cuff. Preston was one of the first towns to be provided with parks or pleasure grounds. The origins of the Miller and Avenham Parks can be traced to the first acquisition of land by the Corporation in this area in the seventeenth century, a development which was noted with favour by contemporary commentators.

Jackson (1623–1701?), subsequently Dr. Kuerden. Born in Cuerden he was educated at the Leyland Free Grammar School and thereafter at Oxford and Cambridge. Taking up the profession of a physician he had settled at Preston by the early 1660s, appearing on the Guild Rolls in 1662 and 1682.[18]

His great passion was for the local history of the region, and to this end he worked tirelessly. With Christopher Towneley, also 'A painefull gatherer and lover of antiquities', he transcribed large collections of family and estate papers, intended to form the basis of the great history of Lancashire which they hoped to publish.

Kuerden seems to have enjoyed free access to the town's ancient records and charters. In 1701 the Corporation ordered:

> that Mr. Roberts, the Town Clerk, take what methods he can to get back the records, writings, and papers belonging to the Town, which were formerly lent to Dr. Kuerden, and that the Bayliffs reimburse him for his charges and paines, and place the same to their accounts.[19]

It is unlikely that anyone before or since has had such intimate knowledge of these materials. Clearly he lacked the resources to carry through such an ambitious project. If his other duties were neglected from time to time, it may safely be assumed that his attention was distracted by more pressing and urgent historical matters. A biography of this great townsman is long overdue.

Kuerden's description of Preston, with his eye-witness account of the 1682 Preston Guild, was eventually published in 1818 with additional notes by John Taylor, who does not seem to have been aware of the identity of the manuscript's celebrated author.[20] After describing the area's climate – 'the ayre [is] of a moderate temperature and healthfull' – Kuerden takes us on a tour of Preston's boundaries from the 'washing stood' at the point where the Swill Brook entered the 'much famed river of Ribell' to Ribbleton, Fulwood, Cadley and back to the river at 'Preston marsh, a little west from the Water Milne'. The Ribble, he says, 'hath been much noted for good salmon fishing (which belongs unto this burrough, within the bondary of their franchises); for into this estuarium the westron ocean twice a day power in its flowing streams which at a springing tide drives up its salt water eastward, a mile or two above the burrough; and passeth through arches of a fayr and one of the statelyst stone bridges in the north of England, called Rible bridge [at Walton], over which leadeth the king's high road from London'.

Kuerden gives an early description of the port which was located near the end of Marsh Lane, at 'a marsh, belonging to [Preston], whither yet, at higher water, a vesall of reasonable burden may arrive from the Westren Sea, guided by a knoweing and well skill'd pylot, though the river below at present is much choaked up with sand, and by the destruction of the

School children 'en fete' c.1910. Festivals have long been a popular feature of civic and religious life in Preston. From the seventeenth century onwards this aspect of Preston Guild began to challenge its more serious economic and political functions.

neighbouring marshes is made more shallow then formerly'; complaints that would be familiar to many involved with dredging the Ribble in later centuries.

The Preston Bushell, used by the Leet's officers to ensure that townspeople were not given short measure.

He then goes on to describe some of the town's principal buildings and streets:

This Burrough is much adorned with its larg square or market-place, as likewise with the streets thereof, which are so spacious from one end thereof unto the other, that few of the corporations of England exceed the same, either for streets or market-place. In the middle of the Burrough is placed an ample antient and yet well beautifyed gylde or town hall or toll bothe, to which is annexed, at the end thereof, a counsell chamber for the capitall burgesses or jurors at their court days, to retire for consultation, or secretly to retire themselves from the comon burgesses or the publiq root of people, as occasion shall require.

The publiq hall hath a decent cheq, and above it an elevated bench, whereat the three portmotes or the two leet days and the grand leet or court of election for new magistrates, sitts the mayor, aldermen, and such gentry as attends those meetings, and likewise at their court of common pleas, held each 3 weeks, for deciding suites and controversies . . .

To this place is likewise adjoined quarterly the publiq sessions for the hundred of Blackbourne and this of Amoundernes where the justice of peace for the county do administer justice, at their sessions for the contryes peace and security of the people, upon all malefactors thither brought before them; . . . Here likewise is held, the election of burgesses in parlement for the Burrough when occasion doth require the same . . . And lastly, this likewise is the place where the gyld mayor, stewards, aldermen, and clerk of the gyld, with much state and grandure, each 20 yeares, hold their gyld merchant.

Under this hall are ranged two rows of

Fishergate c.1830, an engraving by Bentham. The Moot Hall or Town Hall became the symbol of the burgesses' authority. This view illustrates the late eighteenth century building, and its central position on the town's main Church Street–Fishergate thoroughfare. An air of genteel tranquility belies the fact that Preston was a thriving market town and a rising industrial centre.

The old corn mill, Craggs Row c.1895. Though hemmed in by high rise blocks at the north end of Friargate, the Craggs Row windmill survived plans to demolish it during the clearance of the Adelphi district in the 1960s. The vicinity was one formerly noted for its windmills, and was the principal corn milling area of the town. Preston's first cotton mill, located here, was powered by windmill in 1777.

butchers' shopps on either side, and row at either end, where victualls are exposed dayly for the use of man, excepting Sundays, as also weekly on the public market dayes (&c.) Wednesday, and Saturday, and Friday being ever a market for fish, butter, and cheese, as likewise in the evening for yarn; Wednesday likewise being a market for fish, butter, and cheese: And upon Saturday, as soon as light appeare, is the market bell for linnen cloth; when ended, yarn appears, bread and fish of all sorts, butter and cheese; as formerly, the fish all in a row upon the fish stones, and places adjacent; their butter, cheese, and pullen, and potters about the butter crosse, in the end of Cheapside market; and bread nere unto the fish market.

The cattell market ordinarily in the Church-street, and upon the Saturday only; their horse market in the Fishergate, and begins about the ending of their market for cattell.

The swyne market over against the church; their sheep early upon the west side of the Market-square, above the shoomakers' stalls; and the leather cutters, earthern vessell, in Cheepside, and wooden vessell in the west end of the Market-place, below the barley market. The upper corn market, beginning at one of clock, upon the corn bell ringing; here standeth for sale rowes of wheat, rye, groats, in their distinct fyles and orders; below them towards the west is the barley and bean market, places in distinct and well ordered rowes, in which place, before the corn comes into town, was hydes and skinns exposed to sale untill 9 or 10 aclock. Below the fish stones standeth the stalls of hardwaremen, with all sort of iron instruments; in the midst of the Market-place, aside the barley market, are the stalls for brass and pewter; and higher above them, ranges of stalls for pedlars and cloth cutters, hosiers and the like: yet notwithstanding all these varyetys of wares and merchandizes, thus exposed, most of the burgesses or inhabitants of the Burrough have shops about the Market-place and in other streets, in their houses or nere unto their lodgings, were the several companyes of tradesmen dayly expose wares to sale.

This burrough is likewise adorned with a spacious wel built or rather re-edifyed church, for the decent and more comodious solemnization of religious rytes and instruction of the people in sound and healthfull Christian doctrines, and nereunto this church there is likewise built a large and hansom schoole house, for the better education of their children, and bringing them up in humane learning, making them fitter for trade or other better preferment in the world.

And there are likewise 3 other hospitalls or publiq alms houses erected for the habitation of many old, impotent, decrepit, and other of the most needy persons, to preseve them with charity from starveing and extreme necessityes; and these, for many familyes apeece, are placed at the ends of three severall streets for the more comodious assistance.

Adjacent unto which is lately raised a publiq workhouse, to employ the poorer sort of people especially woemen and children in a worsted trade of yar, thereby better to maintaine their family from begging.

A little more remoted from the town stands the ruins of an antient Pryory, formerly built for the relief of begging fryers, or of the minor order cald the Gray Fryers; but what is best thereof now standing is imployed for a House of Correction for the country's use to keep in safety such vagabonds, rouges, theeves, and sturdy beggars, and dissolute persons of no good behaviour, at hard work, under a strict master, with most slender dyet and whipping chear, untill either the publiq Sessions release them, with a naked and bloody farwell, and them for transportation or otherwise be enlarged by the judge & justices of the peace, their order or els retain them with a continando for the countrys safety, until a further punishment or reformation give them enlargement, after a sufficient expiation for their crimes.

Kuerden's description of the streets, buildings and government of Preston provide an excellent picture of a prosperous market town serving the needs of a wide area. In order to bring these streets to life, we can turn to the Borough's municipal records which supplement Kuerden's physical depiction of the town with a huge amount of fascinating social detail.

CHAPTER SIX

Life among
the Prestonians

PRESTON is particularly fortunate that in addition to its series of royal charters extending from 1179, and the run of general Council books and papers which survive from about 1600, the Corporation possesses the Guild Rolls of burgesses and the lists of Guild Orders (or bye-laws) in a regular series from the fourteenth century.

Through the Borough Council the burgesses exercised a measure of local control over the affairs of the town, but it was not always possible to avoid arbitrary interference by the neighbouring magnates. particularly in the early sixteenth century from the Hoghtons. Nor can the method of selecting the council and its officers be said to be in any way democratic or even representative. This led to considerable dispute and repeated attempts to solve the various problems at successive Guilds.

In 1562 it was ordered that the Mayor 'in open courte' was to choose 'two auncyent and discrete and honest burgesses inhabitantes', who having taken suitable oaths on sacred books, were to select 24 of the 'auncyent and discreete burgesses' to serve as a council, and 'one meke and discrete person which they shall thynke to be most to the profett of the said Town and the meynteynynge of the liberties and rights of the same Town', to be mayor. They were to appoint one of the town bailiffs and the mayor was to appoint the other and the town 'serjeant'.[1] The entire council was in effect to be selected by just two burgesses, who were themselves selected by the mayor. Some felt that at least one of the selectors should be chosen by the burgesses, and a sort of compromise was established by the charter of Elizabeth I in 1566, where it was decreed that the second selector was to be chosen by the council members of 'Capital Burgesses'. In practice therefore the town council was self-appointing, and effective power in Preston lay in the hands of a handful of its leading citizens.

Elizabeth's charter piously hoped that, 'The said Borough for all future times should be and remain a Borough of peace and tranquility, to the fear and terror of the bad, and the reward of the good'; but party strife over this fundamental issue reached a climax in 1598, when the Corporation was forced to introduce an interim Guild Order to regulate the election of the mayor until the next Guild Merchant:

> Whereas before this tyme great variance stryffe and contencon hath been hade and moved amongst the Burgesses inhabitantes within this

The charter of King Charles II, one of the several royal charters granted to Preston over the centuries.

towne, for and consernyng the election of officers within the same, to the great greefe and offence of manye of the best sort of people wisshinge the weale and good thereof, and much to the discredit of the sturrers uppe of such contencon, And no small reproche to the whole bodie of the same towne, whereby the good and well geeven are not a little greeved, The wicked and perverse mightelye incouraged by the Countenace of some not so well affected to the good and quyet of the same towne, as in reason and dutie they aught to bee.[2]

Henceforth the mayor was to be appointed from the senior council members, the bench-men or aldermen, on the basis of seniority.

Once appointed a council member held the office for life, unless he was removed for 'bad' conduct; the council was self-perpetuating and 'The general body of the Burgesses had accordingly no voice in, nor control over, the local administration'.[3] The town was an oligarchy dominated by the principal burgess families, and the ordinary burgesses' formal access to power was thus as firmly blocked as the outsiders' access to the town's trade.

Efforts were made to maintain a level of decorum at council meetings, and its proceedings were accompanied by great ceremony. A bye-law of 1582 ordered three days in the stocks for any person 'who shall at any time hereafter Evil intreate or abuse the Mayor or any other his officers . . . by speeche private or publick or otherwyse'.[4] In 1612 members were requested to attend meetings dressed in 'Decente and comlie gownes of blacke cloathe or other blacke stuffe to be maid of the ffashion now used', and they were to attend church on Sunday and sit together as a body.[5] Orders were similarly passed to regulate proceedings during council meetings, at which speakers should use no

opprobrious, reproachfull, uncivill or reflecting words or language [and] whilst any one is speakeing, the rest of the Councell shall all keep silence, and not to use any whisperings privately, or other open discourse one amongst another. [In particular no members] shall contrive or combine together with any other secretly, refractorily and resolutely to make a party against the next meeting, nor shall carry on any private designe for any interest whatsoever.[6]

The surviving Guild Orders provide a clear record of the evolution of the town's bye-laws re-enacted every twenty years. Taken in conjunction with the series of charters these provide a complex mass of local rights and laws. In 1662 the Guild was extended to over six weeks to allow for codification, a complicated procedure covering the regulation of such diverse activities as the keeping of swine, the buying and selling of goods, the duties of officials, and the management of the town's lands.[7]

The Corporation was the ultimate guardian of the Guild Rolls and alone could confer the status of burgess on aspiring apprentices and newcomers, as in 1666 when William Cadman, a stationer of the City of London, was allowed to trade in Preston for two years providing that his

family did not become burdensome 'in regard to the late sadd accident of fire, which hath at present prevented trading there'.[8] The freedom of Preston (i.e. admittance as a burgess) was offered to likely army recruits in 1685 'for the encouragement of such Apprentices, Journeymen, Servants etc., residing in this town . . . as a reward for their loyalty and readiness to engage in the said services'.[9]

A romanticized drawing by Cattermole depicting the 'solemnization ceremony' at the market place during a seventeenth-century Guild.

By the early sixteenth century the Guild Merchant proceedings had become highly elaborate, reflecting the dignity and respect that the council members thought due to them. Dr. Kuerden provided a colourful account of these proceedings in 1682:

> Mr. Mayor, with his Trayn of Attendants, marches in order to the Borough or Town Hall, where all being placed in order, the Sarjent makes 3 Oyes or proclamations that the Grand and unparalleled solemnity of the Gild Merchant is now to be manifested

All this was followed at a feast by much 'good liquor . . . All store of Pipes and Spanish Tobacco, drenched well with healths in Spanish Wine' and 'the best wine or Sack as the cellar will afford', whilst elegantly dressed posters stationed 'one at the foregate, another at the back-gate' ensured that only 'persons of gentry or credit' were admitted.[9]

The records of council proceedings are preserved in the town's celebrated *White Book* which contains the Corporation minutes for over 150 years from 1608.[10] Like all such documents before and since, the *White Book* is full of references to matters of finance and money. In 1609 Thomas Wall was informed that the repayment time for his loan of the 'Townes Money' would only be extended if he could provide additional security, and in 1683 the council recorded with satisfaction its income from the town's fairs: 'The Cleare Toll of ye last sumer faire amounts to £12 10s. 0d. The Cleare Toll of ye Winter Faire amounts to £7 10s. 0d.'.[11] In 1650 the town council became in effect its own landlord by purchasing the ancient rental of the manor from the King, with tenants on the town's lands agreeing to pay five years' rents into a fund to enable it to do so.[12]

The *White Book* contains many references to the comings and goings of council members. In 1698 William Worden gave £10 to the council on his retirement in contribution towards the purchase of a new ceremonial mace, in 1712 Thomas Gradwell resigned, worn down by his 'many yeares violently afflicted with the Gout', and John Kellett was dismissed in 1676 for not attending a meeting for two years and 'Now gone into Virginia or some foreign parts'.[13]

Occasionally the social habits of the townsfolk came under scrutiny. In the puritanical atmosphere prevailing in the first half of the seven-teenth century, measures enforcing the sabbath and restricting the open-ing hours of alehouses were enacted. An order of 1612 abolished the town's traditional Easter banquet, at which the bailiffs 'to their great and excessive charge', had provided: 'Wine, Beare, Breade, Cheese, Ayle, and other banckettinge stuffe and provision, as well ffor the Maior and his Breth-ren the comon counsell and all other ffree Burgesses, as also ffor all Strangeres, Passengeres, and neighbours . . . ' Not surprisingly

> the concourse and assemblie of people att the same times did growe greate, verie turbilente, and unrulie, tending (not onelie) to the breacke of his Ma'ties peace (but alsoe) divers others inconvenience whereof verie likelie to ensue, to the greate prejudice of the whole Corporation and the peaceable government thereof.

In future the Bailiffs were to pay a commensurate sum towards the stipend of the town's schoolmaster.[14]

A century later a new vice acquired by the Prestonians was arousing concern: 'Smoaking and taking Tobacco in the streets, Back Weends and Lanes' of the town. Since several premises had been 'unhappily sett on ffire and consumed to the great hazards and danger of the whole Towne', the practice was henceforth to be banned:

> in any the houses, or shopps within this Borough, wherein is any corne, hay, straw, turves, wood, chips, shavings, fflax, towe, hemp, or any combustible matter, or upon any house during the time that they are building, repairing, thatching, or slating the same

with a penalty for so doing of 5 shillings.[15]

The Four and Twenty

Records of the Preston Parish Vestry, 'the four and twenty' are preserved from January 1645, and the accounts from 1749. Comprising '8 men of Preston towne, 8 men of the Upper end of the parish, 8 men of ye lower-end of the parish', this body had responsibility

Preston's new Town Hall 1867, a lithograph by Armitage and Ibbetson. The tower, with its large clock faces, occupied the corner of Cheapside and Church Street, and was a much-loved local landmark. It bore witness to the zenith of the town's civic pride and belief in 'Preston's progress through its Guild'. The demolition of this building in the early 1960s and its replacement with an undistinguished office block marked, by contrast, the nadir of Preston's post-war redevelopment. Such splendid structures simply cannot be replaced.

for the church's fabric and finances, and occasionally tried to exercise power over the vicar. Damaged during fighting in the town during the Civil War and neglected to a greater extent than usual at that time, the church fabric, and especially the windows, was ordered to be repaired in 1648. After the restoration of the monarchy it was reported that:

> The Church is foule, and uncomely, having not been whitened, washed, nor beautiful for a long time, to the shame of the inhabitants and parishioners, and their discredit among strangers or foreigners repairing on occasion to their church.[16]

The building was to be 'adorned and beautified' and the church wardens were to get the job done 'as well and cheap as they can with some good workman'. The steeple seems to have been the source of a great deal of trouble, with rain pouring in through the decayed lead flashing and rotting the roof timbers. Repairs were specified in April 1680, 'Wythall the wethercock to be placed handsomely in the Middle, and then the whole steeple pointed'.[17]

If the fabric of the church proved a major if often neglected problem, so that the entire roof collapsed in 1770, the adjacent graveyard fared little better. In 1646 it was reported that, 'The churchyard doth in most unchristianly manner lye waste and open being daily spoiled and abused by swyne, for wont of makinge upp the walles and ffences about the same'.[18] The influence of the 'four and twenty' and their connections with the town council and its court leet ensured the adequate punishment of such wrongdoers, and in October 1666 the owners of 26 pigs so apprehended were prosecuted.[19]

Yet it was not only weeds and grass that the herd was rummaging among

> Whereas thers many bones of the dead which lye scattered up and downe in the church, and church yard, which is looked upon as an undecent and uncomely thinge, and which 't were convenient yf they were from time to time gathered and laid together untill, as a full heap or number of them being gathered together, they might be conveniently buried

It was decided to build a charnel house, the 'sexton from time to time to gather the bones together and cart them into the charnel-house'.[20]

Preston Court Leet

In the records of the court leet are preserved some of the most fascinating insights into life in pre-industrial Preston. The court, presided over by the Mayor and its own officials, deliberated on a wide range of administrative and legal matters. A jury of burgesses brought items to the court's attention and participated in the deliberations.[21] The court also appointed a range of officers to put their decisions into effect; the viewers of flesh and fish, ale testers, herdsmen and pinders, and elected agents to keep an eye on their officers and to watch and supervise suspicious newcomers, poor 'fforeigners', and other 'enormities'.[22] In this respect the practice of the court fell short of its dignity, and its proceedings contain the court's repeated threats to prosecute those officers who were not carrying out its edicts to its satisfaction. Occasionally burgesses were presented for refusing to serve as jurors, 'To ye bad example of the ffree burgesses of this Towne', and as officers: 'Thomas Parr, who being duly appointed one of the Viewers of fflesh and ffish . . . did in a very obstinate and contemptuous Manner refuse to take upon him the Excucon of the said office'.[23]

A great deal of work fell to bailiffs whose handful of employees was clearly insufficient to affect the economic, social and public health administration of the town. Furthermore they had to undergo a severe initiation as part of the 'Boundary Riding' undertaken by the Mayor and Corporation. The highlight of this Shrove Tuesday procession around the town's boundary was the jumping of a pond in Marsh Lane, the Colt Hole, into which numbers of the dignitaries fell. The drunken crawl concluded with the whipping of the new bailiffs around the town's pumps. These proceedings having reached absurd levels, and the beating of the bailiffs having developed a clearly vicious streak, they seem to have been abandoned in the 1830s.[24]

In addition to administering the edicts of the court, and supervising Preston's economy, the bailiffs were responsible for the smooth running of farming operations on the burgesses' town lands. Additional duties imposed upon them from time to time included repair of footpaths, streets, wells, springs, the landing quay on the Ribble, and following the manoeuvres of the Civil War, repairs to the floor and windows of the Moot Hall. In 1657, for example, they were ordered to 'cause the ffish stones to be put in good repair before the 13th day of December . . . in paine of 6s. 4d.'. These were the stone benches in the market place on which fish were displayed for sale. Meat was sold from the butchers' stalls beside the Moot Hall, in the 'Shambles'.[25]

The bailiffs were also responsible for maintaining the town's ducking stool, located in a pit in the vicinity of Schleswig and Holstein Streets off Deepdale Road, and used for the punishment of gossips and those detected selling substandard bread and ale; the pillory in the market place; the town's lock-up or prison in the Moot Hall; and the stocks and rogues' post. As late as 1704 it was ordered that, 'The Bayliffes for wont of a Sufficient Ladder at the ducking stool' should provide one or be fined 13s. 4d. The stocks were located in the churchyard and were specially reserved for persons abusing the council, who could be imprisoned there for three days on a meagre bread and water diet with a fine of 6s. 8d. on their release. The whipping post was located in the market place, where flogging of both men and women was carried out.[26]

Accordingly the Great Court Leet of the 25th April 1656 ordered that:

Those persons hereunder named are comon and ordinary hedge

Breakers, and therefore for this offence to bee punished at Mr Mayor's pleasure, either by stockes or ye Rogue's Poste, and if that will not serve turne, that Mr Mayor will be pleased [to order] some more seveare Course for punishment as hee may conceive meete, viz – George Morry's children, George Worden's wife and children, auld Myre's wife, auld Sheppard's wife, James Wasle, George Wood's servants and 'prentices, Thomas Patricke sonne and daughter, John Weengreeve children, Roger Moss children.

George Werden, who at one time served as the town's scavenger, swineherd, sexton and beadle, was clearly overworked, and it is hardly surprising that his services were frequently found wanting:

George Werden is verie negligent in his dutie or office, and suffereth the markett place to continue most parte of the weeke uncleansed, often untill Ffriday in the afternoone, whereas hee aught to sweepe and cleanse the same everie Munday, which this summer tyme will bee verie noysome.

He was accordingly to 'discharge his dutie or be discharged of his place and punished'. In 1656 he was scapegoat once again:

George Werden is continued beidle and scavenger, is very negligent therein, and the Towne is full every day of Country poor, and the said office altogether neglected, to ye discredit of our towne and hindrance of our owne poore. Also . . . ye said George Werden is swyneard, also receiveinge wages for Both and performeinge neither.

The bailiffs were ordered to appoint a new swineherd from among the 'Idle persons' so that 'the townes revinue may not be vainely given'.[27]

The pinders, whose job was to supervise and round up stray animals, incarcerating them in the town pinfold on the marsh (now the site of the Wheatsheaf Inn, Water Lane), were also frequently prosecuted. In 1654 they were accused of hiring out the animals, particularly horses, which they had impounded.[28]

Even the great and good were not immune from prosecution. In 1720 Mr. Mayor (William Gradwell) was fined 3s. 4d., 'for annoying the back street by setting Tubbs and laying wood therein', and in October 'for laying a Midding in ye back Weend to ye annoyance of ye street'. In 1663 the burgesses court investigated the affairs of the 1662 Preston Guild; the mayor was fined £5 for refusing them access to the Guild Orders made that year, and the whereabouts of the £632 11s. 10d. income from the festival was probed. The high officials were required to present:

A particular account in writeing how in what manner they have disposed of ye said £600, and to what uses, yt soe the said Burgesses may be satisfied howe they have discharged ye trust they have undertaken on ye said Burgesses behalfes.[29]

No lapse on the part of the Borough's officers escaped the observant ratepayers. William Jolly, the town's clock tender and bell ringer, was summoned in 1691 'for not ringing eight and four cloke bell according to his duty'. The bells regulated trading on the market; between 8 and 9 a.m. the townspeople had first choice of goods for sale, and 'foreigners' had to wait until 9 a.m.[30] In October 1674 the surveyors of the highways were threatened with fines of £5 each for not repairing the way 'Betwixt Ye Almes houses at Churchgate end and ye Swillbroke, ye high ways in Ribleton Lane, ye Cawsye Rampier betwixt ye more brow and ye horse bridge leading to Caddiley, ye lane called Salter Lane, and ye high way called Ffishergate barrs and ye water side'.[31]

The economy and trade

A central function of this burgesses' court was to enforce their monopoly of the town's trade and to safeguard their rights on the town's lands. The court leet records thus reflect the continued operation of a large part of the provisions of the medieval *Custumal*. Burgesses were still required to take their oaths as prescribed and pay their dues on becoming freemen; they were to erect houses on their burgage plots and keep them in good order; and they were to enrol their apprentices in the correct manner. By 1656 William Bannaster had been prosecuted several times for not rebuilding his house, which he 'Did pretend . . . to have been ruined and burnt by the souldiers in their tymes of warr', and the shopkeepers continued to jostle for position on the pavements in front of their shops: 'John Cottam has in-croached in ye market place by erecting a bulke [a stall] before the shopp window . . . being 2 yrds and a halfe long and one yard broade'.[32]

'Foreigners' – particularly poor foreigners – were to be kept out of the

The old brickworks, Waverley Park, New Hall Lane c.1893. The rebuilding of the timber-framed medieval town in the seventeenth century produced a considerable demand for bricks. The Court Leet frequently prosecuted the brick-getters for leaving dangerous clay-pits unfilled along the road sides, and stipulated the dimensions of the Preston Brick: '10 inch longe, 5 inch broade, 2 and a half in thicknesse' (1685). As late as 1898 the town had 19 brickmakers.

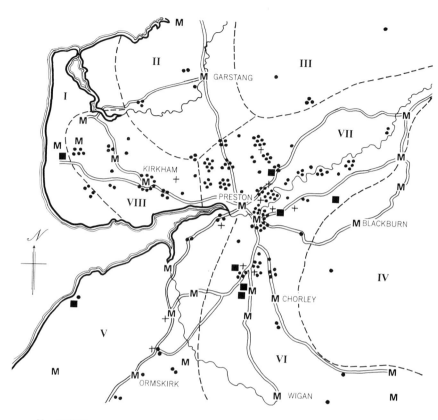

The market area of Preston c.1600 (after H. B. Rodgers, 1956). Preston's rising importance as a market centre reflected its market's position close to the intersection of a number of natural regions. Surpluses could best be exchanged between these local economies at Preston. Those of regions I–V were predominantly pastoral, whilst groups VI–VIII were better balanced with a strong arable component.

M   MARKET
■   HOMES OF PERSONS KNOWN TO HAVE BOUGHT OR SOLD IN PRESTON MARKET
+   STALLENGERS ON THE ROLLS OF 1582–1602
●   OUT-BURGESSES ON THE ROLLS OF 1542–1602
‒ ‒ ‒   BOUNDARIES OF AGRICULTURAL REGIONS
I   WEST FYLDE
II   NORTH FYLDE AND OVER-WYRE
III   BOWLAND FELLS
IV   ROSSENDALE UPLAND
V   SOUTH-WEST LANCASHIRE
VI   CENTRAL LANCASHIRE
VII   RIBBLE VALLEY
VIII   CENTRAL FYLDE

town at all costs, and to detect poor newcomers the court appointed 'Houselookers' to visit premises, seek them out, and evict them from the town. Many local people, however, seem to have been quite prepared to take such people in. In April 1654 a long list of townspeople, including several of its leading citizens, was prosecuted:

Robert Gregson and his wife and children harboured by Mr. William Bannester, Thomas Anderton and his wife and children harboured by

James Wall, John Shorte and his wife and
children harboured by Sir Richard
Houghton . . . Grace Clough and her boy
harboured by Sarah Kendall.[33]

Those taking in such people were to inform
the town's Bell-man at once or face a very
large fine of 40s. The frequency of the houselookers' rounds was increased in 1663 when
Parliament reduced to forty days the length of
time newcomers had to reside before they
could no longer be legally removed, 'and
thereby become settled by lawe in ye towne,
and ye towne be bound to maintain them'.[34]
Poor and idle persons could be sent to the
House of Correction, which stood on a part of
the site of the ancient friary off Marsh Lane.
When this proved inadequate in 1674 a workhouse was established ('To keepe them from
wandering and begging') on the corner of
Bolton's Court and Avenham Lane. This was
literally a place where people were made to
work, producing woollen yarn.[35]

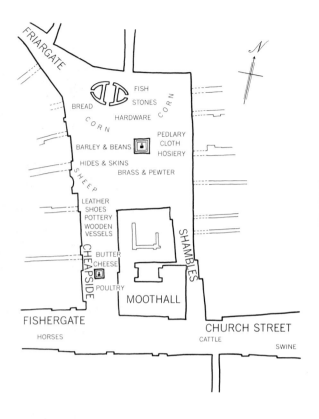

Preston market place in the late seventeenth century.

Once actively resident, newcomers could
not so easily be removed, and proved a further
threat as rivals for the town's trade. Rather
than something to be expanded, trade was
perceived as very finite, so that the more
participants in a trade merely reduced the share for all. Suitable
newcomers could progress from their lowly initial status of 'inmates' and
attain a measure of legal acceptance by paying the required fee to become
'Stallengers', enabling them to trade but not partake in the other
advantages that the burgesses enjoyed. For access to these they had to be
admitted onto the Guild Rolls of the Preston Guild Merchant, and these
contain many examples of people who followed this tortuous process of
social acceptance to become valued citizens.

There was clearly great scope for tradesmen to evade these regulations,
and the court over the years prosecuted large numbers of workmen in all
trades: 'Hugh Rimmer doth entertain in his house . . . one Henry
Gradwell . . . joiner by trade, he not being a ffreeman of this
Incorporacon'; Robert Brindle 'doth make and sell Mault [malt for beer]
within this Towne Contrary to the 11th Order of Mr Catterall's Guild';
'Ellis Makeinge for exercising ye trade of A gardiner within this towne,
not being a ffreeman, to pay 40s.'; and 'Thomas Hoghton, strong-
waterman [maker of spirits], not being a ffreeman of this towne, we do
therefore order to remove forthwith, otherwise to pay ye sume of £10'.
Traders from adjoining towns had to be guarded against; in 1669 Thomas

The fish market, from the corner of Market St., and Earl St. c.1930. Barrett's directory of 1901 lists three fish curers, 56 fish mongers, seven fish salesmen, five oyster dealers and no fewer than 129 fish and chip shops in the town. The market was re-paved, roofed and provided with artificial light in the 1920s.

Cheese show on the covered market 1932. Cheese has long been an important dairy product from the rich agricultural lands around the town and especially on the Fylde. By the 1930s fairs were held on the last Tuesday of each month and competition between family producers was intense. The town's greatest reformer, Joseph Livesey, made his fortune by selling cheese. During the eighteenth century Preston cheeses were exported as far as the West Indian colonies.

Holme of Euxton was fined for selling saddles, and Thomas Cooper of Leyland for selling his ironmongery. In 1658 William Threlfall and others had apparently cornered the market in wooden vessels and buckets.[36]

Of particular interest are such prosecutions concerning the developing textile industry, which was beginning to develop a central role in the regional economy. In 1662 John Greenwood was threatened with a fine of 40s. for allowing 'forreiners to buy and sell and cut cloath in his house'.

The second-hand clothes market c.1906. It was situated on the former fish market, and overlooked by the Farmers Arms *on the corner of Orchard St. and Market St.*

Preston's covered market following its collapse on 6th August 1870. Anthony Hewitson wrote that 'The sight . . . was indeed chaotic'.

The old Black Bull, Friargate c.1970. Preston was a town of inns and beer shops. During the town's puritan phase in the first half of the seventeenth century, opening hours were reduced and night time raids were frequently launched to detect illicit drinking and gambling. During the late eighteenth century the Court Leet took swift action to overcome the harmful moral effects of billiard playing and Preston's single table was ordered to be removed from the town under threat of dire consequences.

Thomas Abbott and his brother were accused of taking in cloth to dye, to the detriment of burgesses, without paying their share of rates ('Scott and Lott'): 'The consequence will be to the ruininge of some famalies, both wife and children . . . our neighbours whose livily hood depend thereon'.[37]

The court also strove to preserve the rights of the consumer. Prestonians had the first choice of goods for sale and efforts were made to drive inferior goods out of the market. Leather goods seem to have come under close scrutiny by the 'Searcher of Leather', particularly those from rival tanners at Cuerdale and Euxton. However in 1685:

> John Hodgkinson, currier and John Hall, Shoomaker, being appoynted Searchers and Sealers of Lether for this Corporacon, doth not discharge their duty in their place, but suffereth shoos to be sold in ye Markett, by Edward Sumpner, that are made up with horse lether.[38]

A close eye was also kept on the size of bricks. Since bricklayers were paid by the number of courses of bricks they laid there were constant endeavours to make them too thin so as to increase the number of courses and therefore the price of the work. In 1685 bricks had to be '10 Inch longe, 5 inch broade, 2 and a half in thicknesse'. In 1653 Roger Woodroofe was accused of illegally exporting one thousand bricks from the town by boat.[39]

The actual sale of goods was also closely regulated. To combat the bidding up and increase of prices it was forbidden for a trader to sell goods which he had bought on the same day. This crime was known as 'Fore Stalling', and like many of these medieval practices has given a word to the English language. In 1663 Henry Blackburne 'Did in open Markett by off John Loxam a veale calfe for the price of 7s. and imediately after upon ye same day did againe sell ye same calfe to Edward Oram, butcher, for 8s.', and Henry Wildinge was similarly prosecuted for buying two sheep within four miles of the town and selling them the same day on the market. Richard Brookfield of North Meols was accused of twice 'forestalling our Markett by buying upp Salmon fish', and John Mosse of forestalling 'a loade of cockles'.[40]

The weight and standard of the Prestonians' principal foodstuffs (bread and ale) was continually checked. The quality of beer was supervised by the 'Alefounders' whose agreeable task it was to visit the beershops and alehouses to sample the quantity and quality of the beer.

In 1667 William Blacoe was fined 6s. 8d. 'for refuseing ye Alefounders a tast of his Ale and abuseing them with bad words', whilst Richard Woods was fined the same amount 'for denying to fill ye townes gallon with Ale for 6d'. He thus seems to have been giving short measure for his sixpennyworth.[41]

Millers' weights were also frequently checked:

> Wee find and present all such persons as have any Weights or Measures and all owners of Milnes [corn mills] shall bring their weights, measures and maulture dishes [measuring dishes] before Mr. Maior or his officers, to bee approved and sealed.

Such theft seems to have been quite widespread, and at the court of October 23rd 1674 it was reported that:

> These Milnrs as transgressors against ye law in takeing unreasonable toll or maulter of Corne, therefore to be punished accordingly – Willm Holme miller to Mrs Eliz Worden, George Bennet miller to Mr John Langton, Adam Morris at Avenham millne, Rich – miller at ye Marsh milne.[42]

Over and above these activities the mayor, bailiffs and burgesses had the power to fix the price of these key commodities through the 'Assize of Bread and Ale', a right confirmed in the charter of Elizabeth I in 1566. The court leet tried to ensure that such prices were kept. Well into the late eighteenth century prices were regulated, and the 'bread riot' seems to have been a common response to bakers trying to raise the price of bread through artificial shortages.

In short, therefore, the townspeople – through the court leet – had considerable power to influence the economic conditions of their town, and although attitudes towards commerce are very different today, the system did enshrine a number of important safeguards for all concerned. Nevertheless, Preston was still, six hundred years after its early charters, the burgesses' town.

—— *Farming operations* ——

Farming remained of great importance to the town and evidence of its social and economic role can be found everywhere in the Court Leet records.

Many fieldstrips remained unenclosed by their owners, for as late as 1691 John Hatch was prosecuted in the Court Leet:

> for plowing up A Land Mark or bocke [Balk: an unploughed strip in an open field used as a landmark] of land between him and James Drinkwater, lying to the north side of the towne, Mawdlands, in the

sum of thirteen shillings and fourpence, if not laid too again before the first of March next.

The grazing of animals required the fencing of strips to avoid straying and damage to standing crops. This needed to be done before ploughing: 'Ye pinders give notice to all ye inhabitants of This Towne that they make their Gardens hedges and Ringe yards before the 5th of March or pay 06s. 8d.'. In 1679 the blacksmith John Baly was fined 13s. 4d. 'for lettinge his fence to lye Downe into a comon feild called Watter Willowes, to the great loss to the occupiers in their corne'.[43]

The townfields, split into individually owned and scattered parcels of strips and fields, thus continued to be farmed from the barns and small farmyards located behind the houses on the narrow burgage plots which fringed Church Street, Fishergate and Friargate. In the adjoining manors agriculture could be made more efficient by the consolidation of holdings into distinct farms, something that was not possible given Preston's fragmented system of landholding based on the burgage plots. The movement of animals to and from distant holdings and the common grazings on the moor and marsh, along the town's thoroughfares, led to many difficulties into which the court struggled to introduce some measure of order.

Very detailed rules were drawn up to manage the common grazings on the moor and marsh, under the management of the bailiffs, pinders and herdsmen. In 1654 the bailiffs were ordered to provide a gate able 'to shutt of itt selfe', for the way to the North Moor, 'To keepe the cattell on the moore, which doe frequentlie breake downe to the marsh, and into mens grounds when the yate is thrown open'. The next year it was decreed that 'Noe Inhabitants within this Towne shall put down their cattle to the Marsh before sixe of ye clock in the morninge, but shall keep them till the Heardsman be ready to receive them'. Geese also caused problems on the commons, and Alex Swansey was fined for rescuing several flocks from the pinder whilst *en route* to the pound.[44] The movement of pigs was entrusted to a swineherd whose ill-paid but difficult job was to move the townspeople's herds daily from the individual town houses to the moor:

> There is a greate anoyance in this towne by swyne both in mens corne and grass, and wee conceive it is occasioned partly by the carelessness of the Inhabitants of this towne, in that they doe not help to bringe their Swyne towards the more, butt leteth them range up and downe the streets; but especially the swynheard comes soe unconstantly and carelessly that the people can scarse have tyme to bring them into the streets, and being past will retorne no more for the preventinge whereof wee present and think fitt that the bailiffs shall cause the said swinsord to blowe his horne from the church gate bars to the fishergate bars [and 'along to the Market Place'] and then retorne back and take the swyne along.[45]

The court also went to considerable lengths to conserve the local 'environment'. When the Peel Moor (the district of the 'Canary Islands' east of Deepdale Road) had been rendered 'verie dangerous both for man and beast' by the brick-clay diggers, their pits were ordered to be filled in 'by people from everie house within this towne . . . when the weather may be convenient for the same'. The court issued a regular stream of orders concerning the repair of roads, cutting of hedges, filling of pits, restoration of ancient footpaths, bridges and platts (footbridges). For example, when the bridge over the Swill Brook was 'gone to decay and ruinated by ye late Inundacon of watters' it was ordered to be repaired and the township of Fishwick was to pay half: if the Fishwickers refused to pay they were to be prosecuted. The interests of the town's Ribble fishery were carefully preserved, the size of fishermen's nets regulated, the shore of the river watched for subtle signs of changes in its course, and the activities of William Ffarington's tenants on the Penwortham shore suspiciously scrutinised.[46]

Farm labourers c.1890. The rich farmlands of the Fylde and west Lancashire have always made an important contribution to Preston's prosperity.

On the moor to the north of the town care was taken to ensure that the drainage ditches were kept clear. The Moor Brook, flowing due west from Deepdale, caused many problems, particularly in the dip near the later English Martyrs' Church on Garstang Road: 'Ye now Bailiffes of this Towne shall stake and wind at ye North Moor Yate, and keep ye brooke in its course which breaks forth and spoils ye high way'. Encroachment on these commons or 'town waste' was firmly resisted.[47]

The court records contain many injunctions for the care of the marsh, a fragile habitat particularly vulnerable to flooding and over-grazing. To prevent erosion and encourage the growth of grass, a series of cauls (embankments) was maintained along the riverside and animals were carefully controlled and supervised by the appointed herders. Activity around the watermill on the edge of the marsh (to the south of Water Lane between Strand Road and St. Mark's Road) was a constant source of anxiety in the 1650s, and Edmund Werdun, the occupant, was frequently summoned in connection with problems with the mill dam and its mill race. Related milling processes such as winnowing and grain drying also caused problems and resulted in further summonses. The pasture was actively encouraged by the court, for in 1679 the pinders were ordered to 'Rake and gather the sticks and wreck from of ye marsh and burn ye same, and spread ye ashes'. The right to graze their animals on the marsh (which seems to have been much preferred to the more distant moor which may have been best suited to cattle) was clearly a valued asset, especially 'To the poorer sorte of ffree Burgesses of this towne'.[48]

Public health?

In seventeenth-century Preston neither effective sanitation nor an adequate water supply was available. Human and animal waste from the pig and cattle pens to the rear of most houses ultimately found itself heaped in the streets to be picked over by wandering animals until someone saw fit to remove it. Water was supplied from a small number of frequently dirty draw wells sunk into the underlying strata. The records of the court leet reveal the constant struggle required to ensure the removal of at least the worst of these middens and obstacles in the streets, and the cleaning of the town's wells.

In 1653 the court was informed that 'Henry Bullow's wife and children, Ellen Alpert and Margaret Welshman doe frequently throw Garbidge in St. Johns Weind, which is a great annoyance to men's Cattell and endangereth the poysoninge of them'. A common practice was to deposit middens beyond the town barrs on either end of Church Street and Fishergate, near the top of Manchester Road and Mount Street respectively. In 1654 a number of prominent citizens were among those ordered to:

> Remove theire middings wch lye without Ffishergate barres before the tenth day of May next, in paine of everie of them 6s. 8d. They nor anie of them shall hereafter lay anie more middings or dunghills there, but on the backside of theire owne barnes.

Anne Ingham, ordered to remove her midden in Church Street in 1653, was still being threatened with dire consequences seven years later.[49]

The records suggest that even the more considerate townspeople, those prepared to sweep the street in front of their houses, usually swept it into heaps in front of someone else's, or left it in the rainwater channels or open drains which comprised the town's drainage system, causing, 'A greate annoyance and disparigment to the governmente of this towne, which formerly have been taken much notice of and comended for the sweete and cleane keepinge of our streets'. Such heaps had subsequently to be removed within three days in lieu of a 15s. fine.[50]

The disposal of dead animals posed problems, and the open street seems to have been a popular remedy. In 1654 complaint was made 'Of carryon, dead swyne, doggs, and other noysome filthie carryon beinge throwne in St. Johns Weend and other Weends and backe lanes belonginge to this towne'. John Greenalgh, blacksmith, and Hugh Gurnall were fined 3s. 4d. each in 1699 'for layeing a dead horse in Alderman Sudell's ditch, in the South Meadow Lane, neare adjoineing to the Publick Road, to the great Annoyance thereof', and in 1685 James Cowp, having 'caused his horse or maire to be ffleaed [flayed] in ye open street', was fined 10s. When Henry Howarth and Thomas Wiggons were accused of hanging dogs and leaving them, unburied, in the lane leading

Marsh, 'They replyed that they would doe it, and if they pleased they would hang them upon ye pinfold rails'.[51]

The old Shambles (roughly between Crystal House and the Miller Arcade on Church Street) was the centre of the town's butchery trade, and seems to have been a particularly dirty quarter. Despite rules to the contrary animals were frequently slaughtered on the premises, leading the court to complain that 'There is A grete and noysome abuse in this Towne by reason of butchers throwing blood, ropps [intestines], and other garbage in the streetes, which is an insufferable annoyance'. In 1721 28 butchers were threatened with fines of 40s. if this practice should continue, and in 1735 Henry Robinson was fined 20s. 'for burning cow claws [hooves] in or near the public streets . . . thereby raising and occasioning a fulsome and offensive smell'. In 1705 William Lorimer was fined 6s. 8d. 'for suffering his meat to corrupt in his shop in the Shambles, being a nuisance to the neighbourhood'.[52]

Despite these alfresco activities a barrel of beef which had broken open and been abandoned by its owners in 'ffryergate' in 1658, 'part of which said Beife was carried upp and downe the streete by doggs and swine, to ye great greefe of the neighborringe Inhabitants', was deemed fit to be given to 'ye poore Inhabitants of this Burrough'.[53]

Rubbish and middens were not the only terrors to be met with in the narrow and unlit streets of Preston, particularly on dark nights. Roaming animals, pigs and savage dogs, were a fairly continuous problem. In 1665 Mr. Joseph Boulton was fined 40s. for his abusive language in refusing to muzzle his 'most insufferable dogg', and John Singleton was fined 13s. 4d. 'for suffring his dogg, being unmusselled to byte Elizabeth ye wife of Thomas Walmesley Butcher, and Jane Walmsley.[54]

Many homes seem to have kept a pig, and these often caused trouble scavenging among the street middens. To restrain them owners were ordered to have them ringed through the snout. Many people refused, 'There is a greate abuse in this Towne by reason of Swyne pullinge mens sacks in peeces, on the markett day, whereof the countery [people] doth much complayne'. The porcine population of Preston, however, often seems to have given as good as it got. George Gregson's wife 'doth keepe an unruly and unlawful sowe, and suffers her to goe abroad in ye streets . . . [which] hath pulled sevrall sackes in ye corne market to pieces'; whilst Luke Greenfield's sow whilst perambulating the streets 'hath pulled ye meat from ye shopp boards of Butchers in ye Shambells, and spoyled their meate'.[55]

Obstacles in the street also proved a threat to life and limb. Many houses in Preston had cellars, and where the entrances were unfenced these posed a danger, especially at night. In 1665 Elizabeth Woodhouse was prosecuted for taking up the pavement in front of her house and digging a saw pit. Large holes also resulted from the sporadic activities of sand diggers and brick-clay getters along the road leading out from the town bars. There was also a danger of walking into articles left in the street: Nicholas Watson was fined 6s. 8d. 'for laying sevrall Timber trees and other wood before his dore in ye ffryergate' causing a great nuisance to the burgesses, '[and] ye hazard of their lives and limbs by falling over ye same in ye night time'.[56] In 1759 the stones for the Penwortham bridge were found to be left lying in the street.

Great efforts were made to ensure that landholders kept their hedges cut: 'All owners of ground to the Maudland land, from Spitle morse to the marsh, may cutt downe their hedges, a man haveing his eye strucke forth within this tenne days'. Much more serious was the fear of fire, and in 1696 William Blackledge's wife was severely fined 'for carrying fire in a paire of tongues, in open street, in danger of fireing the Towne'.[57]

The town's water supply had changed little from medieval times, and Preston's three thousand or so inhabitants drew their supplies from 'Ye minspit well, ye goose well and ye foure draw wells within this town'. Of these the oldest was probably that situated at the bottom of Main Sprit Weind. This water supply had clearly become inadequate by the middle of the seventeenth century, particularly in the poorer parts of the town. In May 1655 the court was informed that 'There is a greate need of sweet water att the Almshouses which is much to the prejudice of the manie poore famalys thereabout'.[58]

The tactful inhabitants of Friargate made a successful plea the following year:

> There are maine [many] complaints of ye Inhabitants in the Lower end of the Ffryergate for want of water, having none but of a great distance or upon leave, which is burthensome and uncertaine, and they being a people to their power as readie to observe and keepe all commands which come from ye Maior and Councill as their fellow inhabitants which have received ye like favour and libertie, not repininge thereat but rejoycinge, onely hopeinge and prayine they may enjoy some priviledge where ye Maior and Councell shall think fittinge and at ye most easiest charge.[59]

The bailiffs, who had frequently to be threatened to make them maintain the existing wells, were ordered to clean and repair 'minspitt well and Goosewell 4 tymes in the year' on pain of a fine of 6s. 8d. each. Occasionally the wells were used by townspeople for washing their produce, thus polluting the water. In 1672 Ellis Makin was accused of washing carrots in the Sike trough in the Avenham fields, and Anne Haworth and others of washing puddings there. In 1697 James Clayton and his wife used the cattle troughs for washing dyed yarn. John Threlfall was fined 20s. in 1717 for 'steeping willows and letting his ducks swim' in a well in Church Street.[60]

In 1729 Robert Abbott and Thomas Kellett proposed a piped system to pump water from Syke Hill to a cistern in the market place and thence to a network of pipes throughout the town. In 1732 Robert Abbott was accordingly summoned for not repairing the 'breaches' in the streets, and again in 1737 when very cold weather burst the pipes. This system evidently proved serviceable if limited, for in 1771 the court threatened

Mr. Thomas Addison, 'for having fixed a water pipe in that part of his house which stands in the Mitre yard, whereby his Majesty's subjects passing and repassing through the Mitre yard are greatly annoyed by the water in windy weather being blown in their faces'.[61]

—— *Civil disputes: fighting* ——

An important function of the court leet was to settle personal disputes among Prestonians. By punishing one or other of the protagonists, and sometimes both, it endeavoured to ensure a modicum of acceptable social behaviour.

In the small town, with its overcrowded and appalling housing conditions, the townspeople can have enjoyed little privacy and even their most intimate affairs must frequently have been common knowledge and open to public scrutiny. 'Eaves-dropping' (standing in the eaves-drop – the space between an overhanging thatch roof and the wall of a house – to listen to the conversations within) and 'hearkening' (listening to other people's conversations) were considered to be quite serious offences. In April 1661 evidence was given that:

> Thomas Silcoke is an Eve dropp, commonly called Eseing Dropps, and stands under mens windows lisoning and carrieing stories betwixt neighbour and neighbour, to the great disquietnes of neighbours and to the evell example of others, therefore to pay, xiijs. iiijd. [13s. 4d].

In 1678 Tildesley Atkinson and Mary Bateson were each fined 6s. 8d., 'for being eseing droppers under James Halls window'. Occasionally their victims resorted to more direct action; in 1654 William Dobson was fined 1s. 6d. 'for a chamber pott emptied and throwne out of his window', presumably onto Margaret Berchall who was fined a similar amount for 'herkinge' at his window.[62]

The wide-ranging town byelaws ensured a frequently torrid time for the officers who had to ensure their implementation, and the carrying out of the court edicts. In 1669 Elizabeth Woodhouse was fined 6s. 8d. for 'striking and abuseing' Thomas Beckonsall, the town Beadle, whilst in 1684 Mr. Roger Bannester, gentleman, assaulted Roger Walshman, one of the town's serjeants, 'In ye execution of his office, by throwing stones at him and knocking him downe and wounding him in ye head, to the hazard of his life'. In 1669 John Preston, gentleman, was fined 6s. 8d. for assaulting the Postmaster, William Worden. Henry Gradwell was fined a similar amount for cursing and swearing at the Mayor and Corporation, 'To the evell Example of others to offend in the like if not prevented'.[63]

The appearance of contrition before the court, and the acceptance of its prerogative, could assist the accused. In 1697 John Shaw, miller at the Windmill which stood close by the site of the present Adelphi Hotel at the end of Friargate, was able to avoid prosecution for grinding corn on the Sabbath by 'Appearing and makeing a Submission'. By contrast Henry Graystocke arraigned for unlawfully keeping his geese and pigs on the marsh – not a particularly serious offence – was fined a massive 40s. for subsequently 'Saying he neither cared for ye jury nor the presentments'.[64]

Women frequently appeared before the court. In 1655 it was stated that 'the wife of William Walmesley doth annoy Thomas Bonny by throwinge his cloaths from off his hedge'. Ellen Haworth was fined 2s. 6d. and threatened with the bridle (a device fixed over a woman's head to prevent her speaking!) for 'Scowleinge and abuseing Mary, the wife of John Higham, with verry uncivell Language, to the bad example of others'. Anne, the wife of Matthew Dickson, 'Who by Informacon of Jennett, the wife of John Preesall, declareth that the said Anne swore two oathes by God', was fined 6s. 4d.[65]

Disputes and fighting occasionally occurred in the Parish Church, perhaps reflecting a religious basis to party feeling in the town. In May 1655 John Salter and John Bolton were ordered to pay 2s. 6d. each, 'for makinge a tusle in the church', whilst in 1657 James Parcevall was fined 1s. 3d. for abusing and attacking William Clerkson whilst at church.[66] When such altercations and slanging matches ran to violence, ladies were also prominent among the participants. Mary Shakeshaft was fined 2s. 6d. for fighting with Margrett Patricke, and the latter 5s. for 'drawing blood of Mary'. In 1657 Margaret Watson was also fined a crown when, during an argument with Richard Tyssinge, she 'struck at him with a board, and did hit him on ye face, and thereof did drawe blood'. By contrast Robert Loxam was fined only 3s. 4d. for 'Breakeing Ellen Gregsons head'. A very large fine of £3 6s. 8d. was imposed on John Smith for a savage attack deemed 'A gross abuse . . . by striking a boy, servant unto Thomas Scholes, with a bunch of keyes, and thereby did breake three of his teethe'.[67]

The part played by drink in these proceedings is open to conjecture, though we do know that in 1653 'Evan Rogerson being drunck did abuse and draw blood upon the bodie of Robert Ingham, and wee doe therefore amerce him in 5 shillings. And wee leave ye punishment of his drunkenness to Mr. Maior'.[68]

Occasionally whole families became involved, as in 1670 when William Charnocke senior, William Charnocke junior, Mary Charnocke and Elizabeth Seddons were ordered to pay 3s. 4d. each for 'fighting and ffliteing [brawling] each other'.[69] Much more serious were the violent disputes involving members of one of the town's leading families, the Mortes, in 1653–4, perhaps related to the sequestration of their estate by parliament in 1651. Seth Morte, son of Adam Morte, the 'Gentleman Mayor of Preston' killed defending the town against the Parliament-arians in 1643, was fined 5s. in 1653 for assaulting William Brewer. He and his brother, Richard, were also each fined 2s. 6d. for fighting each other. On November 2nd he was bound over to appear at the next Court Leet 'and in the meane tyme to keepe the peace of the Commonwealth', on two sureties of £10. These were lost, for despite being publicly summoned to the next session he failed to turn up, and had again been involved in a further breach of the peace with his brother Richard. His other brother, Edward Morte, a grocer, who had similarly been bound over in November 1653, had attacked Alexander Breres in Eaves Lane, Chorley, on the 30th January 1654 'And with his Rapier drawne pursued the said Breres, who leapt off his mare and fled whereupon the said Edwarde Morte stabbed his Rapier into the bodie of the said mare, whereof she presentlyie dyed'. His two sureties of £20 each, Richard Johnson and Henry Kilshaw accordingly lost their money when he also failed to turn up at the Court Leet.[70]

CHAPTER SEVEN

The Civil War

THE late 1630s and early 1640s was a momentous period in English history. A long-standing dispute between the monarchy and parliament over who should have the last word in the government of the country finally spilled over into a turbulent decade of civil war. By the late spring of 1642 disturbing rumours were reaching London of events even in distant Lancashire, amongst them, 'A great number of papists to the vallew of 3 hundred, with swords by their sides, waiting as it seems for more company', on a 'Great plain' seven miles from Lancaster.[1]

Preston, because of its position on the Scottish road and the route into Yorkshire and eastern England, was destined to play a colourful and leading role in the Civil War. At the centre of Catholic Lancashire, as an important centre for the administration of the county and, under the patronage of the Earls of Derby, the town was a rising centre for the local gentry and aristocracy and an obvious royalist stronghold. Indeed, the events of the Civil War years were to confirm and extend the ascendancy of the Derby family in Preston. Yet, equally, the borough council's desire for greater independence in the affairs of the town was also strengthened, and the conflict between these two forces was to be a prominent feature of the political life of the town thereafter. If the country gentry led by Lord Derby and his lieutenants the Hoghtons and Faringtons were to be active supporters of the King, then a policy of at least tacit approval of the parliamentarian cause was likely to prove attractive to Preston Corporation.

The broad religious divisions of the county translated themselves into political zones during the Civil War, for in Lancashire religion was a dominant factor in deciding people's allegiances. The royalist cause was strongest in the old Catholic areas, and in Amounderness 90% of the royalist gentry were Catholic, whilst the parliamentarian cause was much the strongest around the Puritan centres of Bolton and Manchester. Many of the prominent gentlemen of the Preston area took an active part in the early stages of the war, including the Hoghtons and the Faringtons, yet a majority of people tried hard to retain a neutral stance and refused to become involved actively on either side. The true inclinations of the

Ceremonial arch, Fishergate Hill 1885. The arch was erected to celebrate the Prince of Wales' visit to Preston on July 16 1885, en route to the Albert Edward Dock named after him.

The reception of King George V and Queen Mary at the Town Hall 1913. The following year, crowds gathered here for the declaration of the First World War.

Ceremonial arch, Fishergate, 1902 Guild. 'Stanley for Ever' might well be the motto of the great Stanley Interest in Preston. The Earls of Derby continue to have close links with the town, a connection established before the Civil War, and strengthened in 1736 when the Preston Stanleys – distant kinsmen of the Earls – inherited the title. Patten House, which stood opposite Grimshaw Street on Church Street, became an important family home. Although the building was demolished in the early nineteenth century, the link is maintained in the adjacent Derby Street.

townspeople of Preston are difficult to trace, especially since many later proved adept at changing sides whenever convenient. As elsewhere, although the majority of the people in Preston seem to have favoured the King's cause, only a relatively small proportion of them appear to have been particularly committed. Despite the strength of Catholic sympathies, especially in the country district around the town, the established Church had made progress particularly amongst Preston's leading citizens. Accordingly the parliamentarian cause was well represented in the Corporation, and, significantly, the town's M.P.s were parliamentarians. Thus it would appear that the parliamentarians enjoyed greater support among the town's leading families and the Corporation than it did in the town generally, and in turn among the townspeople than in the country districts outside. Yet although the town was predominantly royalist in outlook, whichever party found itself in control of Preston could muster at least some active support.

The summer of 1642 was a period of increasing tension as the supporters of both parties vied for position locally, and as rumours of approaching armies spread wildly throughout the county. On 20th June James, Lord Strange, shortly to succeed his father as 7th Earl of Derby, called a great meeting on Preston Moor to hear the King's case against parliament and to demonstrate support for him. The local parliamentarian leaders Alexander Rigby and Richard Shuttleworth were unable to prevent the meeting being held, but they were able to address their own supporters nearby. Whilst they remonstrated with the future Earl, most of the crowd, estimated by one observer at twenty thousand but probably far fewer, dwindled away leaving a remnant of about 750 committed individuals whose support was broadly split between the two parties.

The High Sheriff of Lancashire and his supporters rode up and down the moor crying 'for the King, for the King', while the rest, as Rigby later reported,

> staying with us we proceeded and declared unto them, that we and others were sent down [by parliament] . . . for the preservation of the peace of this county, and that both Houses, and ourselves in particular, ever had done and ever would doe, all things tending to the safety, honour, and peace of the King's person, and his kingdomes . . . and wished them not to divide between the King and parliament, but to stand for the King and parliament, whereupon with a general acclamation they prayed for the King and parliament.

During these distractions William Farington's steward, William Sumner, was able to spirit away the town's gunpowder magazine and to secure it for the royalists.[2]

In the following month Preston became an important centre of royalist activity. The King's supporters strove:

> to raise up what Souldiery they could and to Garrison such Townes in the County as were eminent and thorow roads as Preston, Wiggan and Warrington. Warrington they maide walled round about making stronger gates and fortifications. Preston and Wiggan they did not make so strong only some Engines maide of tymber was placed in the streets of eyther towne to keep horses out.[3]

The town was thrown into panic when a 'false messenger' reported that a parliamentarian army some twenty thousand strong was on its way. Sir Gilbert Hoghton responded to the threat by sending to 'all his tenants, and commanded them, that they should be readie upon an howers warning, and set a stronge watch about his house'. The parliamentarian reporter of these events concluded with evident satisfaction, 'I thinke there was no brags in our towne for that day. Then they let honest Protestants go through the streets without scoffing at them, and calling them Round heads'.

Yet later in the same week, 'five men gave one Roger Haddock of Chorley very sore strokes and broke his head to the very skull', when he directed a parliamentarian messenger to Lord Derby's house. As the royalist forces mustered on the moor the streets of Preston were not safe for the King's opponents. 'We are beset with papists: I dare not go to the Moore, but my [brother] was there, and they told him he was a roundhead, and swore they would kill him. So he came from amongst them'. At the end of September actual hostilities opened with the royalist attempt to take Manchester.[4]

Coincidentally, the worsening political situation came just as Preston was preparing to celebrate its Guild. The celebrations of 1642 began on 29th August and were held in a town which had become almost an armed camp deep inside the royalist heartland of lowland Lancashire.

Accordingly the Guild ordnances included an order that:

> All inhabitants of the town should, within the space of 3 months, provide themselves with such sufficient arms or weapons for the defence of the town, and the preservation of the public peace, as might be deemed fit by the Mayor and Council, and with the same arms should be ready to assist the Mayor and officers of the Town, upon the ringing of a bell or other summons.

Townpeople failing to provide themselves with a halbert were to be fined 5s., with a musket 40s.[5]

The Council clearly intended that the town's militia should be kept under their own control and not become a part of the forces stationed in the town by the Earl of Derby and Sir Gilbert Hoghton. Early in July the Mayor, Edmund Werden, was believed to be anxious to arrest one of Sir Gilbert's party, Sir Thomas Tyldesley. The latter swore that if the Mayor had done so and refused to release him, his supporters would have pulled down the prison to release him and set fire to Werden's house.[6]

In October Werden's term of office ended and the Corporation met to select his successor. Despite the parliamentary leanings of the Corporation, Adam Morte, a deeply committed supporter of the King who was actively mustering royalist support in the town, was appointed – perhaps following pressure from Hoghton or from the townspeople among whom he was apparently popular. In the event, Morte declined the appointment 'contemptuously' and was rebuked harshly by the Corporation for 'the indignitie and disgrace' of his refusal, 'lest others . . . may become refractory and disobedient' and fined 100 marks. Edmund Werden was appointed to continue in office 'Until the said Adam Morte doe take his oath or until a new eleccon'. Interestingly, the Corporation was to indemnify Werden 'In regard [of] many dangers [that] may arise unto him in execuc'on thereof in theis troblesome times'.[7]

Thus, each party had its own mayor, and both men were the treasurers for their respective forces. Morte was killed defending the town when it fell to parliamentarian forces in February 1643, and Worden was to refuse to surrender it prior to its recapture by Lord Derby for the King a few weeks later.

The hostilities opened in Lancashire in September 1642 with Derby's attack on Manchester, and in November local forces led by Sir Gilbert Hoghton took the field against Blackburn. According to a parliamentarian, a blazing beacon 'Was the signall to the countrey for the papists and malignants to arise in the Fylde and in Lealand Hundred'.[8] This force marched on Whalley to secure the weapons stored there, and went on to occupy Blackburn. A large parliamentarian force was rapidly raised in this parliamentarian district, and after a two hour running fight the royalists were driven away leaving behind their weapons and those recently captured. Sir Gilbert fled with difficulty back to Preston:

> And there makes great defence by chaining up the Ribble bridge and

getting what force he can into the town for his security, out of which the countrie swears they will have him by Godes helpe, with all his adherents, either quicke or dead.[9]

An important meeting was held in Preston on 10th December, presided over by Lord Derby and attended by the main royalist gentry, many of whom had taken up residence in the town. Collectors were to be appointed and £8,700 was to be raised from the county to support the war effort. 'Adam Morte, Gentleman, Maior of Preston', William Farington and the Sheriff of Lancashire were to be treasurers, and Morte in addition was to be a member of a sort of standing council to control affairs from Preston, confirming its importance as a major royalist base. Only Warrington, close to the parliamentarian heartland around Manchester, had a larger garrison.

In the first weeks of 1643, the war in Lancashire became a more serious contest as both sides endeavoured to achieve and maintain control of the main strategic route centres in the county. With the parliamentarian forces in Blackburn reinforced and after the arrival of a force from Manchester led by Sir John Seaton, it was decided to attempt the taking of Preston. The force was able to cross the Ribble bridge in the early evening of 7th February and to assemble in the fields to the south of the town:

> Some companies were drawne by the guidans of those that well knew the towne Towardes the House of Correction to enter there at the Fryars Gate Barrs. Whereas the maine body of the Army came up at a lane at the East Barres where the watter voids the town.[10]

The town's defences were hotly contested:

> Such courage was raised in the Souldiers, that they dared to take hold of their enemies' Musketts put thorow the loopholes . . . And when the Pikes kept them off from the mud walls, yet by breaking thorow an house some twenty entred the Towne . . . then came up the rest of our men . . . chased the enemy and commanded the Towne.

Once through the barricades the parliamentarian soldiers passed along the streets breaking the windows. Among the dead was Adam Morte who had sworn 'He would fire the towne ere he gave it up, and beginne with his owne house'.[11]

The prize was a very considerable one, described by John Tilsley, the vicar of Dean, as being 'To the advancement of the publike work in this County, and not so altogether impertinent to the Kingdom'.[12] Few of the attackers had been killed and a large number of prisoners were taken. Once again Sir Gilbert Hoghton had fled, but his brother had been killed and Lady Hoghton captured. In these events vicar Tilsley could discern the hand of God, 'So soon as matters were settled, we sung praises to God in the streets (Sir, it was wonderfull to see it), the sun broke forthe and shined brightly and hot, in the time of the exercise, as if it had been midsummer'. However, local people summoned to attend before the town's new commander 'Seemed to be joyful but it was dissimulation, for feare, as afterward appeared'.[13]

Whilst Preston's defences were being revamped by John Rosworm, a celebrated military engineer, Lancaster was garrisoned for parliament, and a company led by Captain Sharkey was despatched to capture Hoghton Tower. The stronghold, defended by a number of cannon and a force of musketeers, was granted a parley and surrendered. Whilst the building was being searched for weapons the tower was blown up. Of perhaps one hundred men inside, 'Threescore . . . were afterwards found, some without armes and some without legges, and others fearefull spectacles to looke upon'.[14] Treachery was suspected but smoking in proximity to the gunpowder store was a more probable cause, leading one parliamentarian to bemoan, 'O that this thundering Alarm might ever sound in the eares of our swearing, cursing, Drunken, Tobacco-abusing Commanders and Souldiers unto unfaigned Repentance'.[15]

Utilising the lower river crossings to get around Preston Lord Derby was able to raise a large force in the royalist Fylde, and on 18th March called on Lancaster to surrender. The garrison withdrew to the safety of the great castle, but the town was thoroughly sacked and burned. When news of the royalist action reached Preston a force was sent north to intercept the royalists, leaving the town only lightly defended. In what was for him a rare flash of military genius, Derby waited at Ellel for them to pass by, and seized the chance to march directly for Preston.

The element of surprise was complete, and the royalist army was only detected late at night approaching the end of Friargate, causing panic in the town:

> The friars Gate Barrs was strongly guarded with men, but the nearer the Earle approached the Towne the lesse and weaker it waxed, for the Townes men were generally disaffected to the parliament. And for strangers of the parliament part that were accidentally within it theire care was more how they might provide for their saftie, leave it, and escape, than how to keep it, which many did . . . Many Strangers were cruelly betrayed by base and false Hostlers who had boulted the stable doors uppon their horses . . . Then the Earle's forces comming up to the ffryars Gate Barres discharged that litle peece of ordenance they caried with them, divers times into the towne, the clubmen shouting vehemently. At last without any resistance they entered and their Horse coursed about the Towne to the East end to Ribble Bridge which they guarded that none could fly that way.[16]

The following day, 'The whole Country came in with apparent joy, and many signal affections of their good affections to his majestie, flinging up their hats, and shouting out 'God blesse the King, and the Earle of Derby'.[17] Once again many prisoners were taken. The homes of parliament's supporters were pillaged: 'Master Tildesley was much busied about Mr. Edmund Weorden's house . . . And Mr. Hugh Anderton of Euxton about the shop of Henry Tailor'.[18]

The capture of Preston marked a considerable recovery for the royalist side, and threw the parliamentary forces in the county onto the defensive. The stage was set for the most decisive action in Lancashire's Civil War. In mid-April Lord Derby with Sir Gilbert Hoghton and a force of perhaps five thousand men marched out of Preston to attack the parliamentarian forces in Blackburn Hundred. This army had passed through Ribchester, crossed the river by Salesbury boat, and had almost reached Whalley before it was detected. Having halted at Whalley the force moved off towards Padiham.

Finding themselves massively outnumbered, the parliamentarian commander, Colonel Shuttleworth, and his officers decided to retreat: 'This pleased not the Souldiers then by, That they should turn their backs upon their enimies before they saw their faces'. In spite of their own officers they would rather 'See the enemie and have one bout with them if God will'.[19] Accordingly, in a narrow lane by Read Hall, the royalist advance guard was attacked from behind the stone walls along the lane. The royalists fled, apparently more in surprise than actual defeat, and fell back towards the main force in Whalley. The royalists camped around the abbey were taken by surprise and were unable to organise their defence. The large company of clubmen (largely unarmed and untrained tenants and countrymen), seeing this chaos before them, fled across the river, 'He being most happie that could get through it with most speed and run fastest away'. The force fled towards Preston, and it was said that Lord Derby did not rein in his horse until he reached Penwortham Holme.[20] Shortly afterwards the Earl left Lancashire for eventual exile on the Isle of Man, where he landed on 15th June.

This was a decisive victory for the parliamentarians. Two days later Wigan was occupied and remaining royalist forces were driven from West Lancashire northwards through Preston into the Fylde and northwards again out of the county. During their commanders' temporary absence the parliamentary soldiers pillaged friend and foe alike, particularly around St. Michael's, Bradkirk, Kirkham and Clifton. Preston shortly afterwards found itself host to this force as the men fell out among each other over their stolen cattle and other spoils. In May both Warrington and Liverpool were captured and by June 1643 only Lathom House and Greenhalgh Castle near Garstang were in royalist hands. The Civil War in Lancashire itself was effectively over, troops were sent to fight in other parts of the country, and the long series of sequestrations and seizures of the property of those who had sided with the King began.

With the fall of Greenhalgh Castle – 'thus was Amunderness hundred freed of visible enemies'[21] – and the Countess of Derby besieged at Lathom, parliamentarian victory in Lancashire was complete, yet for a brief but turbulent few weeks in 1644 one of the King's most able commanders, Prince Rupert, wraught havoc in the county as he traversed the north of England with a sizeable royalist force. The siege of Lathom House was lifted; Bolton was besieged and captured with great loss; and

Liverpool fell to Rupert after bombardment and siege. The royalists then marched east in order to relieve the parliamentarian siege of York. Preston did not try to resist as Rupert's force passed through the town, but it is clear that the Prince was not enamoured of his hosts:

> . . . the Prince was not well pleased with the Maior and Officers thereof for they made him a Sumptious Banquet but he refused it saying, "Banquets were not fit for Souldiers". And in requitall of their curtesie he caried the Maior and Bailiff's Prisoners with him to Skipton Castle and there left them.[22]

After three months' incarceration the hostages were released and were eventually paid compensation by the Council.

Rupert continued into Yorkshire and, as he approached York, was joined by the town's garrison. Together they faced a large combined parliamentarian force on Marston Moor, a battle at which Oliver Cromwell's cavalry made a timely intervention to secure victory for parliament. Rupert retreated hastily back through Lancashire. Sir Thomas Tyldesley 'with all the forces of this county and all that escaped at York', having lost

> all their Ammunition in the Battell, and not knowing how to come by more Removed from place to place within the Hundreds of Derby and Amoundnerness till such tyme as they heard that Sir John Meldrum with an army was coming against them.[23]

Preston became a centre of resistance again as the defeated royalists 'fled over the Ribble Watter into the Fylde'. On 15th August a sharp encounter took place along Walton Cop (Victoria Road) and on the Ribble Bridge, when a party of parliamentarian troops and 'countrymen' from Blackburn visiting the fair at Preston encountered a party of the enemy. The following day Meldrum's parliamentarian army rounding up stragglers cleared the town, and the royalist remnant led by Tyldesley fled into the Fylde.

In the Fylde this force was joined by the remains of a group led by Col. Goring who was fleeing southwards, 'Also being a strong number, for (as report was of such as saw them) before the last Companies were marched over the bridge at St. Michaels Church, the first Companie was judged to be at Kirkham'. Goring's men, with their 'Many Strumpets', were responsible for perhaps the most severe looting and plundering in the Preston region. 'They filled the Parishes of Kirkham, Poulton and Lythome, that night, quartering at some House 20, som 40, som 50, and at som 60 men, most of them Horsemen, over night'.[24]

Distracted by rumours of Meldrum's approach the royalists regrouped on Freckleton Marsh: 'Glad was the country soe to be free of them, though most were glad at their coming'. The parliamentary force was drawn up on Penwortham Moor and marched northwards through Preston to intercept them. The royalists had a nervous wait for the tide to fall and so effect their escape across the river at low water. Their respite

was short-lived and on the following day they were dispersed at
Ormskirk. As contingents of defeated soldiers tried to pass homeward
across the district, 'The Fyld country men perceiving [this] they guarded
Ribble Watter always both night and day when the tyde was forth and
some got good prizes by it'.[25]

The great Battle of Preston, 1648

For Preston the first Civil War was over, but four years later, the
town provided the setting for the most significant battle of the
second, when Cromwell caught up with and soundly defeated a huge
royalist and Scottish force under the Duke of Hamilton. In 1647
Hamilton had signed an 'Engagement' with the imprisoned Charles I,
agreeing to raise an army to restore the King. That army was
supplemented by English royalists to make up a ramshackle army of
about twenty thousand men.

After invading England in early July, Hamilton decided to head south
through Lancashire rather than eastwards into Yorkshire, still ignorant
of Cromwell's approach with 8500 well trained men of the New Model
Army. The latter reached Skipton on the 13th and Gisburn the following
day, and at a council of war near Clitheroe decided to press on for a battle
at Preston. Hamilton's army, still ignorant of Cromwell's whereabouts,
was foraging far and wide in the district around Preston. By 16th August
the army was stretched out along the north road, the cavalry was
approaching Wigan but the main body of foot were still to the north of
Preston. Between these elements lay the narrow five-arched bridge at
Walton-le-Dale crossing a Ribble in flood, whilst Cromwell was fast
approaching along the valley. That evening Cromwell camped at
Stonyhurst and, early on the morning of the 17th August 1648, ordered
his advance guard to attack the force of English royalists under Sir
Marmaduke Langdale which was protecting the Scottish flank. By late
morning, battle was entered near Ribbleton windmill, near modern-day
Gamull Lane:

> We advanced betimes next morning towards Preston with a desire to
> engage the Enemy, and by that time our forlorn had ingaged the
> Enemy, we were about four miles from Preston, and thereupon we
> advanced with the whole army; and the Enemy being drawne out upon
> a Moore betwixt us and the Town, the Armies on both sides ingaged,
> and after a very sharpe dispute, continuinge for three or foure houres, it
> pleased God to enable us to give them a Defeat.[26]

Caught completely unawares, Hamilton's failure to reinforce Langdale's
force, which fought extremely well, was critical to the outcome of the
battle, and has never been entirely explained. The muddy road reduced

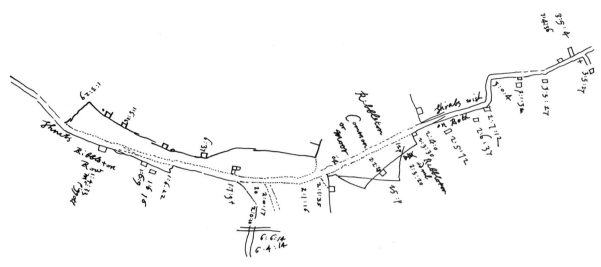

Above: a copy of a sketch map dating from 1684 which is in the Lancashire Record Office (DDX 194/28). This is significant in that it shows the approximate location of the Moor and, in particular, the site of Ribbleton Windmill where we know that the opposing forces of Cromwell and Langdale first made contact.

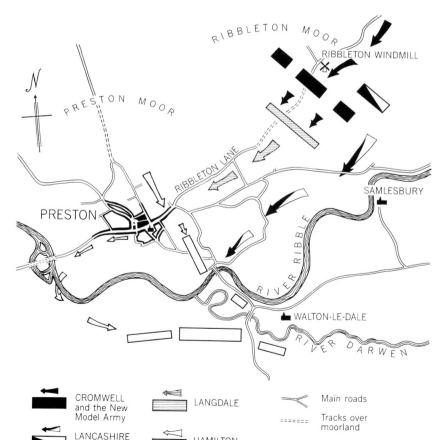

Right: Sketch map showing the disposition of forces during the crucial Battle of Preston on 17 August 1648.

the value of cavalry and Langdale's men were well positioned in the small fields and hedges. Langdale later protested that help from the main body at this juncture could have won the day, but it was still not entirely clear to Hamilton that he was encountering Cromwell's main force. In the event, by late afternoon Langdale's force was destroyed and the road to Preston lay open.

Cromwell's forces, still massively outnumbered, pushed through into Preston. Fierce resistance was encountered on the Ribble Bridge, but with the advantage of the higher ground to the north the parliamentarians were able to clear the crossing after two hours of fighting 'at Push of Pike'. Driving through Walton village the Darwen bridge was captured, and Walton Hall and the houses on Walton Green occupied.

Hamilton himself was brave enough. He tried to make a stand with a small detachment in Church Street, but was forced back and obliged to swim the swollen River Ribble at Penwortham Holme in order to rejoin his army in Walton-le-Dale. Critically, Hamilton's indecisiveness and inability to unite his forces meant that his forces were fatally split. Some of his best forces – the cavalry at Wigan, and Munro's seasoned troops who were at Lancaster – never saw action and were unable to re-unite. Cromwell's men pursued Hamilton's increasingly defenceless men southwards, leaving behind four thousand men to guard Preston with its four thousand prisoners. If Munro was to appear with the third royalist force the latter were to be killed. This Preston massacre fortunately never occurred for, on hearing of the defeat at Preston, Munro turned north

back to Scotland.

The locals now took their revenge on the plundering Scots, attacking the parties of stragglers struggling back northwards. As news of Preston spread throughout the country royalist resistance collapsed. The fate of the monarchy – and the whole political direction of the country – had hinged on this battle at Preston. Following their victory, the parliament-arian army renewed with great enthusiasm their call for the King to be brought to trial for having re-started the Civil Wars. Charles I was executed barely six months later and England became a republic.

The profound political significance of these momentous events may not have been as obvious locally as the deplorable plundering visited on the area by the poorly organised and provisioned Scots – 'the Cariag of Duke Hamilton's Army in their march was very evill, for they plundered extremely', while 'The town of Wiggan, a great and poore towne . . . were plundered almost to their skins by them'.[27] Once again the Fylde was flooded with parties of desperate men. Groups of Hamilton's horse, cut off from the main body of the army by the loss of Preston, 'fled downward into the Fyld country and in great feare, as was thought, parted themselves into sundry roads or waies'. Shortly afterwards a parliamentarian force was quartered in Kirkham:

> Theese were the most theevish Companies that ever the Country was pestered with during the Warr. Notwithstanding they had extraordinary allowance out of the Parish soe that at the least they had 100li for three daies quarter, yet they went most of the Parish over plundering and stealing whatever they could conveniently carry away.[28]

On 9th August 1651 a second Scottish force perhaps fifteen thousand strong led by the future Charles II reached Kendal on a further desperate attempt to recover the royalist cause in England. Two days later Lancaster was occupied, and on 14th August the force entered Preston. This army made only brief overnight stops, passed 'peaceably without plundering or any other violence', and did not try to compel support. Yet although Preston had lately been the site of serious rioting against the parliamentarian government's introduction of excise duties and remained popularly royalist, the future King received no support:

> The young King road through every streete to be seen of the people. Yet it was observed that he received small intertainement there, only one woman who seemed to show more respect to him than all the towne besides, which it was said was some greef to him.

The force passed quickly southwards along the familiar route. As a parliamentarian tract reported:

> Upon Wednesday [13th August] he lodged at Myerscoe, Sir Thomas Tildesley's house, and from thence marched through Preston, upon Thursday [14th], his foot having the van over the Ribble Bridge, that night he lodged at Euxton-burgh, six miles on this side of Preston,

The Battle of Preston, 1648, a painting by Cattermole. The ancient five-arched bridge stood a short distance down stream of the present Walton bridge, adjacent to the network of narrow lanes which ran through the township of Fishwick into Preston on the bluff above. At the bottom of one of these Cromwell is said to have narrowly escaped death at the hands of the Royalists. Defeat at Preston was to be the prelude to the execution of King Charles I.

being Mr. Hugh Anderton's House [Euxton Hall], who was prisoner at Lancaster, but set at Liberty by the Scots. This Anderton is a bloody papist, and one that when Prince Rupert was at Bolton boasted much of being in blood to the elbows at that cruel massacre. The last night [15th], their King lodged at Brine, six miles from Warington, being Sir William Gerard's house, who is a subtle Jesuited papist.[40]

From Warrington the parliamentarian forces withdrew before Charles's army, which was defeated by Cromwell at Worcester on 3rd September.

On 16th August the Earl of Derby, returning from exile in the Isle of Man with a small force, landed on Preesall sands. With the temporary royalist ascendancy in the county established by Charles' passage through he set about raising forces in Preston, where by the 22nd about six hundred horse and nine hundred foot had been assembled. As the main royalist army passed south a parliamentarian force was deployed against the Earl at Preston: 'Such a malignant towne as the like was not in all the county'.

Whilst resting and grazing their horses at Brindle, 'in those low meadows betweene the church and Preston', the parliamentarians were rashly attacked by 'A company of young striplings, Gentlemen's sons with other like them', intent on driving off their horses. Significantly the presence of parliamentarian troops had been 'Made known to some of the Earle's party in Preston by some secret enemy (they being all enimies thereabouts)'. Unaware of the nature of their attackers and suddenly called to arms, the troopers killed or captured all the rustlers, 'save one called Newsham who forsaking his Horse fled into a thick oller tree and there hid himself in the leaves thereof and at night went away'.[30]

On Sunday 24th August, in the silence of the night, the Earl marched out of Preston for the final time, heading for Wigan. Word reached the parliamentarian headquarters at Hoghton Tower the following day, and troops followed in pursuit. The two forces met along Wigan Lane, the road leading out of the town towards Standish. After some of the most severe fighting in the Civil Wars in Lancashire the royalists were defeated, though the Earl was able to escape to report his defeat in person to Charles at Worcester. Eventually captured and tried, James Stanley, Seventh Earl of Derby, was executed beside the town cross in Bolton on 16th October 1651.

The aftermath of war

From 1643 onwards, the property of many former royalists was seized and administered by local committees on behalf of parliament. Relatively few Preston people are listed in the Lancashire Composition Papers but large numbers of the neighbouring gentry appear.[31] Luke Hodgkinson of Preston, yeoman, was fined £27 in 1649 for 'Delinquency, adhering to the forces raised against the parliament in the first war'. Thomas Vavasour, gent, was fined for his participation in both wars, and having a horse, clothing and 'Money in my purse' worth £20 was fined one sixth or £3 6s. 8d. The estates of Henry Preston and Seth Morte were sequestered – the latter resulting in a fatal feud described in the account of the Preston Court Leet.

These measures often caused great hardship, but the system was made even more severe by the corruption of the officials employed to implement it. The local Committee for Sequestrations met in Preston, and local officials seem to have been particularly unreliable. The Goldsmith's Hall Committee had difficulty with one senior official in obtaining the accounts for the years 1643–9. 'He having not long since sent over twoe of his sonns into New England, and what his intentions are in thus leaving the Country, his Accompts not any wise perfected, wee know not'.[32]

In 1648 Captain Richard Winch was sent north to investigate the actions of the local committee. His letters from Preston, where he stayed from 3rd to 30th October, painted an alarming picture of corruption and fraud:

William Awdson of Preston . . . a poore shoomaker, was made a sequestratour: since deserted: hath purchased a great Estate by abuse of sequestrations. Informer Mr. William Bannistor.

One Mr. Clarkson of Preston . . . A Sequestrataur, two of his owne sonnes were prizers of sequestred goods and landes, soe that it will appeare that they bought the worth of £60 for £5. Informers Mr. Henry Taylor and Mr. Henry Leming and others of the same Towne.[33]

Winch's papers also provide a vivid eyewitness account of the district following Hamilton's invasion, describing: 'My paines and travels in a county haunted with notheing but misery and ensueing famine. I cannot put bread and cheese in my mouth under six-pence, and I will assure you wheate is sold in this county 26/6d a bushell'. In August 1651 the Preston Committee had to hide its papers and £2000 cash in hand, on the approach of Charles' Scottish army, but stressed in doing so that 'We are providing for our own security until this northern storm be over and then we shall fall upon busines'.

Isaac Ambrose, Vicar of Preston, was a signatory of the 'True representation of the present sad and lamentable condition of the County of Lancashire' written after Hamilton's invasion of 1648:

The hand of God is evidently seen stretched out upon the county, chastening it with a three-corded scourge of sword, pestilence, and famine, all at once afflicting it . . . There is very great scarcity and dearth of all provisions, especially of the sorts of grain, particularly that kind by which the country is most sustained, which is full six-fold the price that of late it hath been. All trade, by which they have been much supported, is utterly decayed: it would melt any good heart to see the numerous swarms of begging poore, and the many families that pine away at home not having faces to beg . . . to see paleness, nay death appear in the cheeks of the poor, and often to hear of some found dead in their houses or highways, for want of bread.[34]

Indeed, the social and economic effects of the Civil Wars may well have been more profound than the military.

CHAPTER EIGHT

The Jacobites

ON 11th March 1660, the townspeople assembled in the market place to celebrate the restoration of Charles II, amidst a cacophony of musket volleys, drums, trumpets, much bellringing, 'Alacrity and Loyalty'. The Corporation assembled in state and celebrated in the town hall, 'The Mayor in his formalities, serjeants with their maces and halberds, the bayliffs in their gowns, the Aldermen in their furre gowns'.[1] As the order changed once again former disloyalty was not forgotten. However, the town's leading citizens which the Corporation comprised carried out something of a purge of those members who 'Bore arms against the late King and sided with the government and who turned out the loyal members and now engross all the places in the Corporation'. Edmund Werden and seven others were expelled and William Banastre who had been expelled was readmitted. At the Parish Church William Cole was either expelled or resigned, and Preston's former vicar Isaac Ambrose was turned out of his living at Garstang. Their immediate successors leant to the more moderate High Church cause.[2]

During the late seventeenth century the 'rivalry of factions' amongst Preston's leading families began to coalesce into something resembling the emerging national party politics of the day. By the 1680s the dominant Corporation group can be loosely described as 'Tory', taking a strongly royalist, High Church line, as opposed to many of the neighbouring gentry families who were predominantly 'Whig', more Presbyterian in outlook and less prepared to allow full authority to the King. As the Corporation became more Tory, so it probably became more in accord with general opinion in the town.[3] In return, the government of Charles II took careful steps to strengthen the powers of those Corporations under Tory control, and this may account for the granting of a second charter by the King in 1684.[4]

The succession of the Catholic James II in 1685 led to further difficulties. Catholic hopes for religious toleration were high and John Leyburne on his visit to the district in 1687 was able to confirm perhaps nine thousand Catholics, and in 1688 the Jesuits were briefly able to open a chapel in Preston and to conduct services openly for the first time since the Reformation. This period ended abruptly with the exile of James II, and in Preston the chapel was burned by an angry mob.[5]

Prestonians seem to have taken to the developing party politics with alacrity. A curious incident, which for a time developed into a major local issue, provides an interesting insight into this phenomenon. After the 'Glorious Revolution' of William and Mary in 1689, John Birch, the Sheriff of Lancashire, sacked William Tomlinson, the governor of the Preston House of Correction (the workhouse situated in the former friary buildings off Marsh Lane), claiming that he was a Jacobite, that is a supporter of the deposed Stuarts. At the assizes of 1689 Tomlinson disputed these charges and the Justices voted to restore him. The Sheriff refused to reappoint this 'seditious and disloyal person', and obtained royal assent for the appointment of William Higgonson, 'A loyal and sufficient man'. By 1690 Tomlinson had been fully cleared of the charges against him and the Justices visited the workhouse to reinstate him. But Higgonson had barricaded himself in, and a great row with much 'noise and brawling' ensued:

> And as wee have since heard, they had then within the said house an armed rabble to keep the house, and whilst wee were but a little way gone from the place, wee heard a gun or guns go off in or about the said house.

The issue had quite rapidly developed into a major political affair, as each party lined up behind its man. Higgonson remained governor at his death in 1694, whereupon Tomlinson was 'restored' before his dismissal again in 1696.[6]

With the removal of James II in 1688 the Whigs were triumphant and some Tories began to look for a return of the Stuart dynasty, setting the scene for the Jacobite risings of 1715 and 1745. Within this ferment was formed the 'Mock Corporation of Walton-le-Dale' in 1701. Consisting of representatives from many of the local gentry families, and Tory in outlook, this ostensibly social gathering set itself up in a suitable style and conducted its business in mockery of the Corporation of Preston. Along with the high offices of the Corporation this fraternity, meeting in the Unicorn Inn, also benefited from the offices of House-groper, Slut-kisser, Custard-eater, Jester, Ale-Tester etc., for which it is today best remembered. Yet it also had a deeper purpose. The 'Mayor' of 1711, the Earl of Derwentwater, led the Jacobite army to defeat in 1715, and, with fellow Mock Corporation members Charles Chorley and John Winckley, was subsequently executed.

The celebrated Dr. Whitaker concluded that:

> Under this semblance . . . of sport and jollity, there seems to have been concealed a political purpose. The members who appear till about the year 1740, were the Catholic and Jacobite nobility and gentry, and here seem to have concerted their plans for the restoration of the exiled family.

After the failure of 1715 he 'observe[d] a mixture of Whigs, so that as all political confidence must have been destroyed, everything of a political tendency must have ceased'.

Hardwick listed the names of the principal participating families as Towneley, Trafford, Shuttleworth, Farington, Rawstorne, Osbaldeston, Stanley, Holt, Starkie, Parker, Sherburne, Ormerod, Tunstall, Nowell, Hesketh, Gillibrand, Rigby, Blackburn, Patten, Asheton, Atherton, Scarisbrick and Bradsham. In 1715 this highly influential group seemed to offer the Jacobites the hope of strong local support in the Preston district. When such support was not forthcoming from these 'Alehouse Tories' their cause was effectively doomed.[7]

—— *The Battle of Preston, 1715* ——

Shortly after the death of Queen Anne in 1714, the Jacobites began to mobilise their forces to restore the Stuart James III. It was hoped that a rising and mustering of supporters in Scotland could be followed by a march into England, where it would be met by popular acclaim and more recruits in Lancashire, developing a political and military momentum, the Stuarts reasoned, would send the Hanoverians – and George I – packing.

The Scottish army, led by Thomas Forster and the Earl of Derwentwater, mustered at Braemar in early September 1715, and with a force of perhaps eighteen hundred men arrived at Penrith a month later. Against the threatened invasion local defence was organised by Preston's M.P. Sir Henry Hoghton, an energetic 37-year-old Colonel of the Militia and Deputy Lieutenant of the County. As parliamentary leader of the non-conformist interest in Lancashire his loyalty to the Whig cause was never in doubt. He urged his supporters to:

> Raise all the force you can, I mean lusty young fellows to draw up on Cuerden Green, to be there by ten o'clock, to bring what arms they have fitt for service, and scythes putt in streight polls, and such as have not, to bring spades and billhooks for pioneering with.[8]

With a force of perhaps six hundred local recruits Hoghton marched to Lancaster. Here Sir Henry tried to obtain the guns from Mr. Lawson's ship the *Robert*, anchored in the Lune off the bustling port at Sunderland Point. Lancaster's great Quaker merchant refused to release them without a bond for £10,000 and on the approach of the Jacobite army the local force withdrew to Preston. The guns were taken by the Scots and were used to defend the barricades in Preston a few days later.[9]

Having made a colourful entry into Lancaster unimpeded by efforts to demolish the bridge over the Lune, the Jacobite officers set about enjoying the delights of the town:

> This afternoone, the Gentlemen soldiers dressed and trimed themselves

up in their best cloathes, for to drink a dish of tea with the Laydys of this towne. The Laydys also have apeared in their best riging, and had their tea tables richly furnished for to entertain their new suitors.[10]

This expedition does not seem to have been so marked by the plundering which distinguished earlier forays, and the Quaker William Stout later recalled:

It was a time of tryall, and in fear that the Scotts and Northern rebells would have plundered us, but they were civill, and to most paid for what they had; but I had five of the Mackintosh officers quartered on me two days, but took nothing of them.[11]

Whilst the Jacobite officers were distracted at Lancaster the government forces were able to evacuate Preston and to organise their scattered forces south of the Ribble. General Wills was able to secure the bridge at Warrington and to move up to block the Jacobite advance on the Ribble, whilst a second government army under General Carpenter marched to intercept from the east. He had initially deployed for an advance through Yorkshire and, like Cromwell in 1648, had subsequently decided to intercept the Scots at Preston.

The advance party of Jacobite horse reached Preston on 9th November, and the foot arrived on the following day. In the ancient market place James III, the Old Pretender, was declared King. To complete the colourful scene the Scots wore blue and white rosettes and their English allies red and white. The Duke of Marlborough shrewdly guessed that the social and recreational attractions of Preston, the county's principal resort for the gentry, would further delay the advance enabling the government's forces to surround the town. As Peter Clarke wrote in his diary, 'The Ladys in this towne, Preston, are so very beautyfull and so richly attired, that the Gentleman soldiers from Wednesday to Saturday minded nothing but courting and ffeasting'.[12]

The behaviour of its commander, General Forster, appalled the Scottish force, particularly the professional soldiers. No attempt was made to prevent the muster of government forces at Wigan or to prevent their linking up with those from Yorkshire. When news of the approaching government troops reached Preston 'He appeared dispiritted, and then, as at all other times, very unfit for such an important command'.[13] He was particularly blamed for leaving the Darwen and Ribble bridges undefended, though in contrast to 1648 the River Ribble was low and easily fordable in any case. Rather than risk his forces being

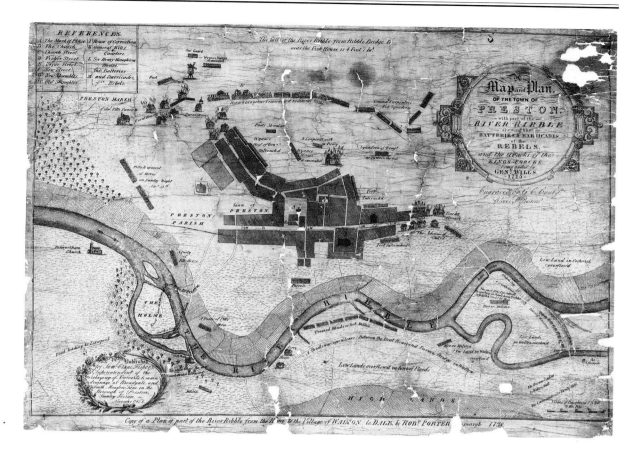

Plan of the Battle of Preston in 1715. In addition to the disposition of troops the plan clearly reveals the medieval street pattern (today the town centre), the tortuous course of the river around Penwortham Holme and the location of individual buildings – notably the House of Correction (the former Friary). Visiting the town in the mid-1720s, Daniel Defoe found the locals still dazed by the intensity of the attack, and the partial burning of their town seven years earlier.

outflanked at Frenchwood, Forster withdrew them into the town which was hastily defended with barricades and trenches. His force was well suited to this type of skirmishing, whilst the opposing cavalry could not be deployed in the town's narrow streets.

On Saturday the troops of General Wills were able to cross the Ribble unopposed, to their amazement, and to block the north and south exits to the town at the ends of Church Street and Friargate. The failure to block Fishergate enabled many of the local recruits to escape across the river to Penwortham in the final stages of the battle. The medieval town was defended by four principal barricades, at the end of Church Street, beside the Parish Church, in Fishergate and at the end of Friargate ('The Windmill Barrier'), whilst most of the force was held in reserve in the market place.

In the early afternoon a direct assault was made on the outer Church Street barrier:

About 2 a clock this afternoon, 200 of Generall Wills men entered the Churchgate street, and the Highlanders firing out of the cellars and windows, in 10 minutes killed 120 of them. The Highlanders also fired the . . . 2 ships guns but the bulletts flew upon the houses, so that no execution was done thereby.

Patten adds that the guns were commanded by a drunken sailor whose first broadside hit a chimney, but whose second effort succeeded in killing many of the attackers.[14]

Frontal assault having failed, the government troops tried to burn the defenders out:

A little time after this a party was sent to burne the houses and barnes where the Highlanders were at the entrance of the said Church Gate street, and accordingly severall houses and barnes were burnt and so forced the Highlanders to move up further into this town. At this time the wind was North, which, if it had been South, the judicious are of opinion that most of this towne wood have been burnt.[15]

One party of troops was able to infiltrate the town by one of the back passages or weinds which characterised its medieval plan, and to capture Patten House, a key strategic point:

A house, whose battlement and battery did command the head of the Hollow Way that leads from the bridge to the town: and the street in the Mercat-Place, and a great part of the neighbouring fields.[16]

Later that afternoon an attempt was made to get around the barricade in Friargate through Back Lane:

At 4 a clock the same day, 300 men were commanded to enter the Back Street called Back Wiend in Preston, and accordingly they made an attempt but the Highlanders placing themselves under Garden Walles, hedges and diches, kiled the Captain and about 140 of his men.[17]

Night fell with the flames from the blazing buildings on the perimeter of the town illuminating the evening sky. To ascertain the progress of his troops Wills ordered candles to be placed in windows of all the captured buildings. To thwart this the defenders followed suit so that in a short time all the centre of the town was lit up. When the Scots were ordered to put them out the order was misunderstood and even more candles were lit, to the amusement of the troops on both sides: 'That night both armies lay upon their arms, but General Forster went to bed. All that night there were constant dropping shots'.[18]

By 10 o'clock on Sunday morning the Jacobite position had been made hopeless with the arrival of General Carpenter's army of 2500 men, who quickly sealed up the boltholes left open by Wills. After further shooting a truce was called for a parley. A fair proportion of the local recruits seem to have made good their escape, but the main force of Scots was determined to fight on, appalled at any talk of surrender. They were clearly in a strong position to inflict severe casualties on their attackers:

The common men were one and all against capitulating . . . Their madness was such that nothing could quiet them for a great while; and it was astonishing to see the confusion the town was in . . . In this dilemma, many exclaimed against Mr. Forster, and had he appeared in the street, he would certainly have been cut to pieces.[19]

Forster, however, accepted the terms of honourable if unconditional surrender at 7 o'clock the following morning. The rank and file laid down their arms in the market place and were marched off to be incarcerated in the Parish Church. With little clothing against the wintry conditions, they

tore apart the pew coverings for use as blankets. The officers surrendered their swords in the churchyard, but the peers were allowed to surrender discreetly, out of public gaze in their former headquarters, the Mitre Tavern. Gentlemen and officers were held in the town's main inns: the Mitre, the White Bull, and the Windmill.

As 'The district where Roman Catholics most abounded' the Jacobites had held high hopes of local support in Lancashire, where a rising of twenty thousand men had been confidently promised. Exactly how much local support was forthcoming is difficult to estimate, and was the source of much rumour at the time, and exaggeration ever since. Nor is it clear how many Prestonians escaped from the town before the fighting commenced.

Few recruits seem to have joined at Lancaster and Jarvis estimated that perhaps five to six hundred men deserted on the march to Preston. At Preston Patten claimed that they were joined 'by a great many Gentlemen, with their tennants, servants, and attendants, and some of very good figure in the country: but still all Papists', whilst Peter Clarke noted that 'Esq Townley, a Papist, joined them here, and Mr. Shuttleworth who lived in Preston, as also did abundance of Roman Catholics'. By contrast Clemesha lists just six local gentlemen, including representatives of the old Catholic families: Richard Townley, Edward Tyldesly and Richard Shuttleworth, with perhaps just two hundred supporters. Although a number of local people were executed for their part in the affair, and the town seems to have been hospitable enough in the circumstances, there was clearly no general rising in support of the Jacobites: Preston had remained loyal to King George.[20]

Nor was aid forthcoming from the local High Church Tories of the Walton-le-Dale Mock Corporation, and the town's vicar Rev. Peploe actually offered prayers for King George before a congregation of rebels! In his account of the rising Patten identified this Tory reluctance as a major factor in its failure:

Indeed that party, who never are right hearty for the cause, 'till they are mellow, as they call it, over a bottle or two, began now to show us their blind side; and that is their just character, that they do not care for venturing their carcasses any further than the tavern . . . I have heard Mr. Forster say he was blustered into this business by such people as these, but that for the time to come he would never again believe a drunken Tory.

The local Tory gentry had felt it opportune, in the event, to stay at home.[21]

What followed the surrender formalities came as a shock to contemporary observers:

After the said 2 Generall's men had taken whole possession of the said Towne of Preston, they with force and armes broke open doors and locks of chambers and clossetts, and the moneys, plate, goods and chattles of most of the *inhabitants* of that towne (who were and still are good subjects to his Majesties King George government) contrary to the will of the owners of the said goods, ffelonyously did steal, take and carry away contrary to His said Majesties peace, crowne and dignity, and also contrary to the laws of this nation.

Patten stated that the 'King's troops began to plunder even before the appointed hour of surrender took place, but that the two generals having been appealed to, the pillage was restrained'.[22]

With its Catholic tradition, Preston was still perceived by the government as hostile territory and savage reprisals were meted out on those local people who had joined the Preten-der's army, and had been captured at Preston. They were tried before a special government commission held at Liverpool in January 1716.[23]

English Martyrs Church on Garstang Road.

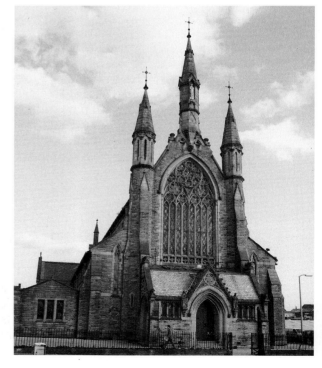

Twelve men were executed at Preston, traditionally near the site of English Martyrs Church in Garstang Road, and four men at Garstang. For their bloody work in the various towns of Lancashire, the two execu-tioners were paid £60, and the Sheriff's accounts include the following entry for Preston:

January 27th: Erecting gallows and paid for materialls, hurdle, fire, cart etc. in execut-ing Shuttleworth and 4 more at Preston (Muncaster, Coupe, Butler, Myerscough) and setting up his head etc. £12.0.4d.[24]

Over fifteen hundred prisoners were taken at Preston, comprising 1,088 Scots and 464 English; perhaps fewer than twenty defenders had been killed compared with almost three hundred of the government troops. Though purchased at a high price the political consequences of the battle of Preston were enormous. As in 1648, so in 1715, events in Preston had once again seen the eclipse of Stuart hopes.[25]

The Young Pretender in Preston, 1745

If the people of Preston and Lancashire failed to come to the support of James III in 1715, there appeared to be an even slimmer chance of their coming out publicly in favour of Bonnie Prince Charlie in 1745. The Young Pretender's army occupied Preston on 27th November and, according to Jarvis, Charles Edward lodged at Mitre Court in the entry to the Straight Shambles. In his private journal, John Byrom wrote, however:

> The Prince lay at Lawyer Starkies at Preston last night [25 Nov 1745] he has marched from Carlisle on foot at the head of his army: he was dressed in a Scotch plaid, a blue silk waistcoat with silver lace, and a Scotch bonnet with J.R. on it.[26]

In his *History of the Rebellion in the year 1745-6*, Robert Chambers wrote:

> At Preston . . . the bells were rung at their entry, probably by the intervention of the Catholics who abounded in the town. Some huzzas attended the reading of the proclamation, and a few recruits were obtained. A Mr. Towneley, a Catholic gentleman, here joined the standard, being the first man of distinction who had done so in England. A council of war was held, at which the Prince . . . prevailed upon the chiefs to continue their southward march. The clansmen had a superstitious dread, in consequence of the misfortunes of their party at Preston, in 1715, that they would never get beyond this town; to dispel the illusion Lord George Murray crossed the Ribble, and quartered a number of men on the other side.[27]

Having progressed as far as Derby the force was obliged to retreat, passing through Preston a second time on 13th December. The Duke of Cumberland's Horse reached the town at 1 p.m. on the same day that the Jacobites had left, thus narrowly avoiding a re-enactment of the battle of 1715. The Young Pretender's force was thus able to leave England intact, before being finally brought to battle on Culloden Moor outside Inverness on 16th April 1746.

Nineteenth-century writers in the romantic tradition were able to assemble a good many tales of Jacobite Preston in the fashion of the day. Principal among these is the story of 'Long Preston Peggy', though whether she was a heroine of the 1715 or 1745 war seems to have been confused:

Long Preston Peggy to Proud Preston went,
To see the bold rebels it was her intent:
For in brave deeds of arms she did take much delight,
And therefore she went with the rebels to fight.

The subject of this Ribblesdale ballad, though in later life said to have manifested 'a strong propensity to indulge in spirituous liquors' and to repeatedly sing the song, has led many earlier writers into 'dangerous speculations' describing her variously as 'buxom' and a 'handsome young woman'.[28]

The Jacobites it seems were ever popular with the ladies, and money demanded from the town was claimed to have been delivered up to the Jacobite headquarters in the White Bull Inn by the mother of Nicholas Grimshaw. Music also looms large in the tradition: the Pretender is said to have entered the town *en route* for Derby to the tune of *The King shall have his Own again*, and on his retreat to the refrain *Hie Thee Charlie Home Again*. Perhaps more accurately, he is also said to have viewed the sites of the siege of 1715 with veterans of the encounter.

Once again neither the county nor the town had risen in support of the Jacobites. In 'occupied' Preston the loyal authorities were clearly put in a difficult position, and both they and the townspeople remained distinctly unattached to their temporary guests. This point is well illustrated by an event recalled personally by James Ray, who had enlisted as a volunteer on the government's side:

> In the road to Preston, I picked up another straggler, following his company; and within two miles of that town I met the rebel post returning with despatches from the army to Scotland, whom I also made prisoner and took from him 49 letters. I conducted him and the above straggler to Preston, intending to deliver them to the Magistrates: but they would neither receive the prisoners nor the letters, for *they feared the consequences of so rash an undertaking*, the rebels being but just gone out of the town; and as I had brought the prisoners into the town they obliged me to carry them out of it.[29]

Ultimately he was assisted by the Corporation, albeit discreetly.

CHAPTER NINE

Georgian Preston

DURING the eighteenth century the economic development of Lancashire reached the critical threshold of the Industrial Revolution. A quickening in the gradual but cumulative processes of growth, based on the textile industry, established the world's first industrial society in the half-century from 1780-1830. In Preston the industrial economy developed alongside the town's continuing market, agricultural and administrative functions: the industrial landscape was superimposed on the medieval town plan: and, in the eighteenth century at least, the town's elite succeeded in maintaining their place and the deference they felt was due to them among the rising industrial throng. Continuity and change, reaction and revolution, innovation and conservatism, are thus the key to the understanding of developments during this crucial period of the town's development.

Visitors in the eighteenth century drew attention to those features of the town which distinguished it from the rapidly expanding industrial centres to the south, such as Bolton and Manchester. Most illuminating is the account left by Daniel Defoe, who visited the town around 1725:

> Preston is a fine town, and tolerably full of people, but not like Liverpoole or Manchester; besides, we come now beyond the trading part of the county. Here's no manufacture; the town is full of attorneys, proctors, and notaries, the process of law here being of a different nature than they are in other places, it being a dutchy and county palatine, and having particular privileges of its own. The people are very gay here, though not perhaps the richer for that, but it has by that obtained the name of Proud Preston. Here is a great deal of good company, but not so much, they say, as was before the late bloody action with the northern rebels; not that the battle hurt many of the immediate inhabitants, but so many families there and thereabout, have been touched by the consequences of it, that it will not be recovered in a few years, and they seem to have a kind of remembrance of things upon them still.[1]

Defoe's picture of a quiet, respectable, regional capital accords well with Celia Fiennes' account of thirty years earlier of a gentrified town of fine

The South Prospect of Preston was produced in 1728 by S. and N. Buck as one of a number of topographical engravings of northern towns.

This early view was intended principally for the gentry and therefore highlights Preston's more fashionable features, as well as the residences of its prominent inhabitants, including Sir Edward Stanley, soon to succeed to the Earldom of Derby. In particular, some of the old burgage plots with their houses, barns and gardens, can clearly be seen along Church Street and Fishergate.

The date of the print is particularly opportune,

THE SOUTH PROSPECT OF PRESTON,

Preston. Said to arise out of the ruins of Ribble-Chester, is a Borough and Corporation of great Antiquity and Note, receiving its first Charter from K. Henry 2.nd which, since hath been confirm'd and additional privileges granted by the succeeding Kings, and Queens. The Body consists of a Mayor, Recorder, Aldermen, &c.
The Present Members of P.t are S.r Henry Hoghton Barr.t and Daniel Pulteney Esq.r

1. Penwortham *The church and priory can be seen clearly. At the Reformation, both the church lands and the priory buildings were bought by John Fleetwood, whose family continued to live there until the bankruptcy of Henry Fleetwood in 1749. The former priory buildings were demolished in 1832 when the Hall was re-built.*

2. Tulketh *In the last century wrongly thought to have been the site of the leper hospital, well outside the built-up area, overlooking the river.*

3. The boat house *Until the building of the first Penwortham Bridge in the late 1750s, the traveller had the choice of a ford over the Ribble at Penwortham Holme or the ferry at Middleforth Green.*

4. House of Correction *This occupied the remains of the friary, just off present-day Marsh Lane. Whittle said in 1835 that 'The demolition in 1539 was so complete, that little remains, excepting some outward walls, painted window mouldings, and gothic arched doorways'.*

5. St. George's Chapel *This fine chapel was first built in 1724. For 120 years it was a chapel-of-ease to the Parish Church until a separate parish was established in 1844. Apart from the Unitarian Chapel, St. George's is now Preston's oldest surviving church building.*

6. The Town Hall *The only known representation of the early Town Hall, which stood on the junction of Cheapside and Fishergate. This building eventually fell down in 1780.*

as it records the town shortly after the Jacobite skirmish here in 1715, and in the year following Daniel Defoe's account: 'The people are very gay here, though not perhaps the richer for that, but it has by that obtained the name of Proud Preston.'

Despite its curious perspectives, the Prospect of Preston shows well the town's topography and location, and emphasizes its position on a shelf overlooking the river valley; the Ribble spills through Penwortham Holme onto the coastal plain and into the estuary, but is itself overlooked by the heights of the fells to the north east.

E COUNTY PALATINE OF LANCASTER

1. {Penwortham the Seat of Henry Fleetwood Esqr
2. Fulcheth.
3. The Boat House.
4. The House of Correction.
5. St George's Chappel.
6. The Town Hall.
7. St Winifreds Church.
8. Avenham Walk.
9. Sr Edwd Stanleys.
10. Ribble Bridge.
11. The River Ribble.
12. {Cuerdale, the Seat of Ralph Ashton Esqr
13. Hoghton Tower.
14. Walton Church.
15. {Walton Hall, the Seat of Sr Henry Hoghton Barr.^t

S. & N. Buck delin.^t et Sculp.^t 1728.

7. The Parish Church *The perspective may over-emphasize the scale of the Parish Church (here captioned by its original name, St. Wilfrid's), but its position of dominance in the early townscape is clear from this engraving.*

8. Avenham Walk *Ralph Thoresby described Avenham Walks in 1702 as 'an eminency lately purchased by the town, where is a very curious walk and delicate prospect'.*

9. Patten House *Edward Stanley* succeeded as Earl of Derby in 1736, and Patten House became the family's Preston residence. It stood on the north side of Church Street.

10. The Ribble Bridge – *for hundreds of years the only bridge in the vicinity of Preston.*

11. The River Ribble *Before the Industrial Revolution 'good Ribble salmon' was plentiful and the fisheries along the Penwortham, Preston and Walton shores were carefully preserved.*

12. Cuerdale *The home of the Assheton family, and close to the site of the remarkable discovery of Dark Age treasure in 1840.*

13. Hoghton Tower *The Hoghtons were important out-burgesses for much of the pre-industrial period.*

14. Walton Church *The Parish Church of Walton-le-Dale.*

15. Walton Hall *The family home of the Hoghtons, which was demolished in 1840.*

buildings and streets.

Visitors to the town during the 1745 Jacobite rebellion left favourable accounts. John Marchant wrote:

> This place from its Situation on a clean delightful Eminence, Handsome Streets and Variety of Company that board here is reckoned one of the prettiest retirements in England. 'Tis a very gay town . . . and is called Proud Preston, tho' not near so rich as Liverpool or Manchester.

James Ray found the town 'A place of the best fashion,' its ladies both beautiful and 'very agreeable,' and its other inhabitants unsurpassed in politeness. He evidently was much taken with the 'handsom[e] church,' 'Spacious Market-Place' with its 'fine obelisk,' and its neatly paved streets, but especially his lodgings with Mrs. Chorley at the *Black Bull*: 'I never met with any better'.[2] Pococke, on the other hand, was perhaps disappointed by his visit in 1750. Though a great thoroughfare, Preston was clearly not among the elite of fashionable places, being, he felt, rather middle-class, and thus 'remarkable for old maids, because these families will not ally with tradesmen and have not sufficient fortunes for gentlemen'.[3]

—— *Preston and the slave trade* ——

In Preston, with its fashionable set, resident gentry, and extensive hinterland, there was a considerable demand for colonial products. In June 1745 the *Preston Journal* reported that:

> A Quantity of choice Rum has been lately imported from the West Indies by Richard Prescott, Grocer in Preston; which will be sold in any quantity, exceeding 2 gallons, at Seven Shillings and Six pence per Gallon.

Fragmentary evidence of the town's participation in the colonial trade has been pieced together from occasional references in the Liverpool newspapers, and from Admiralty records, by M. M. Schofield.[4] The Lancashire coast between the Mersey and the Lune was designated as the Port of Poulton, and in the 1740s local merchants began to trade direct with the colonies from the Ribble and Wyre in their own ships rather than operating through Liverpool or Lancaster. Sailings from Preston were underway by the following decade. The region had a long tradition of trade with the towns of Northern Europe, importing flax, hemp, timber and iron from the Baltic countries, and exporting finished goods in return, whilst operating costs were markedly lower than in Liverpool. A warehouse for goods from Barbados was built at Skippool on the Wyre in 1741, and after 1761 a warehouse at Naze Point, Freckleton, was developed for the Kirkham based trade.[5]

The Preston branch of the trade was conducted by a number of the town's principal citizens and merchants. One such example is William Riddehough, who was appointed town bailiff in 1758, a councillor in 1763, and was admitted to the Guild Company of Mercers, Grocers, Drapers and Haberdashers in 1762.[6] Richard Pedder was Mayor in 1748 and 1756. Of his sons, Thomas was Mayor in 1777 and Edward in 1763, 1770 and 1776. In 1768 a mob threatened to burn Thomas Pedder's warehouse which stood on the west side of the market square.[7] William Riddehough, Richard Pedder, Robert Farrer 'grocer', James Low and James Walmesley are all described as 'Merchants of Preston'.[8] These local interests were well placed to benefit from the expanding colonial trade.

Lloyds List of July 1755 records the involvement of three local ships in the slave trade. The *Betty and Martha* of Poulton, owned by Langton, Shepherd & Company of Kirkham, had landed 65 slaves at Barbados; while the *Hothersall*, owned by J. Birley and Company, also from Poulton, had landed 150 slaves and landed a further 135 slaves in 1756; and the *Blossom* from Preston had bought slaves on the Windward and Gold Coast and subsequently sold 131 at Barbados. Shortly after her return from this voyage her sale was advertised in *Williamson's Liverpool Advertiser*:

> 25th JUNE 1756 FOR SALE AT PRESTON – The good snow or vessel called the *Blossom*, Samuel Gawith commander, burthen 100 tons more or less, built at Preston, and has been one voyage only (on the coast of Africa), a very strong and tight vessel of proper dimensions and every way compleat for the Slave Trade . . . The vessel and her materials may be viewed . . . at Lytham in the River Ribble where she now lies.[9]

Several references to a Samuel Gawith occur in the Liverpool and Lancaster registers. A man of this name made several voyages from Lancaster, and after the sale of the *Blossom* was a master at Liverpool making at least eleven further voyages.

The colonial trade appears to have been particularly hazardous. The *Black Prince* from Chester was lost to French pirates in 1757, and the *Mary* of Lancaster was captured and destroyed by slaves in the River Gambia in 1761.

Although records are fragmentary there was clearly a not inconsiderable involvement in the West Indies trade at this time. In 1754 William Riddehough & Co. shipped goods for sale in Jamaica aboard a vessel actually called the *Preston*. The *Clifton* sailed from Preston in 1750 bound for the Cape Verde Islands where she took on board salt for sale in Barbados. The accounts of a subsequent voyage to Jamaica in 1754 indicate the broad range of local interests involved. She carried shoes despatched by Riddehough and James Low; various small items ranging from inkpots to coffin handles; 91 Lancashire cheeses (of which only three were found to be rotten); and in particular consignments of cloth despatched by the Preston merchants.[10]

When the trade was disrupted by the loss of many ships during the Seven Years War, local investment seems to have turned to the more secure Baltic trade and, significantly, to the emerging textile industry. After the mid-1760s no further West Indies voyages appear to have been made from Poulton or Preston, though the Kirkham interest in the slave trade continued to expand. The Statutory Register of British Ships of 1786 lists 24 Preston ships totalling 1343 tons, owned by 69 different owners in 83 shares.

With the demise of the locally-based trade, merchants switched their operations to Liverpool. In the 1780s the records of Rawlinson Brothers of Liverpool list the export to the West Indies of goods from Preston, Walton-le-Dale, Leyland and Clayton Green. A voyage of 1787 included heavy linen cloth, or 'osnaburghs', used for plantation slaves' work clothing, from the Leyland handloom 'manufacturer' William Pollard (owner of the *Roebuck Inn*) and Henry Critcheley. Repeat orders were won in 1789 and 1790.[11]

——— *Preston in 1774* ———

I n 1774 a detailed survey of land and property in Preston was undertaken by Messrs. Lang, Hawkshead and Porter. Although best known today for 'Lang's Map' of the town, a series of related survey books has also survived in the Derby Muniments.[12] From these it is possible to gain a clear picture of the district at an important date in the town's development, the eve of the Industrial Revolution.

The pattern of land ownership – with its parcels of consolidated holdings spread across the town's fields, and the plan of houses built within the ancient burgage plots – is familiar from medieval times, lending qualified support to Taylor's assertion, made in 1818, that Dr. Kuerden's account of the town was as true of 1782 as it had been of 1682.[13] From the Court Leet records it is also clear that the general pattern of working the townlands, with their arable, meadow and common moor and marsh grazing, persisted, and the farmyard aspect of many of the town's streets survived. Many of the merchants and the better-off townspeople continued to farm their lands in the town fields, and even the less well-off could graze their beasts – goose, pig or cow – on the commons. The town retained a close day-to-day relationship with the land.

In his will dated 2nd March 1759 and proved in 1763, the merchant Richard Pedder, a former mayor and a shareholder in the voyages of the *Clifton*, listed his lands in Preston in much the same way that he might have done centuries before. Among them were his house on the south side of Friargate; two burgages in Friargate with five others on the north

side beside the street's open stream or drain, the 'Brown Channell'; property in St. John's Lane and on Church Street; his warehouse and houses in St. John's Weind; and his fields (lands in the Maudlands, the Oxheys, on Broadgate Lane and Avenham), his church pews, and his cash.[14]

The survey of 1774 describes both land and property separately. The town fields were held in 95 parcels or estates, of which 68 were of less than ten acres, and only those of John Fletcher, Alderman Pedder, John Atherton and Nicholas Winckley were over fifty acres. The highest annual rents were generally obtained for lands in the ancient town fields, indicating both the original exploitation of the best soils by the early farmers, and their continued high agricultural productivity ever since. So successful was the system of land use

St. Georges Church, a lithograph by Croome after Bishop. Hidden by warehouses in Chapel Walks off Lune Street, the Church of St. George is one of the hidden delights of the town. It was erected in 1723 and restored on a number of occasions, and from 1797 to 1862 was host to the Rev. Robert Harris. The adjacent graveyard contains the grave of Samuel Horrocks, brother of John Horrocks, founder of the great cotton firm.

practised that these soils, despite cropping and grazing for literally a thousand years, still fetched high rents and were still among the most fertile soils in the district:[15]

Platford Dales 70s. per acre [to the north of the Ringway between Lancaster Road and Patten Street in the vicinity of the Police Headquarters building]

Square Platford Dale Garden 80s. per acre [to the east of the above on the site of Saul Street baths]

Great Avenham 60s. [to the south of Avenham Lane]

Avenham meadow 57s. 6d. [to the south of Avenham Lane]

Fishergate Field 65s. [to the south of Fishergate adjoining West Cliff]

Maudland Croft 65s. [to the south of Pedder Street, now railway land]

New Hall Lane Fields 60s. [between Stanley Street and Centenary Mill]

Town End Field 80s. [on the corner of Ribbleton Lane and Deepdale Road]

Town End Croft 60s. [on the corner of Stanley Street and Church Street]

Common Field 35s. [Broadgate]

Although fields named 'common field' remained at Broadgate, these had long been divided among several owners. The 1767 survey lists fifteen separate pieces, many of them very small, owned by twelve individuals.

The town's largest landlord in 1774 was Lord Derby whose local estate was then worth about £450 a year, with twenty acres of field holdings worth £98, and extensive housing worth £350 (46 houses and 22 shops). The estate inns (the *Black Bull, Cock and Bottle,* and *Legs O'Man*) and property in the Shambles were particularly valuable.

By this date the process of the infilling of the medieval town plan by

the erection of dwellings and the insertion of side courts on the 'backsides' of the burgage plots, so much a feature of the atrocious housing conditions of nineteenth-century Preston, was already under-way. Ashton's and Gradwell's property in Friargate, for example, comprised '3 dwellings to ye front, 4 backwards'. The houses along Fishergate and Friargate thus became a sort of façade for much poorer-quality dwellings squeezed in behind. A number of surviving narrow ginnels leading through from the street can still be found along Friargate. The narrow weinds to the south of Church Street extending westwards from the Parish Church also contained large numbers of dwellings, and Thomas Woodcock for example owned sixteen in 'Midspit Weind' worth £9 5s. 0d. a year. Shops and warehouses were of great value: Mr. Watson rented from the Corporation a shop under the town hall which was worth £6 0s. 0d., and an adjoining barber's shop worth £1. James Cowburn had '2 Butchers shops and rooms over' worth £4. Large numbers of stables, gardens and orchards are listed. Mr. Bradley's property included twelve

Fete on Miller Park c1890. On Sundays and holidays great crowds took advantage of the town's public parks. The rolling of Easter Eggs on Avenham Park has long been a major local event. By contrast this assembly appears an extremely genteel one. The graceful lines of the East Lancashire Railway bridge can be seen in the distance.

The west side of Winckley Square c.1863. Latterly a part of the Winckley Square convent school, this porticoed building was formerly the home of Thomas Batty Addison, the great political opponent of Joseph Livesey.

gardens worth £4 10s. 0d. a year.

Preston comprised a considerable range of properties. The traditional and abiding love of ale manifested by Prestonians is also represented. The prosperous *Black Bull* was valued at £26 5s. 0d. a year, and 'the brewery' at no less than £31. Valued at £7 10s. 0d. was a coffee house in the Derby estate which provided a more fashionable focus for the town.

Eighteenth-century Guilds

The town's fashionable characteristics and amusements were very much to the fore during the Preston Guilds. Ralph Thoresby, the diarist, was a visitor in 1702. He managed to avoid the worst of the

The junction of Avenham Lane and Bairstow Street seen from Bushell Place c.1863. Gates and gatekeepers were used to good effect to keep undesirable types out of the more select areas.

The south side of Winckley Square c.1863. Amazingly, there were plans in the 1960s to build a multi-storey car park in the centre of Winckley Square, and to route a southern town centre ring-road along the upper edge of Avenham Park. In the event the area has been conserved, retains much of its Georgian charm, and has been the subject of a detailed history by Marian Roberts.

drinking, and the Mayor 'made us a compliment of our freedom, but we thought ourselves more free without it'.

Sept 4th walked . . . to view the Town, wherein are several very good houses, but none so stately as that where the Duke of Hamilton usually resides . . . the town chiefly [depends] upon the quill, here being kept all the courts relating to the County Palatine of Lancaster, as the Court of Chancery . . . We then walked to the fields to an eminency [Avenham] lately purchased by the town, where is a very curious walk and delicate prospect . . . Dined at Lawyer Starkey's with Justice Parker and much good company . . .

Nor were the town's attractions and society connections lost on the diarist Nicholas Blundell, who recorded many visits to Preston in his *Great Diurnall.*

The Guild Rolls of 1722 list almost four thousand individuals and only slightly fewer were recorded twenty years later. The Guild of 1762 was extensively described by contemporaries: 'As Preston is the only Borough Town, in this Kingdom, as far as we have heard, wherein a Guild Merchant has ever been solemnly held, by Royal Charter'.[16] In an age when the town had its own distinct social season the Guilds had become

Avenham Lane looking towards Ribblesdale Place c.1880. Within a very short distance Avenham Lane passes from the mean, overcrowded streets and weinds of the old town to the fashionable suburb of the Upper Walks, a sharp social divide clearly reflected in the townscape of the area.

Stage coach outing from Church Street, 1899. Before the coming of the railway in 1838 Preston was an important coaching centre. In 1836, among others 'The Wonder' ran from the Red Lion Inn to Burnley, the 'Delight' to Lytham from the Castle Inn, and the 'Invincible' ran to Leeds from the Legs O' Man.

major social events in the county.

Preston's earliest newspaper is variously known as the *Preston Journal* or *The True British Courant*. Though little more than a broadsheet containing items of national news and military affairs, it does reveal something of the town's affairs.[17] In June 1745 the printer Robert Moon gave notice that his paper, 'Containing authentic News both Foreign and Domestic will be continued weekly, and may be had at his shop in the Cheapside, Preston, every Friday, for Eighteen Pence per quarter'. The surviving papers contain many local announcements, such as the dates of the Winter Fair, the vacancy for an Usher of Preston School (any applicant to show himself 'well recommended as to his moral Character and that he has a competent knowledge of the classic authors'), plans for a bridge at Penwortham (found to be 'Absolutely necessary for the Benefit and Safety of the Publick'), sale notices, and quack remedies and cures – sold by the father of the town's great artists ('Sold only in Preston by Mr Anthony Devis, in Church St: The true Scots Pills').

In an expansive vein, and anxious to outsell his rivals, John Moon wrote of the 1762 Guild:

> There was, on this occasion, an amazing concourse of People, from many parts of the Kingdom, and from all parts of the County. This spectacle was allowed to surpass any Thing of the kind ever seen in the Country, and exceeded the expectation of everyone present, as well in point of the brilliancy and grandeur that attended it, as in respect of the regularity and decorum with which it was conducted.

In addition to the ceremonial events and main entertainments the town was crowded with singers, dancers, jugglers, tightrope walkers and acrobats, and there were puppet shows, farces and wild beast shows – all the 'fringe' activities associated with the great festivals of today. Some events were held in the new Guild Hall, and the grand balls held in the 'state rooms' of the Town Hall were fully subscribed by up to one thousand people each dance night: 'It is said that the expense of the candles alone amounted to £200'. For the less fashionable, 'Large quantities of Ale and Beer, and cold Provisions of all sorts were ordered to be distributed among the Populace each day'.[18]

Notwithstanding the collapse of the Town Hall in 1780 and warnings of 'large groups of Housebreakers, Pickpockets and Sharpers' heading for the town, the plays, concerts and popular amusements were once again at the forefront of the 1782 Guild. This celebration marked a significant watershed in the history of the festival, for with the decline of the economic and political rights of burgess-ship conferred through the Guild Merchant the Guild began to take on the characteristics more of a popular carnival and ceremonial entertainment.

The 1782 proceedings were recorded in the *Manchester Mercury*:

> We hear from Preston that no expense is spared to render their approaching Guild agreeable. The New Town Hall, which has been some time in building, is now finished in a most elegant and masterly manner: it adjoins the Guild Hall, which is also very handsome, being decorated anew.

Perhaps to the chagrin of the fashionable set in Liverpool and Manchester it was generally conceded that 'Preston might truly be called the Region of Pleasure. Several people of the first fashion were here, and a great many of the middling rank'.[19]

—— *The Devis family of painters* ——

During the early eighteenth century the Devis family of artists were prominent in the town. Anthony Devis settled in Preston around 1710, and in 1729 was elected as a councillor. The town's most famous artist, his son Arthur, was born in Preston in 1711. In 1742 he married Elizabeth Faulkner in London; she bore him 22 children, of whom only six reached adulthood. Among them were Thomas Anthony (1757–1818) who specialised in portraiture and subject painting, and Arthur William (1762–1822), a favourite of Sir Joshua Reynolds.

Arthur William, the nineteenth child, embarked on a tour of the world, was shipwrecked in the China Seas and established himself as a portrait painter in the British possessions in India. Though instructed by his father it is said that 'he evinced a genius for painting from early childhood'. His important works include *Portrait of Warren Hastings (1785)* and *The Death of Nelson* (1806) in the National Maritime Museum. His work was exhibited at the Royal Academy in 1781-82, 1791 and annually from 1796-1821. Arthur Devis's step-brother Anthony Devis junior (1729–1816) was born in Preston and was elected to the Corporation in 1753. He travelled extensively in Britain, producing hundreds of fine topographical drawings, and his work was exhibited at the Royal Academy in 1772 and 1781.

Precisely when Arthur and Anthony Devis left Preston to pursue their careers is uncertain, but Arthur is said to have been mistaken for the Young Pretender in the town in 1745. This may not be literally true, but a pair of miniatures in the Harris Museum does suggest that he and the Prince had a strong physical resemblance. As artists serving a limited market among the gentry, the Devis family must have travelled extensively.

Among Arthur Devis' works of local interest are *View of Hoghton Tower* (1734), for which he was paid six guineas; portraits of Robert Gwillym of Atherton, William Farington of Worden, Ralph Assheton of Cuerdale (1742), General John Burgoyne, and Nicholas Fazackerley, MP for Preston 1732–67; a self-portrait of 1742; and a family group showing the Heskeths of North Meols and Tulketh Hall. The Ribble, Hoghton Tower and St. Leonard's Church, Walton-le-Dale, are the background to *Lady and Gentleman on a Terrace* (1754) and it has been suggested that the couple may be Mr and Mrs Starkie of Frenchwood House.

Among the Harris Museum's more curious items is a model tomb, acquired in 1936, containing cuttings of the hair of Arthur Devis and his wife along with her wedding ring. Together with the town's architectural masterpiece, Winckley Square, the paintings of the Devis family form a rich artistic link with Preston's own Age of Elegance.[20]

The Derby Interest

The top of the social pyramid in Preston was unquestionably occupied by the Earl of Derby and the Stanley family. Beneath lay the Hoghtons, Faringtons, Rawstornes, a myriad of lesser gentry, the town's aldermen and councillors and their wives, and the more prosperous merchants. Before the Industrial Revolution threw up new fortunes to challenge the old order, the Derby interest directed the even tenor of the social and political life of Preston, which was something of a regional capital for the Derby family. S. W. Urbanski, in a masterly study of Preston politics, has identified three key elements of the Derby domination: their extensive property in the town; valuable patronage; and their great prestige and long-standing association.[21]

The Derby estate in Preston by the end of the eighteenth century comprised ancient land holdings; property brought into the family by the marriage of Sir Thomas Stanley and Elizabeth, heiress of Thomas Patten; and blocks of property bought systematically during the second half of the century, perhaps to bolster the family's political interest. Land holdings in Preston dated back to the establishment of the earldom, to lands granted in 1489 by the King to Thomas, 1st Earl of Derby, 'In order that the Earl and his heirs may be more honourably to sustain the state and name of Earl of Derby'. Among these lands, 'lately forfeited' by James Harrington, were those in 'Preston in Amounderness, 2 burgages, 4 acres of land, and a rent of 2s. 6d'.[22]

During the sixteenth century the Derbys accumulated a vast Lancashire estate, with extensive land holdings in the Fylde. The *Inquisition* on the death of Ferdinando, 5th Earl, held in 1595 lists '2000 Messuages, 200 cottages, 20 watermills, 10,000 acres of land, 3000 acres of meadow, 6000 acres of pasture, 2000 acres of wood, 8000 acres of moor and moss, 6000 acres of heath and furze'.[23]

In this broad context the Preston property itself was of limited significance, but the town had considerable political and military importance as the 'capital' of Lancashire, and was the county town in all but name. Preston could return two MPs who would be supporters of Lord Derby in Parliament, and in times of strife was an important potential stronghold. During the Civil War it had been very much Lord Derby's town. As a fashionable resort and regional capital, Preston was a natural centre for the North-West's greatest magnates to exercise their political authority and social leadership. In addition the Earls seem to have been genuinely popular among the townspeople, as the career of James Stanley, the 7th Earl, during the Civil War had shown. The long-

The Derby Room, Bull and Royal Hotel, 1900. Built at the expense of the 12th Earl of Derby, the Assembly Room was one of the most fashionable salons in early nineteenth-century Preston. Whittle wrote that 'Sedan chairs are in constant requisition during the winter assemblies'. The room was used for balls during the Preston Rose Week and other public events.

standing, if occasional, feuds between the Corporation of Preston and successive Earls do not seem to have extended to the general populace.

This link was greatly strengthened in 1688 by the marriage of Elizabeth Patten to Sir Thomas Stanley of the Bickerstaffe branch of the family, MP for Preston 1695–8. Their son Edward was born at Preston in 1689, was Mayor in 1731, and on the extinction of the main line of the Stanleys succeeded as 11th Earl of Derby in 1736.[24] With this marriage the Stanleys acquired Thomas Patten's estates in Preston, including Patten House – a fine building admired by Dr. Kuerden, Celia Fiennes and Daniel Defoe. The house stood opposite the top end of Grimshaw Street, set back about thirty yards on the north side of Church Street. The house seems to have been a popular family home, and since the early 'Preston Stanleys' were deeply involved in the town's affairs it became the natural centre of what thus became the great Derby Interest in Preston.[25]

The estate papers reveal the major expansion of family property in the town. Much of this was housing, but land holdings became important as industrial sites and house-building plots in the early nineteenth century, proving a valuable source of ground rents. From the surviving estate rentals it is possible to trace the increase in the annual rental value of these properties, and occasionally their sale later in the nineteenth century for large sums. For example Lutwidges, purchased for £4546 in 1787 and a lucrative part of the Preston estate, was worth £415 in 1790, rising to £703 in 1810, and by 1830 £1150 *per annum*. Thus although the Industrial Revolution eventually undermined the Stanleys' political position in Preston there were compensations in the greatly increased value of their Preston estate.

Accordingly the income from the Preston estate was steadily rising by the end of the century, from £1300 in 1796 and £2900 in 1797, to over £4000 in 1798 with the development of the Dale Street industrial premises. By 1801 the rental was worth just under £5000 (£3500 net of costs), of which John Watson's factory contributed £2800. In 1803 Watson bought the factory from the estate and the revenue fell accordingly to about £2500 per year. During the same period the annual revenue from the Derby estate in Lancashire was approaching £100,000, perhaps £75,000 net of costs. The importance of the Preston estate lay, however, in the political leverage it could exert. Direct pressure could be exerted over the wide electorate through the estate's role as landlord, controlling the rents and leases of a large number of dwellings.[26]

By 1790 the value of the Preston house and small business rents in three hundred lots was approaching £1500 per year, and rose to £2379 in 1810, £2876 in 1830 and £3488 in 1840. They came largely from a great variety of small and often sub-divided premises concentrated in the main residential blocks in the centre of the town: on either side of Church Street; in the vicinity of Lancaster Lane; and on the east side of the market place. The estate included many of the town's inns and probably a majority of its butchers' shops, particularly those located in the Shambles. With the development of the textile industry, mill premises were added to this list, notably the Church Street factory built for John Watson and known as Lord's Mill. In these years, therefore, there cannot have been many commercial activities, or even aspects of everyday life, for which the Derby estate did not at some stage exact payment of rent – at least in theory. A survey of 1819 reveals a depressing picture of rent arrears: in a list of rentals totalling £670 annually arrears had reached £963, and against many names is written, 'Money will never be got'[27]

In addition to direct controls over rents and leases, the Stanleys could exert more subtle influence on the town's affairs through patronage. This could take forms besides actual expenditure in the town: gifts to local charities, sponsorship of sport, or their presence at major social events. Although at least a section of the Corporation may have resented what they saw as the Derby interference in their affairs, the Derby Interest obviously brought them direct and considerable financial benefits, and was the price they had to pay for the large array of purchases from the town's markets and shops required for the upkeep of Patten House, and its stream of well-to-do visitors.

The Derbys' patronage of social events is perhaps best exemplified by the Preston Guilds, but could extend to much more modest affairs, such as Lord Stanley's coming of age celebrated in April 1796, and sporting events. Well into the nineteenth century cockfighting was a fashionable sport, and was organised in conjunction with the Preston Races. By this date the cockpit was located at the bottom of St. John's Place, and also served as a Sunday School. Anthony Hewitson described the proceedings:

> The rabble were not admitted to this place when fighting was going on. The results were shouted out of the windows to the crowd below. An old woman, named Jenny Bell, who lived near the building, used to get the killed cocks for sale.

This cockpit closed in the 1830s following the withdrawal of the Stanleys from the town after Orator Hunt's great election victory.[28]

Preston Races were run on the moor as early as 1695. Held annually here from 1726 they fell victim to the rivalry between the Corporation and the Derby Interest from 1786–91, when the latter organised rival races on Fulwood Moor. Thereafter they were held here until 1833. With the Stanleys' breach with Preston the races ended. Racing was revived on Penwortham Holme during the 1842 Guild and were held there until permanently discontinued in 1848 after fighting between troops and police.[29] During the early nineteenth century the principal event was the Preston Gold Cup, won each year from 1815 to 1821 by Mr. Riddell's *Doctor Syntax*.

A relic of another fashionable sport can still be seen in the pavement at the south-west corner of the market square: the lead stump of the tethering post for the town's bull. The *Preston Journal* of September 1808 describes a bull-bait at Fishwick, from which the onlookers gained such pleasure from the barbaric proceedings that the dogs were pulled off the bull to 'fight' again the following day, but 'To the disappointment of a number of gentlemen, and the grief, we doubt not, of the owner, the bull died in the night'.[30]

Thus by the late eighteenth century the Earl of Derby's estate in Preston was considerable, the Stanley family led the town's fashionable circles and patronised its major sporting and social events. There can be no doubt that the town gained financially from the residence in it of one of the North's principal landed magnates. In return the town was expected to give the Earl its political support by returning his two nominees to Parliament.

——— *The 'Great Election' of 1768* ———

The political roots of what came to be known as the 'Great Election' went back over a hundred years. After a disputed parliamentary election in 1661 the Committee of Privilege and Elections reported to the House of Commons:

> the question being, whether the Mayor and Twenty-four Burgesses had only voices; or the Inhabitants at large; the committee was of opinion, *that all the inhabitants had voices in the election . . .*

Thereafter the Corporation determined that all resident in-burgesses had the vote, and considerable interest focused on the status of the burgesses in the Guild Rolls.

This political settlement prevailed until the remarkable election of 1768, which brought to the surface the main conflicts in Preston society at that time: between Council and townspeople; the burgesses and 'foreigners'; the Corporation and the Stanleys and Hoghtons, and all the various religious denominations against each other. As Abrams concluded, 'few election contests so implacably bitter or so desperately ferocious have ever been waged in this country'.[31]

The Corporation nominated Sir Peter Leicester and Sir Frank Standish to represent the Tory interest, whilst Lt. Colonel John Burgoyne, the husband of Lady Charlotte Stanley, was put forward to support the Whig cause with the non-conformist Sir Henry Hoghton. The writs for the election arrived in June 1767 and the poll opened at 10.40 a.m. on 21st March 1768. The interim period was dominated by 'The Canvass', in which each side used bribery and violence to draw up their lists of voters. John Burgoyne in particular seems to have been deeply involved and was subsequently fined £1,000 for his activities. Despite these efforts, when the canvass was finished the advantage was seen still to lie with the Tories. Thereafter the proceedings lurched towards mob rule:

> It was found that the town of Preston did not furnish a sufficient

contingent of fighting men for this warfare; and large bodies of farm labourers, delph men, and others were brought into the town from the neighbouring estates of the Earl of Derby and Sir Henry Hoghton, to fight under the flag of Colonel Burgoyne; whilst the colliers upon the estates of Sir Frank Standish, and the labourers of other local Tory squires, were fetched up to make reprisals in the interest of the two Tory baronets who were candidates.[32]

St. Mary's Catholic Church in Friargate was set on fire, and the Mayor, Mr. Moss, was put under the town pump by Burgoyne's thugs. A letter from Preston dated 21st February was printed in the *Gentleman's Magazine* for March 1768:

> The contest here is attended with imminent danger. I have just escaped with many friends. The country is now up in arms. As the town is abandoned by our men, the cry is 'Leave not a freeman alive'! God knows where this will end. I think tonight or tomorrow may be fatal to many. This is shocking work in a civilised country.[33]

Ultimately, as this state of affairs was brought to the attention of the authorities in London, Burgoyne's men forced ten of the leading Tories to sign a statement absolving them from any blame for the troubles. The presence of a huge mob threatening to fire his warehouse may have made Thomas Pedder, for example, more inclined to sign.

The 'electorate' were to present themselves openly in groups of ten Whigs or Tories, and the vote was to continue in tens until neither side could muster further votes. The voters passed between strong-arm men into the Town Hall, where before a panel of officials and lawyers they stated their vote – providing that they could demonstrate their right to do so. Both Lord Strange and Burgoyne were generally in attendance, but the Tory candidates kept away for their own safety.

The nature of the franchise qualification immediately became crucial. If it could be restricted to the resident in-burgesses (who were named on the Guild Rolls) then the Tories would win. A wider franchise, including *all* adult male residents, would assist the Whigs. The eligibility of each potential voter was thus carefully scrutinised. 'Witnesses' were produced by both parties to contest questionable cases, and their evidence, along with the voting intentions of those people rejected as voters, was carefully recorded in the poll book. This is virtually a directory of the male inhabitants of Preston at the end of the 1760s, and is thus a priceless source of the local history of the period:[34]

> Thomas Dewhurst
> Charge with having a bastard child and fined £5. This was paid for him by supporters of Leicester and Standish.
> Evidence of Thomas Turner: 'The first time I saw him was at the Boars Head – he say'd he would gladly have boon o'th 'other side – but he must vote for those who cleared him of the bastard child.'
> Vote Admitted: Voted for Leicester and Standish.

James Hall
Evidence of John Cardwell 'He is a seafaring man, he lives in Preston, has been a pilot lately – he has a share of a flat [a boat] and brings coals to Preston in it.'
Evidence of Nicholas Walmesly 'He has sailed aboard my vessels.'
Vote Admitted: Hoghton and Burgoyne.

Evan Health Jun
Objected to as not being a man: claimed to be 'More of the female than the male.' Had him inspected by an apothecary 'privately and prove the contrary.'
Vote Admitted: Leicester and Standish.

Many 'voters' clearly had no right to the Preston vote, and had recently entered the town in the hope of selling their vote. Liverpudlians, Longtoners and Huttonians seem to have been particularly culpable in this respect. On Friday 25th March the rejection of a large number of his supporters led Colonel Burgoyne to remark that, 'He should not be surprised after what he had seen this Day, if the best Vote in Preston was refused'.[35]

By the eighth day of the poll the Whigs, falling behind, played their trump card. They claimed that the forgotten parliamentary judgement of 1661 that 'All the inhabitants . . . of Preston have voices in the election' meant all male inhabitants. Many of the rejected votes were thus valid. At the close of the poll the Mayor judged that the Tories had clearly won by 565 votes to 489, a majority of 76. The result was contested and given the strong Stanley party in Parliament the Whig claim was upheld, leading to the reversal of the poll by a majority by 1147 votes to 567. Leicester and Standish were turned out of their seats and Burgoyne and Hoghton installed in their places.

The implications were immense: seven years before the Declaration of Independence, 22 years before the French Revolution, and 150 years before the Act of 1918, universal manhood suffrage had been established in Preston. The dispute between the two elitist groups had thus resulted in the vote being thrown open to the masses, and Preston (along with Westminster) enjoyed the most democratic franchise in England. The judgement effectively destroyed the Corporation's ability to regulate the electoral roll, and significantly reduced the political importance of the Guild Merchant.

CHAPTER TEN

The early cotton masters

THE rapid expansion of the Lancashire cotton industry in the decades after 1770 followed centuries of steady development in the local manufacture and trade in both woollen and linen goods. In 1700 the Town Council informed Parliament that, 'The making of linen cloth hath for many ages been the settled trade of their neighbourhood and is the sole dependence of hundreds of families', and in 1674 a 'workhouse' was established to put to work the 'wandring and begging' poor of Preston – many of them children. It was located on the corner of Bolton's Court and Avenham Lane, and a 'master workman' was to instruct the inhabitants in the 'art, science, craft or mystery . . . of greasing, carding, spinning and workeing the sade wooll into yarn.' Those who did not care for this opportunity of advancement were to be sent to the House of Correction, 'There to be whypt and sett to hard labour and receive due correction for their idleness'.[1]

Preston's development was influenced by its location. Its market-orientated economy gave it wide contacts with the surrounding area where handloom weaving was expanding slowly, and Preston's position meant that it naturally developed as a local centre from which the 'putting out' system was organised. Later, with cotton extending its grip on Lancashire's textile industry, Preston became established in the mechanised spinning of yarn to meet the demands of a wide handloom weaving hinterland. At a time when a single loom could absorb the output of around half a dozen spinners, there was clearly a strong incentive for technical improvement of the spinning process.

Richard Arkwright was born in Preston on 23rd December 1732. His family has been traced in the Fylde back to the Middle Ages. They were enrolled at the 1562 Preston Guild, and during the seventeenth century lived in Back Lane, off Friargate. Richard was apprenticed to a Kirkham barber, and then in 1750 moved to Bolton, his home for the next eighteen years. He prospered as a peruke (wig) maker, and in 1762 became in addition landlord of the *Black Boy*. His son, also Richard, was born in 1755, and in 1768 the family returned to Preston.[2]

During these years Arkwright became obsessed with the possibilities of spinning yarn mechanically, to the despair of his wife who saw his

business neglected and who ultimately left
him. In association with Thomas Hayes
(Highes) and John Kay, a machine was finally
developed while Arkwright was living in
Preston in 1768. The secrecy surrounding
their stay at the Rev. Ellis Henry's house in
Stoneygate is revealed in Arkwright's description in the poll book of that year:

Richard Arkwright

Evidence of Mr. Henry [Headmaster of the
Free Grammar School in Stoneygate] 'Let
him some Rooms in his House – has
resided there since January – at 7 guineas
per Annum – making a machine to find
out the Longtitude.'

Evidence of Jno Kay 'Has known him 12
months – is a servant assisting him in
making a machine. Knows not where he
came from – but by Lr from Manchester –
works about a machine – knows not what
it is for, but believes to find out
Longtitude.'

Another account describes him as a 'Barber
working on clockwork'. The fears of interlopers stealing his machine, or of
mob action (such as had greeted the first spinning jennies) were not
misplaced as events were to prove. An old story relates how two crones living
in an adjacent thatched cottage mistook the whirrings of the prototype for
Arkwright and Kay dancing a reel to the devil's bagpipes!

By the early summer of 1768 many of the practical problems had been
solved. A flax-spinning wheel, the Saxony Wheel, was adapted to spin and
twist the fibres as they passed between successively faster moving pairs of
rollers. Although this device had original features several rivals subsequently
came forward protesting that Arkwright had stolen their inventions – as
indeed the shrewd Prestonian probably had. Arkwright and Kay moved to
Nottingham, and with financial backing from Samuel Need and Jedediah
Strutt, a partnership and first mill was established. The spinning frame was
patented in 1769, and power for this first venture was provided by a horse gin.
This proved to be inadequate and it was decided to relocate the enterprise at
Cromford where adequate water power could be harnessed.

The long narrow mill at Cromford became the prototype for all that came
after it, and all the preliminary production stages were also mechanised and
patented, including carding and roving. Seeing production in terms of an
industrial process, Arkwright thus laid the basis of the modern industrial
system, and ensured that he alone had the rights to operate it. His principal
workmen were bound by long contracts, and every effort was made to prevent

*Arkwright House,
Stoneygate, 1946. Dating
from the early eighteenth
century, when it was built as
the house of the Grammar
School master, the building's
world fame is due to the
activities of Richard
Arkwright, who lodged here
briefly in 1768, during which
time he perfected the
mechanism of the Water
Frame. Its subsequent history
has been chequered,
although restoration in
recent years has ensured the
survival of a building which
may justly claim to have
been one of the birthplaces
of the Industrial Revolution.*

his mechanics escaping to other concerns. A vigorous pursuer in the courts, Arkwright thus maintained a close control over use of his machinery which was strictly licensed or 'franchised'.

Taking care not to over produce and so lower prices, Arkwright quite quickly amassed a huge fortune which was invested in Government stocks, leading him to boast that he could pay the National Debt. His patents which held back his rivals, and thus the overall progress of the industry, were overturned in 1785. Leaving court and overhearing one of his jubilant rival manufacturers remark, 'That's the last of the old barber,' he is supposed to have replied, 'I have a razor that will shave you all!' And 'shave' them he did, for his fortune at his death was estimated at about half a million pounds. The *Gentleman's Magazine* noted that Sir Richard had: 'Died immensely rich, and has left manufactories the income of which is greater than that of most German principalities'.[3] His son inherited the family acumen, rising status and wealth which by his death he had extended to somewhere between three and seven million pounds. The place in history of the greatest Prestonian has been precisely yet succinctly stated by his biographer R. S. Fitton:

> The founder of the factory system, he was the creator of a new industrial society that transformed England from a nearly self-sufficient country with an economy based on agriculture and domestic manufacture, into the workshop of the world.[4]

With its lack of fast flowing streams, Preston did not possess the water resources Arkwright's Water Frame required, and the town's early mill production was based on Hargreaves' 'Spinning Jenny' and Crompton's 'Mule', powered by hand, windmill, or horse gin. To the south of the town, however, a number of good watermill sites were exploited from this

Handloom weavers' step houses, Mount Pleasant, 1952. The step houses consisted of a simple two-up, two-down cottage with a semi-subterranean cellar. The cellars might contain up to four looms, requiring the combined labour of all the inhabitants of the house. After the 1840s, with the introduction of the power loom, most cellars were sublet to poorer tenants.

Mule-spinning inside the Big Factory 1835. Notice the small child sweeping beneath the moving drawing-carriage on the right.

Powerloom-weaving inside the Big Factory, 1835.

period along the River Darwen, at Hoghton Bottoms, Samlesbury Bottoms, Roach Bridge, and perhaps Higher Walton. Indeed, with the mills higher up at Darwen and Blackburn, the modest River Darwen had a good claim to be one of the most heavily undustrialised waterways in the world at this time.

Together with the mechanisation of the spinning process and closer control over the weaving side of the industry came major developments in the cloth finishing process, particularly bleaching and printing. Walton-le-Dale, with its plentiful water resources along the Darwen, was an important and nationally early centre of these related activities. The

Clayton family of Bamber Bridge had premises on the River Lostock by the later eighteenth century, and Edward Clayton is usually regarded as the first recorded calico printer in Lancashire on the strength of a reference in the Walton parish register in 1764. During the 1780s the firm of Livesey, Hargreaves and Co., which had premises at Bannister Hall and Mosney in Walton, took the lead in the mechanisation of the cloth printing process. Developed by the Scotsman Thomas Bell at Mosney in 1783, it was introduced to counter wage demands from the hand printers. In addition to these premises the firm had 'Bleaching grounds at Hoghton Tower' (Hoghton Bottoms), a large mill at Clitheroe, a factory, warehouse and offices at Manchester, and a London warehouse. The company had its own coal pit at Standish to provide fuel, and employed large numbers of handloom weavers as out-workers.

It was claimed that they employed large numbers of the population in Preston, and were 'the means of giving bread to 20,000 persons' (including dependants) when the firm crashed spectacularly in 1788. Perhaps eight hundred workers were employed directly, with a large number of handloom and domestic workers employed indirectly.[5] With the failure of Livesey, Hargreaves and Co. in 1788, the local cotton industry came to be dominated by the two great Preston firms of John Watson and Co., and John Horrocks.

—— *John Watson and Sons* ——

The first spinning mill in Preston was built by William Collison (or Collinson) about 1777. It was located on the corner of Walker Street and Moor Lane beyond the end of Friargate on the outskirts of the town, on land owned by Ralph Watson (Mayor in 1772, 1777 and 1784). The factory was initially powered by a windmill before progressing through a horse-power phase to become perhaps the first steam-powered mill in Preston. Pre-dating the development of the spinning mule, it seems likely that this was a 'factory' or shed containing spinning jennies, or perhaps machinery for the pre-spinning processes such as carding. Hewitson, however, records that 'the mill was, it is said, fitted up with Arkwright's spinning machinery'. Shortly after this development Collison was formally joined in the venture by John Watson, a linen draper who had been a town councillor since 1764. On Collison's death the firm came under the control of John Watson.[6]

After 1785 Watson developed two spinning mills outside the town, at Roach Bridge on the River Darwen and at the Penwortham factory in Factory Lane, Walton-le-Dale. A Sun Insurance Co. policy of 1792 valued the Roach Bridge mill and its machinery at £1,000 each.[7] Both of these concerns appear to have used apprentice or orphan labour, it is said from the Foundling Hospital in London. In his autobiography Joseph Livesey

The Big Factory, Fishwick, an engraving from Baines' History of the Cotton Manufacture. *One of the largest cotton mills of its day, known locally as the 'Big Factory', the mill was operated by Swainson and Birleys. Related by marriage, the Birleys were long established Kirkham linen merchants, whilst the Swainsons had been pioneer bleachers and printers at Higher Walton in the late eighteenth century.*

described them as:

> Poor, squalid, deformed beings, the most pitiful objects I think I ever beheld . . . apprenticed to a system which nothing but West Indian slavery can bear analogy [and living in] a wretched physical condition, with crooked legs from standing 12 hours at a time.[8]

On Sundays the children were paraded a considerable distance to church at Walton and Samlesbury (where Watson built a special double gallery at the back of the nave to hold them). They were known as 'Wat Apprentices' and were dressed uniformly in brown coats with yellow collars and cuffs. This distinctive mode of dress must have given them a semblance of smartness and, of course, greatly facilitated their recapture in the event of their escape.

Notwithstanding these spinning facilities Watson was unable to meet the demand of local weavers and began to buy yarn from more distant producers, among them the young John Horrocks of Edgworth.

John Watson and Co.'s most celebrated concern was the Lord's Factory in Church Street, which was subsequently owned by William Ainsworth and Co. In June 1795 the Earl of Derby acquired the premises in Dale Street in the former Town End Field from Thomas Leeming, purchasing additional land from Thomas Pearson later the same year.[9] Whether Thomas Leeming, timber merchant, built the factory on his own account or on behalf of the Earl is unclear, but there does not appear to be evidence of its operation by him. Part of the factory contents was purchased by John Watson who became the tenant, while the rest was acquired by the Derby estate after arbitrators had valued it in November 1796. The inventory of 'Divers machines, Engines, utensils and articles used in and about the Spinning and Manufacture of Cotton', includes a wide range of smithy, metalworking and machine tools, in addition to eight double and three single mules, drawing and roving frames, and a considerable stock of spare parts, all acquired for £1,319 4s. 11d.[10] A part of the premises seems to have been subsequently used for the manufacture of mill machinery.

The financial affairs of the Preston factory are difficult to unravel, since Watson was one of the Earl's leading political agents in the town, and 'political' expenses were often used to balance rental payments. It is clear however that in the years up to 1803 the factory became an important element of the Derby estate's Preston rental, and the estate cash books reveal sizeable payments to John Watson to pay for improvements to the buildings and to purchase further machinery.[11] During these years the firm was acquiring machinery from McConnel and Kennedy – five mules in 1796 and six in 1797. Despite this expansion the Preston firm was still unable to meet all demand for yarn itself, and purchased over £9,000-worth of yarn from the same company in the years 1796–1801.[12]

In June 1803 John Watson purchased the extensive premises outright. The Estate Journal records:

Sold John Watson the factory and cottages in Dale Street, Preston . . . The two factories steam engines etc. for £4,175 to be paid by instalments annually of £1,000 and until the whole is paid to bear interest of 10% *per annum.*

The cottages and vacant ground in Dale Street as particularly described . . . for £5,643.4.0d . . . to bear interest at 5% per annum.[13]

Watson did not pay for the premises directly: rather the purchase price was added to the loans previously advanced to him. Accordingly his debt to the estate rose from £1,750 in 1802 to £11,328 4s. 0d. in 1803. In the following years he was able to pay the interest and reduce the outstanding debt which had fallen satisfactorily to £7,987s. 14s. 0d. by 1806.[14] Mutual self-interest and steadfast Whig solidarity in the face of competition from the political and commercial enemies John Horrocks and Preston Corporation, had produced an unlikely partnership between Preston's leading cotton manufacturer and the Derby Interest.

By 1807 at least a measure of control of the Watson firm seems to have passed to Watson's sons, John Watson junior and Joseph Watson. An indenture drawn up in 1806 as part of a guarantee to his sons' creditors lists among John Watson's private estate a town house and warehouse in Church Street, property in the fields at the lower end of Fishergate, land in Fulwood, Penwortham and Walton, housing in Ribbleton Lane, land along Marsh Lane, property by the site of the old friary with 29 tenants, and 'Cottages known as Starch House' in Back Lane.[15]

In 1807, 'through some trade mishap or pecuniary difficulty' he was declared bankrupt. The Watson empire came crashing down, bringing with it the partnerships of which he or his sons were members.[16] The crash followed the failure of a number of Preston firms in the earlier part of the year. In addition to the Watsons, their partners David Ainsworth (Watson, Ainsworth and Co.), Paul Catterall and James Kay (James Kay and Co., with Paul Catterall and David Ainsworth 'Machine Makers and Dealers') and Thomas Ainsworth of Blackburn, had to appear before Commissions of Bankruptcy. Accordingly John Watson junior's household goods were sold off at his house in Church Street in December, and Paul Catterall's a week later.[17]

The subsequent sale of their industrial assets provides a clear picture of the scale of their Preston operations as the town's first great cotton manufacturer: premises in Dale Street ('those two extensive, newly erected and well built cotton mills or factories . . . with a powerful steam engine . . . and 60 cottages'[18]); Moor Lane ('two spacious factories for spinning cotton and . . . a wind corn mill'[19]); a machine-making workshop and the contents of a firm's warehouse (containing over 10,000 'pieces', almost 10,000lbs of yarn and '400 dozen of very choice old wines, chiefly port and madeira'[20]). Although the Watsons were ruined, both the Ainsworths and Catteralls survived to form Preston cotton dynasties. They took over the Church Street mill and for most of the first half of the nineteenth century their business was to remain second only to that of the Horrockses in importance.

By 1808 John Watson was a debtor in gaol at Lancaster Castle. On 8th September 1813 the *Blackburn Mail* announced: 'Died on Monday week in London, John Watson Esq., formerly a very eminent manufacturer in Preston'.[21] Letters of Administration granted to his daughter describe him as 'John Watson, late of Penwortham . . . Gentleman'. His personal estate and effects were valued at less than £20.[22] He has subsequently been largely forgotten, and the credit for the establishment of the Preston cotton industry has gone to John Horrocks. Yet it is in a Victorian account of John Horrocks's career that John Watson's most fitting epitaph is perhaps to be found: 'John Watson may be regarded as the leading spirit of his day in the founding of the Cotton Industry of Preston'.[23]

—— *John and Samuel Horrocks* ——

Born in 1766, John Horrocks was the youngest of two surviving sons in a family of eighteen children. His father was a Quaker, and a relatively prosperous manufacturer of high quality mill stones at Edgworth, near Bolton. The family home, a fine building, still dominates Horrocks Fold a short distance along the lane from Thomasson Fold. This was the home of Thomas Thomasson, a man of enormous ability and foresight with a very clear vision of the economic future, whose influence was to be critical in the establishment of the Ashworth as well as the Horrocks cotton empires.[24]

Many details of John Horrocks's early life are confused. He is stated to have attended a boarding school at Manchester, although Thomasson is usually credited with his education and the discovery of his remarkable mechanical talent. John Horrocks had the good fortune to be born into a family financially able to educate him and to allow him to follow his talents into the developing cotton trade. From Thomas Thomasson he acquired the mechanical and theoretical skills which were the foundation of his early success. But over and above these factors, the textile industry had reached a critical stage of development which did not exist twenty years earlier, and was scarcely to occur again: 'It was a time of pith and moment which presented unparalleled opportunities to men of foresight, energy, skill and enterprise, such as John Horrocks'.[25]

He was clearly a man of great vision, a gifted improviser, persevering, capable and willing to undertake much physical work. Doubtless brusque and sharp of speech by turn, he was also a superb judge of character and ability, a motivator with the patience to encourage his apprentices – many of whom were to become great men in their own right. He was a formidable man of business, and a gambler able to withstand the colossal business pressures he must often have been under. Able to 'get things done' quickly by the most direct route, it seems that he did not tolerate time-wasters or the faint-hearted gladly. Perhaps most remarkable of all, during the great period of expansion of his firm he was a young man, in his late twenties and early thirties. An associate of William Pitt and one of the first manufacturers to have a seat in the House of Commons – he was MP for Preston from 1802 – he clearly had a highly influential career at the national level ahead of him, but in 1804 he died in London after a short illness at the very early age of 36. During his thirteen years in Preston he had amassed a personal fortune of at least £150,000.

The increasing industrialisation (and growing competition) around Bolton and Manchester, of which Horrocks must have had experience, pushed him in the direction of Preston where his yarn was already being put out by Watson. Since the latter was older than Horrocks, and the two were probably well-matched in terms of stubbornness, it can be no surprise that a disagreement over prices produced a bitter schism which for a time became as political as it was commercial. That the two walked arm-in-arm through the streets during the 1802 Preston Guild celebrations seems to have been a subject of genuine amazement. After some years of trading in the town, Horrocks moved permanently to Preston in 1791.

In January 1791, with his new wife, he rented a small property in Turks Head Court, off Church Street. Although carding was undertaken on these premises, it seems spinning was carried out domestically, probably on jennies. From its inception the business seems to have aimed at the higher quality end of the textiles trade, and to have enjoyed a ready demand for its fine yarns among the local handloom weavers.

In partnership with George Bolton, of the Preston banking firm of Shuttleworth, Claytons and Moore, work was begun on a factory. Although

small by later standards it seemed a radical
departure to the Prestonians of the day, and
Bolton withdrew his money in alarm. At this
moment of crisis a partnership was established with Thomas Greaves and Richard
Newsham. Horrocks was to remain free to
operate as a merchant in his own right, and
the expansion in Preston was able to
continue. The Yellow Factory in Dale Street
was probably completed in 1792; it was seven
windows long and five storeys high, and was
to be the nucleus of what became the Yard
Works. The factory was so-called because of
its faded whitewash; by contrast Watson's
supporters called the freshly painted Penwortham factory the 'White Factory'!

The pace of expansion was phenomenal. Preston has seen nothing like
it before or since, and Watson's capacity was probably outstripped within
four years. Investment and expansion must clearly have been carefully
co-ordinated. This was no piecemeal growth; rather it was the systematic
putting together of a super-giant of the cotton industry.

John Horrocks' first mill, the Yellow Factory, was built in 1791. Though tiny by later standards, the Yellow Factory was a huge investment for its day, causing Horrocks' backers to withdraw their money in alarm. Though powered by a horse-gin, the mill proved to be the foundation of Preston's largest cotton firm – 'Horrockses – The Greatest Name in Cotton'.

Though distorted by the inconsistent trading conditions caused by the
Napoleonic Wars, the firm's cash books reveal the large profits made in
most of the early years of the nineteenth century. In 1799, for example, a
company turnover of £105,000 produced profits of £55,000, representing
perhaps somewhere in the region of £15 million today, and towards the
end of the wars the firm again registered high profits: £36,735 in 1813 and
£52,923 in 1814.[26]

By 1833 the firm had nine mills employing thirteen hundred spinners
and four hundred weavers, in addition to an unknown (but very large)
number of indirectly employed domestic handloom weavers. These
developments were not, however, without their setbacks:

> On Thursday night last (Feb. 18 [1796]) a most dreadful fire happened
> in the Cotton Factory belonging to Messrs. Horrocks, at Preston, which
> burnt with such fury that in about two hours the whole of that extensive
> building, which was allowed to be the completest Factory of this kind in
> the Kingdom, was totally destroyed. Very fortunately, the wind was in
> such a direction as saved the adjoining Cotton Factory of the Earl of
> Derby, and the other extensive works adjoining; happily no lives were
> lost; and we understand the building burnt was insured to nearly the
> full value, supposed by some to be £6,000, by others, £16,000.[27]

In addition to the expansion of bricks and mortar came the
development of commercial and managerial skills to run the enterprise, a
process which has been traced by Sylvia Birtles.[28] In 1794, after a period
managing a mill in Blackburn, John's brother Samuel came into the firm,
rising to the post of manager of the Preston operation, and freeing the

Centenary Mill, New Hall Lane, c.1910. Though one of the first mills of modern concrete and steel construction, Horrockses Centenary Mill (1892) retained the fashionable architectural facade deemed tasteful by the shareholders of the day. Together with Cliff Mill and Tulketh Mill, the Centenary Mill marked the last phase of the construction of large spinning mills in the town.

The Yellow Factory, Yard Works, an engraving from Hardwick's History of Preston. *This print gives a good impression of the huge scale of the premises, and the extent to which the pioneer Yellow Factory came to be overwhelmed by subsequent developments. Mill chimneys can be a good guide to the age of a mill. Square-sectioned ones like this usually date from before 1860, and round ones predominate thereafter. The local race to build the highest chimney was probably won by Higher Walton mill at 240 feet.*

founder to concentrate on the London office and its mercantile connections. On the death of his brother, Samuel Horrocks took over the running of the firm on behalf of trustees, but on the lines laid down by John. In 1802 their brother-in-law John Whitehead was brought in to assist Samuel, ultimately becoming a partner. Thomas Miller, a small farmer with an interest in textiles, and also from the Bolton area, possibly joined the firm as early as 1795 and became a partner in 1801. After the death of John Horrocks he developed the firm, which from 1815 until 1887 was styled 'Horrockses, Miller and Co.' He was succeeded after his death in 1841 by his son, the second Thomas Miller, the greatest of the mid-Victorian 'Cotton Lords of Preston'. On his death in 1865 the early family link in the firm's management came to an end.

Several of the early company apprentices were to establish firms of their own, often with the assistance of Horrockses. John Bairstow, a one-time apprentice in the Bolton warehouse, established the firm of Horrocks, Bairstow and Co. Richard Riley, a foreman in the mechanics' shop of the Yard Factory, and a joiner, John Paley, established – with John Horrocks's help – a machine shop and foundry in Heatley Street which provided the parent firm with engines and machinery. In 1802 John Paley moved into cotton in his own right, establishing the Royal Sovereign Mill and Bank Top Mill, and his own mill-owning dynasty.

An apprentice, William Taylor, married one of John Whitehead's daughters and established the first Tulketh Mill in 1835. The Turks Head Court premises were taken over by Isaac and George Horrocks, who having been joined by another former Horrocks apprentice, George Jackson, established the firm of Horrocks and Jackson.[29] Taking all these family, personal, commercial and financial connections together, and with the exception of the Watson firm, it has been fairly said that at the time of his death John Horrocks virtually was the Preston cotton industry.[30]

The handloom weavers

Despite the progressive mechanisation of spinning and other processes, the late eighteenth century was the golden age of the handloom weaver. Although they were no longer the independent artisans they had once been, and by the 1780s and '90s were very much under the control of the putters-out who supplied yarn and collected finished pieces, the handloom weaver was an immensely important figure. The availability of cheap yarn made possible a major expansion of cloth exports, and there was a great need for weavers to meet the demand. Plain weaving could readily be taught and looms acquired relatively cheaply, and there was a great expansion of the industry in the Preston district. As Lawrence Rawstorne of Penwortham later recalled: 'At the time that weaving was at its tip-top price . . . all other considerations gave way to it. A good handloom weaver would then earn his 30s. a week or even more: he would perhaps work half the week and drink the remainder'.[31] In 1799 Preston Corporation, eager to share in the handloom bounty, converted the House of Correction into a weaving shop and its captive inhabitants into an industrious workforce. By 1821 they were making a profit of almost £1,400 per year for the ratepayers.

The economic effects of the textiles boom reached out from the spinning towns such as Preston into the weaving countryside. As John Holt remarked, 'The rate of wages is in proportion to the distance of the townships from the seats of manufacture'.[32] Where competition for labour was greatest, wages were highest, and the migration into the towns gathered pace. Since Preston was on the edge of a large rural district – the Fylde – the town enjoyed a constant stream of unskilled and cheap labour and as labour was usually reckoned by the 1820s to be roughly 30% of production costs, the town enjoyed a clear advantage over its more clustered rivals. In this way the lack of local coal supplies (perhaps accounting typically for 5% of costs) was more than compensated for.

From the 1790s specific building societies were formed to provide purpose-built cottages over weavers' shops, the so-called step-houses. Important local examples include Club Row in Longridge, Union Street and Bradshaw Street in Leyland, and Club Street in Bamber Bridge (whose inhabitants 'excelled in fighting, vice and profanity').[33] Large numbers of similar dwellings were provided in Preston, whose most celebrated colony of handloom weavers was housed by Horrockses in 'New Preston', at the Stanley Street end of New Hall Lane:

William Shakeshaft's map of Preston 1822. This map clearly illustrates the intensive development around the Yard Works, the line of the Lancaster Canal, and the spread of housing onto the ancient townfield strips along Avenham Lane. Colonies of handloom weavers' houses had grown up around the north end of Friargate, and at 'New Preston' in New Hall Lane. Within the confines of the old town the construction of houses upon the gardens of former burgage plots had produced appalling conditions of overcrowding. Growth of the town had simply not kept pace with the growth of its population.

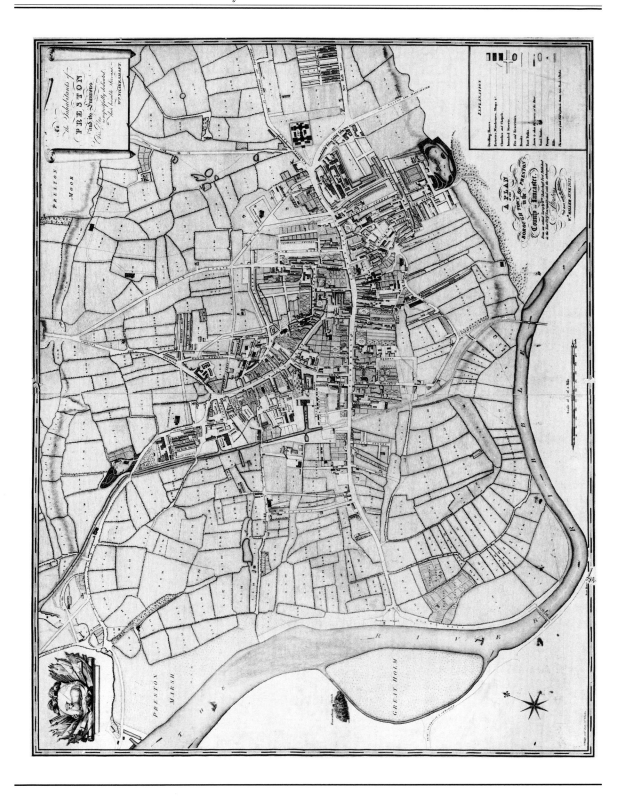

The male denizens of 'New Preston' were, in the old days of handloom weaving, an exceedingly rough lot. They could earn good wages after playing 2 or 3 days a week. In their leisure time, or in the time in which they did not care to work, they used to swagger about in top boots, and extract what, to their minds was enjoyment, from badger baiting, dog-worrying, cock-fighting, poaching and drinking. A pack of hounds was, in the days we are talking about, kept in 'New Preston' for the recreation of the people.[34]

'New Preston' was a comparatively novel development, for there specialised loom shops were laid out as separate buildings between the rows of houses, perhaps in preparation for the use of power looms:

The power-loom was not invented until long after Mr. Horrocks' decease, but when he built the cottages and weaving shops at New Preston he had some notion of arranging for his looms being propelled by steam, and he often observed that, to supply the market with cloth, the agency of steam would have to be applied to the loom.[35]

In 1807 a memorial to the government from the Manchester Interest, calling its attention to the valuable work of Dr. Cartwright in developing an early form of power loom, was signed by the Preston manufacturers Horrocks and Co., J. Watson and Sons, Paul Catterall and Co., Sidegreaves, Leighton and Co., and Riley, Paley and Co. Andrew Kinlock,[36] another pioneer of power loom development, lived many years in the town before his death in 1849.

A recent study by Nigel Morgan has revealed the marked extent to which the development of handloom weaving transformed the geography of Preston. A poll book of 1830 records almost fifteen hundred weavers individually by name, to which must be added their helpers and wives, indicating a figure of perhaps five thousand people directly involved in the trade. The study also suggests that over one thousand houses were given over to weaving, perhaps a quarter of the dwellings in the town in 1821. Two major concentrations of such houses have been identified, between Church Street and Frenchwood (particularly Albert Street, and the streets betwen Oak and Silver Streets), and to the east of the Lancaster Canal at the lower end of Friargate (especially Heatley Street, Mount Pleasant Street, Canal Street, Kirkham Street, and Ladywell Street).[37]

In addition to 'New Preston' close by the Yard Works, Horrockses also developed a weavers' colony beside the Spittals Moss factory, centred on Kirkham Street. A similar relationship may have existed between Watson's Moor Lane Mill and Singleton's Row. Nineteenth-century commentators noted the care with which Horrocks located his mills in areas apparently convenient for the weavers. In fact weaver accommodation was developed close to the spinning mills to enable the firm to exercise closer control over production.

Thus the parallel development of factory spinning and domestic weaving brought about significant changes to the town plan, establishing a pattern of mill-led urban growth which was to dominate the evolution of the town as late as the opening of Tulketh Mill in 1905:

> The erection of each of [Horrocks's] factories was necessarily attended with the building of cottages in their vicinity. Shops and houses, and places of business, and then other mills, rose in various quarters: streets extended and branched out: fields and gardens became covered with bricks and mortar . . .[38]

Around Preston, Horrockses developed a system of warehouses which effectively drew together and centralised much of the loom production and demand for yarn of the town's hinterland. Analysis of the early company ledgers reveals two main groups of warehouses; a northern group (Kirkham, Plumpton, Blackpool, Garstang and Longridge), and a southern group (Ormskirk, Wigan, Chorley, Croston, Leyland, Longton and Hutton).

From 1820 onwards, although demand for cloth continued to expand rapidly, weavers' wages fell fairly consistently. The weavers were unable to restrict newcomers entering their trade (by long apprenticeships or membership of unions), leading to an oversupply of weavers. Wages accordingly fell. Indeed the cheapness of labour may have delayed the full introduction of power-loom weaving, which began to make significant inroads only in the 1830s and 1840s. Henceforth manufacturers increasingly concentrated production in their own power weaving sheds, using the handloom weavers only as a reservoir of production in times of excess demand. The boom days over, the handloom weaving trade became synonymous with 'the iron teeth of poverty'.

In 1834 Preston weavers gave evidence to the Royal Commission appointed to inquire into their conditions. Robert Crawford estimated that the Preston district had about thirteen thousand handloom weavers, with perhaps forty thousand people dependent on the trade. A weaver working ten or twelve hours per day could weave one cut per week, earning five to six shillings for it. Although the operation of power looms in the town was increasing, the local weavers blamed the masters and 'embezzlers' for their plight. John Lennon spoke of their living and working conditions: his rent was two shillings per week for 'A cellar that holds two looms, one bed room and a small kitchen'. The Commission could only suggest that the weavers find alternative employment, and ensure that their children did not enter the trade.[39]

After 1840 handloom weaving declined rapidly, but in the country districts around the town the trade was to survive often well into the 1860s. For a long time power looms were unable to compete in very fine or complex fabrics, whilst in villages such as Longton no alternative work was available for the rural poor. Writing towards the end of the century the Rev. Brickel, vicar of Hoole, wrote: 'I thank God that as in other places, so in Hoole at last, our young people have given up the handloom, and have found better wages with the power-looms at Walmer Bridge'.[40]

The cotton masters and the Derby Interest

The rapid rise of the cotton masters had produced an economic force at last capable of challenging the great landed interests in the politics of the town. In establishing a wide franchise to defeat the Corporation, the election of 1768 had the unforeseen effect of giving the mill masters enormous political influence and leverage over the voting intentions of their employees.

The feud between the Corporation and the Derby Interest reached new heights during the late 1780s and early 1790s, producing something approaching a real schism in the town. Separate horse races were held, and separate hunting meetings organised with distinct Whig and Tory packs of partisan hounds (the P.U. or 'Preston United' pack, and the U.P. or 'United Preston' pack). Even in the face of the very real threat of invasion by the French, separate 'Volunteer' forces were raised to defend the town – the Tory Royal Preston Volunteer Force (commanded by Nicholas Grimshaw) and the Whig Loyal Preston Volunteers Force (commanded by John Watson). Even the sedan chairs then in vogue among the town's ladies displayed similarly sectarian loyalties, and the chairmen sported collars in their party colours.

Whilst John Watson was a Whig and an important local agent of the

View of Avenham and the Tram Road c.1860. Seen from the garden of the old vicarage, this view shows the engine house of the tramway, the wooden tram bridge and Ladies Walk, bereft of its modern canopy of trees. The meadows which eventually formed Avenham Park can be seen, with Jackson's farm in the middle distance. Shortly after this photograph was taken construction of the park proper began, employing large numbers of cotton workers made unemployed by the Lancashire Cotton Famine.

Derby political cause, John Horrocks was quickly drawn into the local Tory camp which dominated the Corporation. Chosen as a burgess in 1794, he served as Town Bailiff in 1794-5, was elected a Council member in January 1796, and became an Alderman in 1799. The role of the Derby estate as a virtual sponsor of the Watson firm at this time was widely believed to be an attempt to counter Horrocks's influence among the town's rapidly emerging working class. Both the aristocratic Derby Interest and the clique of old families who comprised the antiquated Town Council thus sought to ally themselves with the rising textile interest.

At the election of 1796 John Horrocks duly represented the 'Corporation and Manufacturing Interest', but after an election of eleven days he retired beaten, the poll being: Stanley 772, Hoghton 756, Horrocks 742. Long before the next election was due it was clear that Horrocks would be almost impossible to keep out, and so a cynical compromise was reached between the two parties whereby each would put forward one candidate. Though this all but abolished the democratic principle it carried six successive elections. In 1802 Sir Henry Hoghton retired and John Horrocks and Lord Stanley were returned. On Horrocks's death his seat was taken by his brother Samuel. During his years as one of the town's members Samuel's only contribution to the proceedings of the Commons was claimed to have been an unguarded 'Oh,' whilst a book of his parliamentary speeches hawked about the town was found to contain blank pages.

The remarkable acceleration of social change represented by the rise of John Horrocks thus presaged the end of the Derby Interest. A new Preston was in the making, far removed from the quiet tenor and genteel ways of its aristocratic past. Preston became not just another classical mill town, but *the* classic mill town.

The east side of the Market Square c.1875. These buildings were demolished to make way for the Harris building, whose foundation stone was laid during the 1882 Preston Guild. The large anchor indicates Blue Anchor Court, one of the maze of ginnels which typified this historic part of the old town.

The Town Hall and Market Place c.1870 (engraving). In addition to the market place and the Town Hall, the old buildings, later to be demolished to make way for the Harris Library, Museum and Art Gallery, can be seen. Notice also the narrow entrance to Glovers Court at the top of Cheapside.

CHAPTER ELEVEN

The making of a mill town

THE great increase in Preston's population – from 11,887 people in 1801 to 69,361 in 1851 – was directly related to the growth of textiles. This rapid expansion, reaching 40% per decade in the 1830s and 1840s, had very profound and far reaching consequences on the fabric of the town; in the 1840s alone, accommodation for an additional 18,500 people had to be found. In the absence of planning controls and building regulations grossly inadequate housing was hastily thrown up to accommodate the mill workers. The principal control on housing was the amount of rent prospective tenants might be expected to be able to pay. The potential gain of landlords and builders dictated the evolution of the new industrial environment. The consequences of this unregulated and speculative growth were horrifying.[1] By the mid-century the 'improvers' could claim with some justification that the town was fifty years behind the progress of other industrial centres:

> In the consequences, the comforts, and the embellishments of life . . . It is a place slow in improving, and seems to consist only of people intent on amassing wealth by commerce, manufacture and speculation.[2]

Well into the twentieth century Preston was still paying the price for the rapid and unregulated growth of a hundred years earlier. Throughout much of the nineteenth century the town was killing large numbers of its inhabitants.

Numerous contemporary central and local government reports, surveys and local newspaper accounts attest to the appalling living conditions prevalent in most of Preston for much of the nineteenth century. In 1842 the Rev. John Clay, Chaplain to the House of Correction, produced a detailed statistical analysis of the town's death rate in his *Report on the Sanitary Conditions of Preston*. This influential study considered the causes and social implications of high mortality:

> Notwithstanding the natural advantages of Preston, the condition of

The industrial landscape: Greenbank and Moor Brook Mills c.1925. Adelphi Street may be seen in the bottom left foreground, and Garstang Road with English Martyrs Church in the top right-hand corner. Greenbank Mill, established by John Hawkins in 1836, was one of a series of mills sited on the line of the Moor Brook. The photograph shows the close relationship between industrial premises and housing in a landscape which, though it has come to typify the North of England, was in fact a product of a fairly brief period at the end of the nineteenth century.

the dwellings of the lower classes has been but little attended to, and in consequence of the inefficient sewerage, the scanty supply of water . . . the unremoved collections of animal and vegetable matter, and the general absence of the means of ordinary cleanliness, disease is engendered or aggravated, and the mortality materially increased.

Preston housing from the Rev. Clay's Report. In this example the back passageway to the houses had been turned into a great open sewer.

The difference in the life expectancy of the town's better-off and poorer inhabitants in the mid-nineteenth century was stark:

We have seen that the wealthy, who live in the best cleansed and best ventilated districts, have, from the time of birth, a probability of life extending to more than *47 years*; but that the poorest class – surrounded by the miasmata generated in filth and putridity, crowded into rooms into which pure air never penetrates, and into beds utterly and in every way unfit for their purpose, with minds sunk in ignorance, and with affections (social and family) uncultivated, with their children exposed to the unrestrained influence of disease, improperly fed, and drugged with narcotics by ignorant and indolent nurses – have their chances of life bounded by a limit extending little beyond *18 years*.[3]

In 1861 a reporter working on a series entitled *The Condition of Our*

Towns for *The Builder* magazine visited Preston. He noted the squalid courtyards and the open sewers of the old town, as well as the consequences of factory-led expansion in the new:

> New Mills are built without roads. The Queen's Mill, newly built on this moor, has neither roads nor drains; and the rain and waste streams have formed lakes around it of coal-ash mud, which the operatives must ford to enter the mill. A landowner here provides his houses with drainage and water closets: but, unfortunately, the want of playground obliges the children to play where they may, and the closets soon got out of order; and this pioneer movement was abandoned, and the reign of the cesspool returned.

In 'New Preston' and along the still largely rural New Hall Lane, he reported:

> More mills, and more unhealthy houses for the operatives . . . more mills, and more mud; a row of houses with a man weaving in a cellar in one of them, a great stagnant swamp, with a brick yard in it and a square dung heap; an isolated row of houses in Skeffington Road, with pools of drainage spread before them; more mills, more mud, more dwellings propped up while building, with 5 feet of drainage water in the cellars and a foul ditch at the rear.[4]

—— *The new Preston* ——

The expansion of the town during these years has been recorded in a large number of contemporary maps and plans.[5] Principal among these for comparative purposes are Lang's Map of 1774, Shakeshaft's map of 1808, Baines' Plan of 1825, Myers' Map of 1836 and, after 1840, the various editions and scales of the Ordnance Survey maps.

Initial development was largely confined to the fringes of the medieval town adjacent to the new factories, at Spittals Moss, Canal Street and Singleton's Row beyond the end of Friargate, to the south of Church Street in the vicinity of Frenchwood Mill, and at 'New Preston' on New Hall Lane. With the exception of these districts and the construction of the Lancaster Canal basin behind the Corn Exchange, William Shakeshaft's map of 1808 differs little from that drawn by Lang in 1774.

By 1824, however, a large working-class district had grown up to the south of Church Street and wholesale development was underway along Avenham Lane. Here, rows of narrow houses were crammed within the boundaries of the medieval fields. Redevelopment and new building within the old town had also intensified, producing tightly packed and congested weinds and housing between the Parish Church and Cannon Street. In this very short distance, a matter of only a few moments'

walk, Nigel Morgan has identified fifteen alleyways and rows of housing jammed into the former burgage plots and gardens of the Church Street houses. Here the dwellings of a large resident population jostled for space with slaughter houses and industrial premises of all kinds. Similar conditions have been identified in the back courts of Friargate. In marked contrast to these slums, but only a short distance away, the town's most fashionable district had been steadily evolving since 1799 around Winckley Square.[6] Class lines were thus very finely drawn in the urban landscape.

During the 1830s development extended to the former agricultural lands around the town, described in the Preston Tithe Map and survey. This process was outlined by Charles Hardwick in 1857:

> The Park estate, belonging Saml. Pole Shawe Esq., was opened for building land about the year 1822; Green Bank estate and Ox Heys estate, belonging to the late William Tomlinson and Thomas

Horrockses, Crewdson and Co.'s Yard Works, and Park Road, c.1925. The multi-storey spinning blocks lie at the centre of a vast expanse of single-storey weaving sheds and water lodges. This enormous industrial site had its own internal railway and gasworks. A scale model of the site, made in 1913, may be seen in the Harris Museum. To the north of Church Street the familiar pattern of housing and mills reaches out towards Moor Park.

The Preston skyline from Penwortham c.1905. The forest of cotton mill chimneys illustrates the tremendous extent of industrialisation in Preston. What this photograph does not show is the cloud of factory smoke which hung over the town on calm days.

Tomlinson, esqs., in 1834, to which was added, in 1856, by purchase from John Myers, esq., 100 acres from the Moor Hall estate; Maudlands estate, belonging Edward Pedder, esq., in 1834; Peel Hall estate (135 acres), belonging to the trustees of Gen. Fletcher in 1846: Lancaster Road and Harrison's Hill, in 1835; Freehold Park estate, Fulwood (45 acres), in 1850; Hole House estate, in 1855, about 30 acres. In 1851, Swainson, Birley and Co. opened 7 acres, purchased from Lord Derby; and Edward Stanley esq., opened, in 1852, several detached fields in the vicinity of Fishergate. The estates of Tulketh and Ashton (100 acres), the property of J. Bray, esq., E. Pedder, esq., and Jno. Able Smith, esq., were opened for building in 1853.[7]

It was the general practice for the landowner to retain ownership of the ground on which the usually terraced houses were built, providing a significant expense for their tenants as well as a lucrative source of income for themselves as 'ground rents'. Perhaps the best example of this process was the laying out of the extensive Moor Hall Estate in 1855 by J. J. Myers on behalf of the Tomlinson family. Within a rectangle formed between the lines of the railway and Garstang Road, and on the north and south by Eaves Brook and Moor Brook, he laid out a grid pattern of streets: Plungington. Housing was not built as an estate, but rather in separate house plots, sold piecemeal to a large number of builders and related tradesmen over subsequent years.[8]

By 1850 most of the town centre, once dominated by gardens and orchards, was intensively built up. The only exception was the open space called Chadwick's Orchard, near the present market. Mills and housing were pushing outwards towards Preston Moor and the marsh, and developing between Marsh Lane and Fishergate, whilst housing was extending deep into the Avenham fields. Though much of Deepdale, Ribbleton Lane and New Hall Lane remained open fields, a major new factor in the town plan had emerged – the railway.

Thirty years later the development of the great rows of terraced houses and factories, which came to typify the northern mill-town landscape, had begun to emerge along Plungington Road, Ribbleton, and New Hall Lane. The Market Square also began to acquire a familiar look; the new Town Hall was erected in the 1860s and work began on the Harris Museum and Library after the 1882 Guild. The Harris Reference Library was to be particularly important in the facilities it was to offer generations

Opened in 1824 at a cost of £11,000, the Corn Exchange was the scene of polling during Orator Hunt's great election triumph six years later, when entry to the hustings in the interior market area was blockaded by the 'Huntites' and 'Blackfeet'. Though principally the site of the town's corn market, the streets adjoining the building were the site of a number of smaller markets.

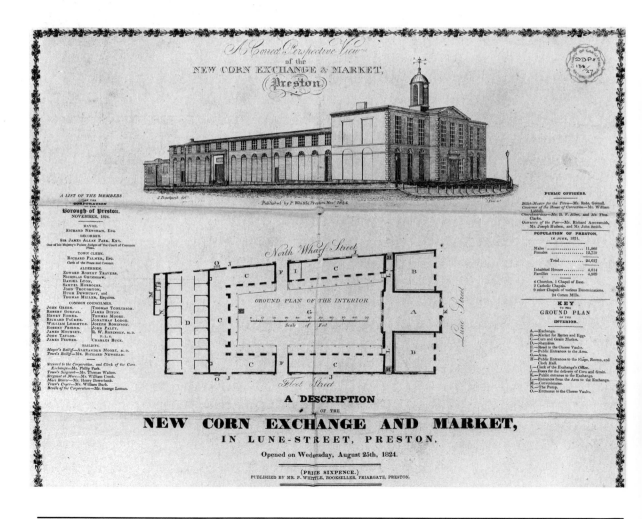

The interior of the Public Hall c.1930. For the 1882 Guild the Corn Exchange and Market were extended by the addition of the Public Hall. The Hall was a central element of town life prior to the development of Preston's ring-road in the early 1970s. In 1932 the Hall was described as 'the most elaborate and convenient building for all kinds of public assemblies, concerts, balls etc., in the north of England.'

Exhibition in the Public Hall c.1860.

of self-taught Prestonians.

By this date Moor Park Avenue had been laid out as the southern boundary of Moor Park, and Strand Road was established across the marsh between Water Lane and Fishergate. The moor and marsh thus shared the fate of the Avenham fields as Preston swallowed up its ancient town lands, and continued to reach out hungrily towards once outlying communities. New housing standards began to improve, existing housing was upgraded, and the worst of the slums were cleared during the construction of Corporation Street. Ashton, Ribbleton and Fulwood emerged as fashionable suburbs following the development of the tramway system after 1879, and expanded rapidly in the years up to the First World War.[9] Urban growth, powered first by the textile industry and then by railways and the Dock development, produced the familiar townscape of industrial Preston – the town as it existed until the early 1950s.

This form of urban growth caused many social problems. After 1800 the provision of houses did not keep pace with the growing population, leading to atrocious conditions of overcrowding in many districts of the town. This problem was perhaps at its worst in the 1850s, when the gross increase in population was greatest. Although the development of the great estates of terraced houses in the 1880s and after improved the overall position, it did little to alleviate existing overcrowding, so that the mortality rate remained very high. An even more serious problem was the town's lack of adequate services – sanitation, drainage and clean water supplies – a clear consequence of the lack of earlier planning and building controls.

Important landmarks in the emergence of such controls were the establishment in 1850 of Preston's Board of Health and the Preston Improvement Act of 1880.[10] Although the Board had only restricted powers over house building, and did not think the appointment of a medical officer worth the expense, it did begin to tackle the problem of sanitation. Despite the great efforts around the middle of the century to improve the town's water supply with the construction of the reservoirs at Longridge, supplies were insufficient for the Board to enforce the provision of water closets in new houses. Adequate sewers did not exist, and the use of earth closet privies was to be the rule for most Prestonians well into the next century.

Progress, however, began to be made. In the

Notice of sale of houses in Fishergate 1780. The growth of Preston in the early years of the Industrial Revolution was marked by overcrowding in the old centre. Often, as in this case, small houses were simply crammed into the gardens behind the larger properties on the street front.

To be Sold,
By Auction;
At *Mr. COOPER's,*
The BULL INN, in PRESTON;
On *Wednesday* the 29th Day of *Nov.* 1780;
At Seven o'Clock in the Evening;
According to such Conditions as then will be Produced.

The Inheritance in Fee, of and in

TWO Dwelling Houses, with the Appurtenances, situate on the North Side of the *Fishergate*, in *Preston*, in the Occupation of *George Whittle*, and *Mary Cowsell*, with Eight other small Dwelling Houses at the Back, in the several Occupations of *Mary Walton, Stephen Thompson, Mary Byrom, John Pilkington, Henry Topping, Margaret Dewhurst, Dorothy Page,* and *William Townley;* containing in Breadth to the Front 9 Yards and 1 Foot, or thereabouts, and in Depth backwards 40 Yards, or thereabouts.

The Tenants will shew the Premises, and further Particulars may be had of Mr. *Lodge*, of *Preston*.

PRESTON: Printed by *W. SERGENT*, where may be had STAMPS, on Parchment or Paper, the greatest Assortment.

Ribbleton Hall 1860. As Nigel Morgan has argued, the quality of housing in Victorian Preston was a reliable indicator of the income of the inhabitants – rich as well as poor.

face of much opposition Dr. Pilkington was eventually appointed part-time Medical Officer in 1874, becoming full-time in 1882. As the town's death rate approached forty per thousand, Councillor Myers argued against the appointment, reflecting a widely held view at the time: 'Preston was a most healthy town: but it was their own filthiness, and their own carelessness and recklessness that had brought them into such a state'.[11]

The struggle to establish adequate building regulations and bye-laws was similarly long and hard, and had to be fought in the face of strident opposition from the town's landowner developers, notably Sir William Edward Murray Tomlinson, MP for Preston 1882–1906. The 1880 Act enforced the use of better building materials, the construction of higher, lighter houses, and the provision of a front door step so that the ground floor had to be raised above the outside street. Houses were to be provided with backyards, for privies and water closets, to which entry was to be available by a rear access road. The eventual success of these efforts can still be seen in the large numbers of good-quality late-Victorian terraced houses which still predominate in extensive areas of the town.

Yet the bitter heritage of the boom years of the nineteenth century remained a seemingly intractible blight on the town. Outbreaks of contagious disease, including cholera and smallpox, were almost endemic at times. Between 1880 and 1900 Preston was fifteen times top, and three times runner-up, in the national table of infant mortality. In 1893 the infant mortality rate in the town was 268 per thousand: Salford, Birmingham, Manchester and Liverpool all managed to do better.[12]

—— *From tramway to railway* ——

Alongside the expansion of the textile industry came considerable improvements in the transport system – stage coach travel on better turnpike roads, the moving of heavy goods by canal, and the development of the railway system. From 1790 onwards these forces also began to shape the emerging mill town, to become an important source of employment, and to confirm Preston's ancient role as a major centre of communications.

In the early eighteenth century long-distance transport was still limited. The great traveller Arthur Young described the Preston–Wigan road, now the A49:

> I know not, in the whole range of language, terms sufficiently expressive to describe this infernal highway. Let me most seriously caution all travellers who may accidentally propose to travel this terrible country, to avoid it as they would the devil, for a thousand to one but they break their necks or their limbs by overthrows or breakings down. They will meet with ruts which I actually measured four feet deep, and floating with mud only from a wet summer! What must it therefore be in winter?[13]

From 1771 a stage coach ran between Preston, Wigan and Warrington. Three years later the fare to ride inside the Preston–Liverpool coach was a hefty 8s. 6d. In the early nineteenth century the trip to Blackpool by a luxurious 'mailcart on springs' still took 6½ hours and cost 4s. 6d.. Substantial improvements and the turn-piking of local routes greatly increased the stage coach trade of Preston's hostelries. The entrance to the town from the

This photograph shows the last man through the gate at the Lea Gate toll bar c.1900.

south, Preston brow, was cut, and in 1824 Blackburn New Road was built, using the new river crossing at the bottom of Brockholes Brow. In 1823 72 coaches arrived and departed from Preston each Wednesday, and by 1830 this number had increased to 81.[14]

Although plans for the linking of Preston and Lancaster to the projected Leeds and Liverpool Canal were put forward as early as 1760, and James Brindley was employed as consultant in 1771, little was achieved before the 1790s.[15] Preston had connections, via the Douglas Navigation and the coastal trade, with the industrial and coal producing districts to the south, but it became increasingly important for Lancaster that it be linked to the national canal network. In the midst of the 'Canal Mania' the Lancaster Canal Act was passed in 1792. John Rennie, the greatest civil engineer of his day, was appointed engineer to the Canal Company and planned to cross the rivers Lune and Ribble on aqueducts. The Lune crossing cost almost £50,000 and although it remains one of the wonders of the Industrial Revolution, its great expense led to the shelving of plans for a Ribble aqueduct. Surviving plans reveal that the Ribble crossing would indeed have been a marvel. The canal was to descend 222 feet through 32 locks from Walton Summit to a great embankment across Walton Flats and thence to the huge aqueduct itself.

By 1797 boats could sail from Tewitfield Locks near Kendal to Spittals Moss at Preston (the portion still navigable today), and south of the Ribble the Whittle tunnel linking the branch route to the Leeds and Liverpool Canal near Johnson's Hillock was nearing completion. In 1799, however, the company – fearful of the likely cost of the aqueduct – opted for a 'temporary' tramway to fill the gap. By 1804 it was complete: goods were unloaded at Walton Summit onto trucks, and drawn by horses to the canal basin behind the Corn Exchange in Preston. The route was via Ladies Walk, the tram bridge, the edge of Avenham Park and the tunnel under Fishergate which is now the access to the Fishergate Centre car park. Stone sleepers and short iron rails (or 'plates') can still be found along its course, although the old engine house at the Belvedere in Avenham Park, which pulled the trucks up the steep Avenham incline by chain, was demolished in 1868.

The canal strengthened Preston's links, particularly with the agricultural district to the north, and had a considerable influence on the siting of early mills. Two of Horrocks's early factories, the Spittals Moss factory and the Canal Street factory, were located directly upon it. It was later a source of circulating water for the great steam mills built along it in the mid nineteenth century, notably Shelley Road mill. Although now cut off near Aqueduct Street this section of the canal still retains something of the 'Canyon of the Mills' feel of the Weavers' Triangle district in Burnley.

The canal basin behind the Corn Exchange became an important and very busy centre of commerce and particularly of the coal trade, and this area thus became an important node of development. Indeed with the exception of the Yard Works complex, early industrial expansion was particularly concentrated on the western side of the town, a district adjoining and bounded by the canal. The vitality of the concern is further illustrated by the fact that not only could the canal boats (notably the famous *Water Witch*) compete with trains even for passenger traffic, but

The North Union Railway Bridge 1863. Though later widened twice, this structure remains an imposing monument of the early railway era. During its construction there were great fears for its safety when the river froze over, and the bridge was not completed when the first passengers on the Preston–Wigan line nervously passed over it in 1838. It gives some impression of what Rennies' postulated canal aqueduct might have looked like, whilst through the arches can be seen the viaduct of the East Lancashire line, subsequently transformed into an embankment.

The entrance to Miller Park c.1920. This ornate viaduct carried the East Lancashire Railway line through the town's Avenham and Miller Parks. During the steam age the railway was a very noticeable aspect of the town's life, occupying a massive area next to the town centre.

the canal company subsequently took over Lancaster & Preston Junction Railway.

The moulding of Preston's emerging town plan and the stimulus to its industrial economy were consolidated by the early railways. By 1838 Preston had connections with London and the cities of the south, and ten years later had emerged as the mid-point on the London to Glasgow route. The railways emphasised not only the town's local and regional importance, but also its national significance as a communications centre. Of enormous intrinsic interest in themselves, the early railways made a major contribution to the development of the town, with their marshalling yards and Ribble bridges. Until well after the Second World War few parts of Preston were out of earshot of the railway.[16]

The town's early railway companies were frequently at odds with each other. Trains were run illicitly on lines belonging to rivals and accidents were not uncommon. As late as 1896 competition between the west coast line and its rivals on the north–south route resulted in the down Scotch Express leaving the rails in the town's most spectacular rail smash, in which one person was killed. For a long time Preston had several railway stations, causing great inconvenience to travellers. Until 1844 the lines of the hostile Preston–Lancaster and Preston–Wigan companies faced each other on either side of Fishergate, and each hindered passengers from their trains trying to connect with trains of the other company.

The spirit of these early pioneers was later recalled by an old Preston engine driver:

> Alongside the line at Scorton was a big field celebrated for its mushrooms and many times a train was stopped while the driver, fireman, guard and even passengers alighted to gather the edible. An extra spurt afterwards made up for lost time.[17]

The construction of the town's first railway, the North Union line to Wigan, was followed avidly in the press. The engineering works were of a scale never before seen in the district, and the construction companies struggled to complete their contracts on time. As the completion date neared, three thousand men worked day and night in shifts. In May 1838 something akin to a pitched battle took place between the Irish navvies and the Farington mill hands, in which perhaps five hundred men took part, and one man at least was shot dead.[18]

From September 1835 a great viaduct began to arise over the Ribble. It was 872 feet long, 28 feet wide and 68 feet high above the bed of the river; it contained 675,000 cubic feet of rusticated ashlar brought from quarries in Whittle, Longridge and Lancaster, and cost £40,000. The cutting at the northern end through 'The Cliffe' was 29 feet deep, and the

ACCIDENT
TO SCOTCH EXPRESS
PRESTON. JULY. 13ᵀᴴ 1896. (COPYRIGHT)

The Preston rail crash, July 1896. Rivalry between the railway companies on the Anglo–Scottish routes resulted in excessive speed by certain express services, and this was the main cause of the crash at Preston. The interesting story of the railways around Preston has recently been the subject of a book by Gordon Biddle.

embankment on its southern approach was forty feet high on a base ninety feet wide and contained 464,431 cubic yards of earth in its ¾-mile length. In all the line cost £500,000, or £21,000 per mile. The travelling time to Wigan was cut from three hours to under half an hour, from Preston to Manchester to 1½ hours, and to Liverpool 1¾ hours. On Wednesday 1st November 1838 the line was opened. Despite the need for a push from its passengers and the discovery that for much of its journey the brakes had been left on, the first engine duly arrived in Wigan. The return trip to Preston was accompanied by much ceremony:

> Loud huzzas greeted our arrival, the bells sent forth their sonorous peals, the Union Jack was unfurled on the Parish Church, the standard of St. George floated on top of the Mayor's Mansion, and a band of music played in the gardens.

The Directors and guests then repaired to a dinner 'of the most luxurious viands . . . served up in a magnificent and luxurious style'.[19]

Progress of the cotton industry

Throughout much of the nineteenth century the cotton industry was the main driving force of economic growth in Preston, creating both a new town and a new industrial society in it. The firms and their off-shoots established by Horrocks and Watson continued to dominate the local spinning industry, though the pace of earlier expansion was not maintained. By 1820 only nine further mills had been built, but after 1803 all new mills were steam-powered, and by 1821 all the town's mills were run by steam.

During these years Preston's favourable location in relation to rural labour became an important factor in facilitating further growth, and by the middle of the century 52% of the town's inhabitants had been born elsewhere. By 1836 the town had 42 mills employing perhaps one fifth of its population. The 1830s and '40s were perhaps the industry's most significant period of expansion in Preston, and contrast with the later peaks of expansion in neighbouring towns such as Blackburn (1860s) and Oldham (early 1900s). The period is perhaps best exemplified by the erection of Swainson and Birley's 'Big Factory' off New Hall Lane, while in 1845 William Ainsworth announced the construction of 'the largest power-loom weaving shed in the world'.[20]

Capacity rose from 310,000 spindles in 1832 to 500,000 in 1842, when the largest firms were Horrockses, Miller and Co., Ainsworth and Co. (29,234 spindles), Swainson, Birley and Co. (37,240), John Paleys (50,796), Richard Gardner (43,214) and Paul Catterall and Sons (23,996).[21] A survey undertaken by the Inspector of Factories, Leonard Horner, in 1842 reveals the range of premises:

15 Spinning Mills
15 Combined Spinning and Weaving Mills
3 Power Weaving Factories
5 Doubling Mills
4 Mills closed.

These employed 707 spinners, 1,725 piecers, 7,500 power loom weavers and 523 overlookers. After the depression of the 1840s the upward trend resumed, and ten years later the town had 64 mills and over one million spindles, employing perhaps twenty thousand people, supplying the developing markets in India and China. Setbacks in these distant and volatile markets or any interruption to the supply of cotton could mean disaster for a community almost entirely dependent on textiles.[22]

Massive profits made in the eastern markets during the boom years just before the American Civil War led to further mill construction and employment in the district rose to 25,000. By 1880, however, the great period of expansion in the Preston industry seemed to be over, as Anthony Hewitson noted:

For some time, the cotton trade at Preston has been in a dull retrograde state. Neither the enterprise nor the activity manifested a quarter of a century ago is now apparent. There are no new mills put up in these days. Weaving sheds and kindred structures have increased in number. But it is almost 20 years since an additional mill was erected in Preston.[23]

Although Horrocks, Crewdson and Co. embarked on an ambitious series of takeovers and rebuildings around the turn of the century (including Fishwick Mill and Centenary Mill), Cliff Mill and Tulketh Mill were the town's only ventures in the construction of enormous 'Oldham' type joint stock spinning mills in the years before the First World War. The thirty years between 1830 and 1860 thus mark the golden age of mill construction in Preston.

The nature of the cotton manufacture also underwent considerable develoment. By 1830 handloom weaving was still the largest sector in British manufacturing industry despite the steady encroachment of the power loom. Spinning companies began to employ their surplus steam power in weaving, and single-storey weaving sheds thus became another familiar feature of the townscape. The middle years of the century were also the golden age of the combined firm (spinning and weaving), but by the end of the century the two processes were drawing apart again, and distinct spinning and weaving companies became the norm. In contrast to domestic weaving, which was largely a male occupation, the workforce in the new weaving sheds and mills was dominated by women and children. In 1816 almost three-quarters of the workforce at Horrockses was under 18 years of age, and by 1850 women accounted for over half.[24]

Mule spinner in the Yard Works c.1920. The spinners were the aristocrats of the mill workforce, and the trade was one of the bastions of male supremacy. His bare feet were a natural response to the oily floors. These graceful machines can still be seen in operation in the Museum of the Lancashire Cotton Industry at Helmshore.

The mill architecture of Preston

This pattern of development left a distinct imprint on mill architecture, to such an extent that old cotton hands could tell much about a town's history from its industrial buildings. In a detailed analysis of this aspect of Preston's industrial heritage, T. C. Dickinson has placed many of the old landmarks in their chronological and architectural context.[25] Mills built in the 1820s and '30s included Fishwick, Greenbank (the location of one of the town's worst fires, in 1861), Moor Brook, and the first factory at Tulketh. The 1840s saw the running of Brookfields, Brookhouse, Oxheys, Croft Street and Murray Street Mills, and the 1850s New Preston, Arkwright Mill, New Hall Lane Mill and Shelley Road Mill. Mills built in the 1860s include Queens Mill, Alexandra Mill, Moor Park Mill and Caledonian Mill. The town shared in the mid-Victorian enthusiasm for high chimneys, square-based ones being the fashion before 1850, round ones thereafter. The chimney at Brookhouse topped two hundred feet and included half a million bricks. Greenbank Mill approached 250 feet, and Higher Walton 270 feet.

The very large spinning mills of the years before the First World War included Centenary Mill (with a revolutionary steel frame, built at a cost of £125,000), Cliff Mill in Dundonald Street, and Tulketh Mill (with its wonderful 2,400 h.p. engine – the engine house is still one of the town's architectural gems). Tulketh Mill originally stood in open fields, and by the 1930s it operated almost 140,000 spindles, its reservoirs held 1,750,000 gallons of water, and the condenser used 1,750 gallons of water per minute. The trend towards separate weaving plants at this time was marked by the construction of Stocks Bridge (1904), Progress Mill (1906), Emerson Road (1907), Bute Mill (1910), Embroidery Mill (1910-13), Raglan Street (1912) and Waverley Park (1914).

Important architectural factors in these years were the availability and provision of ever larger steam plant, and the increased use of iron and steel framing. As greater weight could be supported within the structure, the external walls supported less, so windows could become larger and more numerous – providing another aid to mill dating. The great expanses of brick walls which typified mills of the mid-century, such as New Hall Lane Mill, were superseded by virtual walls of glass, as at Tulketh Mill and the side extension to New Preston Mill.

In the manufacturing district to the south of the Ribble a similar evolution can be seen in Calvert's Flatts Mill, Withy Trees Mill and Stone Mill started in the 1830s, Higher Walton and Orr's Mill built in the 1850s and '60s and the splendid steel-framed Bamber Bridge Spinning Company's New Mill of 1907 with its very fine 2,000 h.p. 4-cylinder triple expansion engine.

CHAPTER TWELVE

The making of livings

THE Industrial Revolution swept aside the medieval restrictions enshrined in the Preston Guild Merchant and, in addition to the de-regulation of trade and industry and the replacement of skilled labour by machine manufacturing, there came a fundamental change in the relationship between employer and employee. The close day-to-day relationship which had formerly often existed between a tradesman and his apprentices and assistants was clearly impossible to maintain in the great cotton mills, where a single manufacturer might employ many hundreds of hands. In what was almost a pure market economy, relations between the two sides – capital and labour – became increasingly bad, at times amounting to civil war in their acrimony. Thus the competitive edge of the new industrial society was most keenly felt in the making of livings.

Preston's ready source both of cheap foodstuffs and labour from the Fylde meant that mill wages were generally among the lowest in the county, at least in the first half of the nineteenth century. Since the 'lists' or rates of pay in neighbouring towns reflected the various local conditions it was generally believed that an advance in wages paid in Preston would push up the rates in the rest of the industry. Accordingly Preston became a great battleground, with both sides receiving aid and support from the adjacent towns.

The Cotton Lords of Preston

In the first half of the nineteenth century control of the cotton industry lay very much in the hands of the cotton masters and their families, the Cotton Lords of Preston. A popular song, named after them and written during the 1853-4 Lockout, ran:

The working people such as we,
Pass their time in misery,
While they live in luxury,

The Guild Arch in
Fishergate 1862.

The Cotton Lords of Preston.
They're making money every way,
And building factories every day,
Yet when we ask them for more pay,
They had the impudence to say,
To your demands we'll not consent,
You get enough so be content,
But we will have the Ten per Cent,
From the Cotton Lords of Preston.[1]

The 'Swells of Fishergate' were often the founders, or the sons of founders, taking a deep and personal interest in the affairs and progress of their firms. Frequently reviled as tyrants by their workpeople, and an unassailable force collectively, as individuals they made little impact on affairs beyond their town. However, their deaths were marked by extravagant displays of grief by their work people – at least if contemporary newspaper accounts are to be believed.

Greatest of the Cotton Lords was Thomas Miller (1810–1865). The son of the elder Thomas Miller, he exercised vast personal influence through

William Ainsworth's villa on the corner of Cross Street and Winckley Square c.1862. During the nineteenth century many of Preston's leading citizens and millowners, such as William Ainsworth, lived in the vicinity of Winckley Square. Although this house has been demolished, Thomas Miller's house still stands at the north-east corner of the Square.

the firm which at his death operated ten mills, 155,970 spindles, 2,865 looms, twelve steam engines (540 h.p.), and employed three thousand 'hands' to spin 104,000 lbs. of yarn and weave 227 miles of cloth each week. The Yard Works was the largest 'single site' in Lancashire, perhaps even in the world. His death caused great consternation among the Horrockses workforce, and all the town's councillors and clergy followed the former alderman's funeral procession around the town. Some 2,500 of his former employees walked in ranks from the Yard Works to line the route from the Corn Exchange to Miller's splendid Italianate-style town house at the top of Winckley Square, before his body was put on to a train for burial at Lytham.

To many of the Horrockses workforce he must have indeed seemed a father figure. Around 95% had been employed by the firm since childhood, and of eleven hundred workers in the weaving department of the Yard Works 250 had been employed over twenty years, and six hundred over sixteen years. His role as leader of the Preston Masters during the Great Lockout forgotten, his obituary stressed his generosity during the late Cotton Famine. The mills had continued to run half-time and had avoided closing, the reduced wages had been subsidised from his own pocket and he had contributed to the Preston Relief Fund. Thomas Miller was also 'An ardent lover and warm patron of the fine

A mid-Victorian group c.1862. Members of the Pedder family in the grounds of Whinfield House, Ashton.

arts. His gallery of paintings by modern artists is one of the best selected and most valuable in the Kingdom'. In addition, 'A firm and conscientious supporter of Liberal principles,' he had given freely to churches and schools, and presented the land for Miller Park to the town. Investing in fine art and an extensive estate in the Fylde, this second generation master, son 'of a good practical weaver,' had clearly ascended into the ranks of the landed gentry.[2]

The fortune of John Paley (1767–1855) was similarly established in the John Horrocks era. After being apprenticed to a wheelwright at Pateley Bridge in Yorkshire, he became a joiner at the Spittals Moss factory in 1792. In 1799, in partnership with Richard Riley, he established the firm of machine-makers sponsored by Horrocks, before moving into cotton directly. His great success thereafter was attributed to his 'Persevering industry, indomitable energy, and unvarying punctuality, accompanied by many strict habits of providence'. A town councillor and magistrate, he was succeeded in the firm by his son John Paley junior (1798–1857), also a councillor and alderman.[3]

William Ainsworth (1807–1862) was the Glasgow University educated second son of Thomas Ainsworth, a partner of John Watson. With his elder brother, he joined his father in the running of the Church Street mills, and in a cotton mill at Backbarrow near Ulverston. For some years before his death he had been sole proprietor. He was a Liberal, a councillor and a magistrate.[4]

A member of a family of twelve, Charles Swainson (1780–1866) was also the son of an early manufacturer, Charles Swainson senior, a putter-out. With various partners he developed calico printing and bleaching at the Bannister Hall printworks at Higher Walton, before moving into cotton and linen production in association with the Birleys of Kirkham. As principal of the firm of Swainson, Birley and Co., he operated the 'Big Factory' at Fishwick. He alone of the later Preston masters attempted a parliamentary career, being defeated at Preston in 1841. Ten years earlier he had thought it prudent not to contest the seat with 'Orator' Hunt. In evidence to a commission inquiring into the construction of the proposed Fleetwood, Preston & West Riding Junction Railway, given a few days before his death, he described himself as 'A Worsted Manufacturer, Cotton Spinner, and Linen Manufacturer at Preston' employing one thousand hands. Resident at Cooper Hill, Walton-le-Dale, Swainson was a prime mover in the village's Relief Committee during the Cotton Famine, and he was described in his obituary as 'A friend and benefactor of the Poor'.[5]

Edmund Birley (1817–1895) was born into an already long-established textile dynasty. The son of William Birley and Mary Swainson, he left Rugby School in 1842 to join the family business in the Fishwick Mills, then among the largest and most advanced in the world. His obituary assured the reader that 'His manner, at times, might appear somewhat brusque, but under a dignified and stern exterior he had a tender heart'. He was elected to the Town Council in 1855, became an alderman in

1858, Mayor in 1866 and was Guild Mayor in 1882. A magistrate and staunch member of the local Conservative Association, 'There were no rival claims to leadership so long as he was at the head'.[6]

After John Horrocks, perhaps the most remarkable of the Preston mill owners was John Goodair (1808–1873), indeed 'A self made man, the architect of his fortune'. Though, once again, the son of a manufacturer, Goodair found himself 'in the Chorley streets at the age of 13' when his father's business failed. He found work as a warper. At the age of 22 he became manager of a fancy silk and gingham factory in Preston, putting out to handloom weavers in the Croston and Ormskirk district, then an area noted for its silk trade. In 1836 he transferred to the cotton trade: 'He worked very hard, was at his business early and late, and, caring nothing for luxuries in either eating, or drinking, or clothing, he saved money and steadily extended his trade connections'.

Perhaps more importantly he had a hard-working wife. In 1843 he established a power loom shed at Brookfield, and larger premises and further mill acquisitions followed. His son Richard followed him in the trade. He was a member of the Town Council and Public Health Board, represented Preston on the Manchester Central Relief Committee during the Cotton Famine, and was 'a very great authority on the Cotton Trade'. He was knocked down and killed by a cart whilst visiting Manchester, and his rather splendid tomb still dominates the churchyard at St. James Church, Brindle.[7]

Obituaries of working men are extremely rare in the Victorian press, but in 1880 the *Preston Guardian* recorded 'the death of an old Townsman' – George Cowell (?–1880), a former weaver and one of the leaders of the Preston cotton workers during the Great Lockout of 1853–4: 'Through his efforts on behalf of his fellow workers he was compelled to leave town, and from here he went to Manchester, where he has worked earnestly in the cause of Tee-Totalism'.[8]

—— *A life in the mills* ——

Frequent lay-offs, unhealthy working conditions, extremely long hours of work, and accidents resulting from unguarded machinery were hallmarks of cotton mill employment in the first half of the nineteenth century. The gradual improvement of conditions was won through the steady persistence of the factory reformers and pressure from the early trade unions. Over and above these efforts lay the simple lesson of experience: a less tired, healthier and less accident-prone workforce ensured a greater return on investment.

Parliamentary papers and inquiries, especially Royal Commissions, are an important source of information on factory conditions at this time.[9] Horrockses, Miller and Co., one of the leading and largest manufacturers, gave evidence to the 1833 Royal Commission on Factories.

Their statement reveals working conditions in mills run by a model employer of the 1830s. During the previous twelve months, 310½ days had been worked – that is, every day apart from Sunday, with single-day holidays at Christmas and Easter: 'Our time of working for all ages in the cotton manufactory is 69 hours per week, i.e. 12 hours for 5 days and 9 hours on the Saturday. The mechanics work only 60 hours per week'. The company did not work at night, and its hours of work were evidently not regarded as onerous, for it specifically stated: 'We have no practical knowledge of the effects of working long hours'. Ventilation was extensive and had lately been improved, whilst machinery was guarded:

> Any injury, therefore, to the limbs or fingers of those employed very seldom happens in our works, and never but through gross carelessness and neglect.

For the efficient running of the industry Horrockses felt it essential to introduce children to the work at an early age: 'We have always found those hands who have been introduced young to be the most skillful workers'. Whilst the restriction of working hours 'would very much injure the workpeople, by reducing their comforts and means of support',

Mill mechanics c.1905. Employment opportunities for men were comparatively restricted in the mills, particularly in the early nineteenth century. Most mills, however, had their own workshops employing considerable numbers of mechanics to repair and maintain an enormous number and variety of machines.

Weaving shed group c.1910. Life in the mill was not without its lighter moments, and local and national festivities were marked by the enthusiastic trimming up of the workplace. This photograph clearly illustrates the large number of young people employed and the dominance of women in the workforce.

A weaver in a Preston mill c.1920. By the early twentieth century Lancashire weavers claimed that they wove until breakfast to meet British demand, and for the rest of the day to supply the world. Yet by 1914 the first signs of the decline of the trade were already perceptible.

foreign competitors and firms not enforcing the reduced hours would gain at the expense of the law-abiding. Indeed, many parents asked for their children to be taken on whilst very young:

> To show the anxiety there is on the part of the parents to get their children introduced into cotton factories where proper order and discipline are observed, we can produce several instances of children above ten years of age, having worked six, seven, and even nine months, without any wages, to insure the first vacant situation.

The company did not have a policy of enforcing corporal punishment, and both overlookers 'too intemperate in their bodily coercion of children under their charge' and parents improperly chastising their own children, had been dismissed.

In many respects the company was ahead of its time, and thus rather atypical of much of the Preston industry. They provided washing and changing facilities for their workforce, offered housing accommodation, and later pioneered nursery schools.

——— *The Spinners' Strike of 1836* ———

Before 1830 a leading part in labour affairs in Preston was taken by the handloom weavers. Agitation for higher wages in June 1808 caused 'much excitement and unease' when 'the cotton weavers of the town assembled on the Moor in great numbers, in order to consult and induce their employers to raise wages'. The magistrates ordered up the 84th Regiment and arms were distributed to 'volunteers', but beyond marching to and from the Ribble Bridge and Preston Moor – the principal places generally frequented for political meetings – the military were not required. The town was the scene of large demonstrations for similar ends ten years later, in 1818, in which twelve hundred people are said to have taken part.[10]

The 1820s and 1830s saw very significant developments in the town's cotton industry, with profound implications for its workforce. The masters were very forthright in the assertion of their authority to manage without consultation and the outcome was exceedingly bitter, and indeed bloody, labour relations. Over all loomed the near collapse of the handloom weaving trade. In 1821 the spinners had a 10% cut in wages imposed upon them and despite a three-week strike were forced to accept it. The introduction of new machinery led to threats of trouble throughout industrial Lancashire in 1826; in Preston the military were called out, and loyal hands manned the mill roofs with paving stones to repel attackers.[11] Following one of 'Orator' Hunt's visits to the town in 1831, 'radicals' enforcing the closure of the town's mills to further industrial demands attacked the town's prison, the House of Correction:

Captain Anthony, the governor, having been previously apprised of the doings of this lawless herd, and anticipating an attack upon the prison, planted in front – on a walk which at that time ran in a straight line from Church-street to the entrance – an 18-pounder carronade (a short cannon) charged with grape shot . . . The mobbers at length forced their way through the outer wall gate; and, seeing that matters were now beginning to assume a serious form, Captain Anthony, standing by the side of the carronade, with fuse in hand, vowed, in very emphatic language, that if any of them dared to come forward . . . he would fire. The firmness of his attitude cowed the would-be ruffians, and they gradually withdrew from the front, and proceeded into the town. Next day some soldiers belonging to the 80th Regiment arrived at Preston, and the town was preserved from further mob disturbance.[12]

The building was subsequently strengthened against future possible attack by the addition of four martello towers.

The two most important labour contests during the nineteenth century were the Spinners' Strike of 1836 and the Great Lockout of 1853-4. Copious accounts of these events can be found in the local press. Although both originated in 10% wage claims by the work people, both disputes were dominated by the issue of the legitimacy of trade unions and the refusal of the masters to have any truck with them. As well as being forthright in his personal abuse of the Preston owners, there is no doubt that the Chartist, Alexander Challenger, met with much popular support in his assertion that: 'The Cotton Lords of Preston are the greatest tyrants in the country. It is well known that they grind their workmen down more than any other persons, getting their work done cheaper, and therefore they can undersell their neighbours'.[13]

The great strike which began in October 1836 was estimated to have cost the town almost £110,000 and Whittle estimated the figure of those out of work at fifteen thousand.[14] Normal working was resumed on 5th February 1837 following the exhaustion of union funds, the employment of 'knobsticks' (non-union labour usually imported from outside the town), and the introduction of labour-saving machinery. Some two hundred of the most ardent strikers were carefully blacklisted. The turning point had come in December when, as union funds dwindled, the masters re-opened the mills offering employment and the 10% to those who would sign a written declaration renouncing the union.

The Preston Chartists

A coherent political response to the harsh economic realities of working life during this heyday of industrial expansion, came in the form of the Chartist Movement. The Chartists were feared by the masters as an extreme, if not revolutionary, force. They saw political

Drawing-in at a Preston mill c.1950. In addition to weaving and spinning many workers were employed in the preparatory stages of manufacture, which were usually extremely complicated processes requiring much manual dexterity, skill and keen eyesight.

reform as a key to social reform and sought to accomplish it by convincing Parliament to adopt the six points of their Charter, nearly all of which have subsequently been adopted. Chartism has been described as a 'snowball movement', growing as it absorbed a great variety of local movements and agitations against injustices. Accordingly its nature differed from one part of the country to another. In Preston it was dominated by the handloom weavers and to a lesser extent the factory workers. The terminal depression in the former trade, harsh working conditions in the latter, and opposition to the new Poor Law introduced in 1837, combined with a genuine working-class radical party in the town to define the political horizons of Preston Chartism. One of the local leaders, Richard Marsden, a handloom weaver and 'White Slave' of Bamber Bridge, has been the subject of a study by J. E. King, which illustrates the course of the movement in the town.[15]

Shortly after the collapse of the 1836 strike the great national Chartist leader Feargus O'Connor sought to emulate 'Orator' Hunt's success in contesting the Preston seats for the Radical cause. His failure was followed by the formation in 1837 of the Preston Operative Radical Association. The Radicals soon had two hundred members and their own reading room. They were instrumental in organising the great Preston demonstration held on 5th November 1838, which in many respects was the high water mark of the local Chartist effort. An enormous procession dominated by local trade unions with eight bands and forty banners, left Chadwick's Orchard *en route* for Preston Moor, where it was addressed by O'Connor and Richard Marsden, who spoke of the need for working people to reclaim their rights.

In February 1839 Marsden represented Preston at the great National Convention of Chartists held in London, and spoke eloquently of the atrocious conditions in Lancashire. He claimed that in one street in Preston twenty muskets had been purchased. Since the town remained quiet this was perhaps no more than hyperbole, but the rack of firearms long displayed as a curiosity in the head office of Horrockses may have been bought at this time. When the House of Commons rejected the Charter petition the convention called a general strike. The 'Sacred Month' began in Preston on 12th August and lasted for three days.

The severe economic depression of 1842 brought a revival of the movement, but in May 1842 a second petition with three million signatures was thrown out by Parliament. The celebrated 'Plug' strikes began in July, and by early August spread rapidly to Lancashire. Bands of men entered mills and drew the plugs of the steam engine boilers, stopping work and enforcing a general strike. On Friday 12th August the movement crossed the Ribble and reached Preston.[16]

Early on Friday morning, following meetings at the Orchard, groups of strikers went from factory to factory 'turning out the hands' and stopping the mills. As the clearly shaken local press reported:

> The movement was altogether one of such a sudden nature, that the civil authorities, although alive to what was taking place in the neighbouring towns, had no idea of any commotion taking place immediately amongst ourselves . . .

On the following day, Saturday 13th August – Preston's 'Black Saturday' – an attack was made on Sleddon's Mill at 6 a.m. and the hands were turned out. Further disturbances followed with fatal consequences:

PRESTON RIOTS : FIRING UPON THE PEOPLE

> At about 8 o'clock, as the mob were proceeding up Lune Street, near the New Market, they were met by a body of Policemen and the military. The crowd commenced shouting and throwing stones. An Captain Woodford making towards them, as if to arrest one of the parties, he was knocked down. One of the constables in endeavouring to assist was struck a violent blow on the arm with a stick, and on the chest and in the face with stones. An attempt was made to reason with the parties, and they were informed that if they did not disperse, and cease their riotous conduct, orders would be given to fire upon them. The Riot Act was read, and the police having been beaten back, the order to 'fire' was given, and several were wounded.

The *Preston Chronicle* for that day was just going to press, and later editions carried further details:

> At this time, 12 o'clock, quietness has been restored, but of course there is a great ferment in people's minds, and business is almost at a standstill, although it is our chief market day.
>
> Half-past 12, we hear that 8 have been wounded: 5 mortally – Notice

is posted on the walls that the Riot Act has been read.

The rioters had gathered between Wharf Street and Fleet Street at the bottom of Lune Street brow, facing the authorities who blocked Lune Street higher up, near the Central Methodist Church. Both John Bairstow and the Mayor, Samuel Horrocks, had tried to reason with the crowd, who were pelting the soldiers with stones brought by women and children from the canal wharf behind the Corn Exchange.

After repeated orders to disperse, and dire warnings of the likely consequences, the Riot Act was read by Horrocks, who was hit by stones as he did so. Groups of rioters had tried to get behind the military from the top of Fishergate, and the authorities were scarcely in control of the situation. A second, more respectable crowd had assembled to follow the proceedings, and it seems that everyone expected to see the soldiers fire blanks. In the event live ammunition was used; twenty shots were fired, the shocked crowds rapidly dispersed, and the jury at the inquiry returned a verdict of 'lawful killing'. Four men were killed and three seriously injured.

Local Chartists took pains to distance themselves from the events, issuing a placard against the masters and justifying the movement:

> Cannot the workmen plainly perceive that there is no limit to your reductions, whilst anything remains to be taken . . . Now the working community lie at your mercy – such mercy as it is, they being permitted only to exist as a prey to your rapacity. Daily they feel its effects: and each month, nay each week, tells its tale of added woe, in your further encroachments on their wages.

Several mills re-opened on the following Monday, breaking the general strike, and the town remained quiet until Wednesday, when word reached it of the approach of a mob from Wigan and Chorley. This relief force after closing the Farington, Bamber Bridge and Walton Mills, and comprising 'a large body of Navigators, as they are called, that is excavators employed in making the railway, colliers, weavers and others . . . armed with bludgeons and other deadly weapons . . . such as large iron bolts, iron bars, knives and scythes', was dispersed by the police on Walton Bridge with the military looking on. The crowd panicked and fled. As Thomas Banks later recalled:

> Away they went racing and chasing over Darwen Bridge. An old friend of ours, Scotch Bob now in Bolton and has been for many years, was almost run down by a policeman, but being fleet of foot he out-ran his pursuer a very few yards till he reached the banks of the River Ribble at the high bathing place. The policeman was about to seize him when Bob plunged into the river and swam across and escaped. So ended the Plug drawing and rioting of 1842.[17]

In a letter published a few weeks later in the Chartist newspaper *The Northern Star*, Richard Marsden described himself as writing from 'our humiliated town of Preston, where the well-known Peterloo tragedy hath just been re-enacted'.[18]

In October 1842 the Rev. Clay, Chaplain to the House of Correction, produced a statistical analysis of the 96 persons committed for the riots in Preston and district. Poverty, illiteracy and ignorance of the scripture he identified as important contributory factors in their lawlessness. Only 22 earned over 15s. per week, sixty were unable to read, and only five were even 'acquainted with simple outlines of our Saviour's history'.[19]

Preston lock-out, a contemporary cartoon. 'Knobsticks' were people imported by the masters to run the mills in the places of the workpeople who were either locked out or on strike. Often imported from workhouses in Ireland, they were not infrequently waylaid by union officials, given a meal and put on the next boat home. George Cowell was the leader of the Preston operatives, and the 'Mr. Large Firms' included those of Thomas Miller and William Ainsworth.

—— The Great Lock-Out ——

The Great Lock-out of 1853-4 has been the subject of a detailed analysis by Dutton and King. Karl Marx, writing in the *New York Daily Tribune* just six years after completing the Communist Manifesto, claimed that 'The eyes of the working classes are now fully opened: they

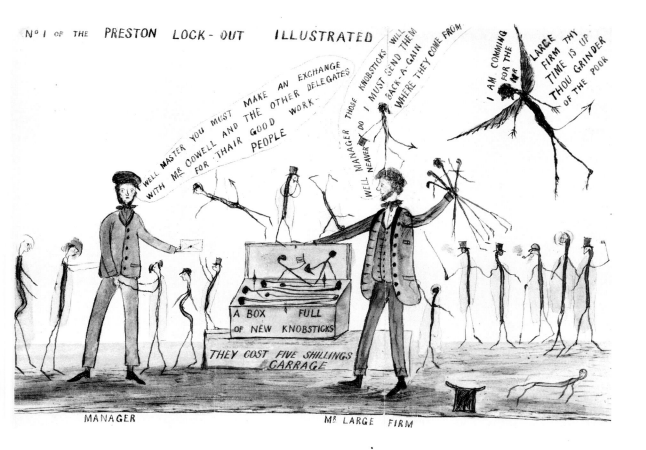

begin to cry 'Our St. Petersburg is at Preston' '.[20] Faint shadows of the events made their way into Dickens' *Hard Times* and Mrs. Gaskell's *North and South*.

After 'a great struggle upon the wages question' at Stockport, mill workers in several towns gained an advance in wages. The Preston masters paying wages estimated to be 20% below average rates held out, but eventually conceded the restoration of a 10% cut they had made in 1847. Only a handful of firms refused, and in these the agitation continued.

The Preston masters responded by closing all the mills and locking out their workforce. They regretted:

> to find that the operatives have put themselves under the guidance of a designing and irresponsible body . . . To this spirit of Tyranny and Dictation the Masters can no longer submit, in justice either to the operatives or themselves; and hence they are reluctantly compelled to accept the only alternative left – to close their mills, until those on strike are prepared to resume their work, and a better understanding is established between the Employer and the Employed.[21]

The dictat dated 15th September 1853 was signed by the members of the Masters' Association, who had provided stiff financial guarantees against coming to separate settlements. The 36 firms included Horrockses, Miller and Co.; Paul Catterall and Son; John Paley junior, Ainsworth and Co. (William Ainsworth was Secretary of the Association); Swainson, Birley and Co. and John Hawkins and Sons. From the Walton annexe of

Mr Alex Foster with family, motor car and chauffeur c.1900. Alexander Foster of Tinniswood, Tulketh Road, was a director of the cotton firm Daniel Arkwright Ltd., and operated Arkwright Mill in Hawkins Street. As one of the town's leading citizens in the early twentieth century, he was Deputy Chairman of the Preston Magistrates and Chairman of the Board of Management of Preston Royal Infirmary.

the Preston industry, Miles Rodgett, William Bashall, William Calvert and Richard Eccles had signed. The masters were in a strong position, for the cotton boom of the earlier 1850s had run its course.

From October 1853 onwards an enormous campaign on behalf of the Preston operatives was launched and contributions flooded in from all over the country. During a severe winter between fifteen and twenty thousand people were out of work. In February 1854 the masters re-opened their mills in an effort to force a return to work on their terms. Pickets were placed on the mills and the lock-out became a strike. Their strategy having failed, the masters began to try to find 'knobstick' labour to run the mills. A party of poor emigrants despatched from Ireland *en route* for the mills was captured at Fleetwood, given a good meal at the *Farmer's Arms* and escorted home by union officials. As union funds began to run out a trickle back to work began, and on May Day 1854 a huge meeting of ten thousand operatives gathered by Walton Bridge to ratify a return to work. Major strikes occurred again in 1869 (against wage reductions), 1878 (when the Preston operatives were locked out for assisting their friends in the 1853–4 contest, the Blackburn operatives) and 1912.

—— *Radical Preston* ——

Harsh economic realities in a predominantly working-class town with one of the widest electoral franchises in the world were conducive to colourful parliamentary politics. In 1820 Henry Hunt, the great English radical, challenged the Derby/Corporation alliance. The election took place while Hunt was awaiting trial at York for his role in the 'Peterloo' meeting in St. Peter's Fields, Manchester in 1819. After thirteen days of polling the coalition prevailed comfortably, and 'Orator' Hunt was subsequently sentenced to 2½ years confinement in Ilchester Gaol.

By the time of the election of June 1826 conditions had changed markedly. Samuel Horrocks and the Stanley nominee retired, and the Corporation decided to withdraw from its official sponsorship of candidates. In fact the antiquated Corporation was increasingly margin-alised in the new conditions which prevailed, and was swept away by the Municipal Corporations Act of 1835 which formed the basis of the modern system of representative local government. The Whig–Tory coalition thus came to an end after 24 years.

The family seat was contested by E. G. Stanley, later to become the 14th Earl of Derby, a leader of the Conservative Party, Prime Minister on three occasions (1852, 1858 and 1860) and architect of the 1867 Reform Bill. One of his opponents was William Cobbett, the Radical politician and brilliant writer, particularly celebrated for having brought Tom

Paine's bones home from their exile in America. The contest between the great aristocrat and famous radical wit was a national event: 'Almost during the whole election, the town presented a complete Saturnalia. The immense sums expended, especi-ally in the public-houses, produced the inevitable result – rioting and destruction of property'.[22]

The authorities had taken the precaution of arranging for a party of dragoons to be stationed at Kirkham, and when things boiled over on the third day of polling, signals were sent from the top of the Parish Church tower. An observer in his garden at Kirkham saw the flag and troops arrived in an hour. Cobbett came last in a poll of four candidates, but he shrugged off the defeat with his usual humour: 'Gentlemen, I have done much good to you by coming. I have sweated your tyrants – I have bled them. I have made the silly Honourable throw £15,000 among you and that's no joke!'[23]

Henry Hunt again contested Preston in the election of July 1830, the first after the Catholic Emancipation Act. Again he was well beaten. In December a by-election had to be held to confirm E. G. Stanley in his seat before he could take up a government post. The Preston radicals wanted Hunt to stand again; he consented, but only if he headed the poll at the end of the first day. New electoral practices gave considerable scope for fraud, whilst Stanley's supporters were perhaps complacent after their recent easy victory. When the hustings opened the Huntites and the Black Feet (working-class mechanics, supporters of Hunt, so-called from their distinctly stained footwear) took over the Corn Exchange. At the close of the first day the Orator had his lead.

The Stanley voters had a very rough time. The *Preston Pilot* described what happened to one of their Five-shilling Men (named after the price of their vote):

> In one instant several hundreds were upon him, the ejection from the Booth and the area became the work of a moment, and in as short a space of time the fragments of his apparel were to be seen flying about in all directions amid the shouts and exultations of the delighted multitude.[24]

In fact by the standards of the day the seven days' poll was peaceable enough. Many Prestonians voted more than once, for an electorate estimated at 6,291 in 1832 polled 7,122 votes. The outcome was a national sensation: Hunt 3,730, Stanley 3,392. Amazingly, Stanley's support for a very moderate Reform Act had turned local Tories against him, and in favour of the extremely radical Hunt, whom they had supported with both votes and money. The Orator issued his supporters with silver medals bearing the words, 'One of the 3730 Electors of Preston – The Grateful Tribute of the People of England' and 'H. Hunt esq. M.P. for Preston, Dec. 24th 1830 – The Time is Come'.

Two years later in the first election after the passing of the Great Reform Act, for which Hunt had been a leading speaker and advocate, the Preston electorate showed their gratitude by turning him out and

Frederick Arthur Stanley, 16th Earl of Derby, Preston Guild Mayor 1902. Five years before the death of his brother, the 15th Earl in 1893, Frederick Arthur had been created Baron Stanley of Preston. Queen Victoria apparently thought highly of 'Freddy Stanley', on whose death the title and estate passed to his son Edward George Villiers, the Lord Derby of the first half of the twentieth century, who was celebrated as 'The King of Lancashire'.

electing a Stanley in his place. Yet the Derby influence of old was at an end. The town was never forgiven, patronage was withdrawn and Patten House was sold. After his defeat in 1830 E. G. Stanley had issued a public letter of farewell:

> Gentlemen, a parliamentary connection has, for many years, subsisted between your borough and the family to which I belong, which I had hoped had not been unproductive of advantage to the town of Preston. The rupture of that connection has been your act. I acquiesce in your decision, and shall make no attempt in future to renew it.[25]

The end of the Derby Interest?

Between 1820 and 1837 three leading Radicals of the day contested the wide franchise of Preston, it being one of the few seats in the country in which they stood any chance of success – Henry Hunt, William Cobbett and Feargus O'Connor. The town had a large working-class electorate and active trade unions, yet from 1859 until 1906 both of its representatives in Parliament were Tories. Clemesha in 1912 addressed himself to this apparent paradox, reaching three main conclusions which are fundamental to the understanding of the town's politics: radicalism had no deep roots; Edward Stanley's subsequent leadership of the Conservative party drew former Whigs (Liberals) and old supporters of the Derby Interest with him; and voting patterns reflected religious divisions.

Religion was particularly important. Clemesha argued that perhaps half of the population was Church of England, a third Roman Catholic, and the remainder Nonconformist, and that the majority of churchmen were Low-Church Anglicans. This group, having 'a firm belief in the virtue of the established church, and a determination to resent and resist any proposals that would tend to undermine it from its privileged position', and under the leadership of the Vicar of Preston the Rev. John Owen Parr, had firmly turned against the Liberals after Gladstone's move to disestablish the Church of Ireland.

Clemesha concluded that:

The politics of churchmen in Preston are consequently of a Conservative or – to use a more accurate term – of a Tory type. They have an ecclesiastical bent and the political aspect of the town bears some resemblance to that of Belfast or Liverpool, though it is happily not distinguished by those exhibitions of bigotry and intolerance which have given an unpleasant notoriety to the places just mentioned.[26]

Since the Liberals were not very successful in harnessing the Catholic and Non-conformist vote, and echoes of the old Derby Interest were now on the side of the Conservatives, Preston's parliamentary representation in the second half of the nineteenth century was very reminiscent of the Preston Corporation/Derby alliance of 1802–26.[27]

Efforts to establish a distinct Labour Party provided a separate avenue of representation, one not so deeply rooted in old local loyalties. In 1893 the Independent Labour Party was formed at Bradford, and a branch was established at Preston shortly after. In 1895 the town's first Labour candidate was soundly beaten. At the Boer War election of 1900, 'the well known Socialist and Labour Leader, Mr. J. Keir Hardie' was nominated for Preston and also for Merthyr Tydfil. Notwithstanding his great prestige, Hardie was rejected at Preston but successful in Wales.

In 1906 J. T. Macpherson of the Steel Smelters' Union, 'a fluent and powerful speaker, who quickly became very popular amongst the operatives of the town' stood for the Labour Representation Committee with Harold Cox, 'one of the most lucid and brilliant exponents of the case for Free Trade' representing the Liberals. As part of the great Liberal landslide of that year both candidates were elected, defeating the veteran W. E. M. Tomlinson and John Kerr. Labour's hold on the town was precarious, however, and in 1910 the Lib-Labs lost both seats.[28]

—— *Sectarianism* ——

The social history of Preston in the later nineteenth century and the early twentieth is marked by a strong taint of sectarianism, though the town's Catholic community had existed from before the Reformation and in the early nineteenth century Fr. Joseph Dunn ('Daddy Dunn') was one of the town's leading and most respected citizens. The Catholic community grew with the town, and although from the 1840s large numbers of Irish people settled in Preston, they still accounted for perhaps only 4,300 of its 22,000 strong membership in 1851. From the 1860s the Whitsuntide walks became a focus of sectarian rivalry and occasional trouble. On Whit Wednesday 1868 a number of Orangemen were bodily ejected from an Irish enclave in Milton Street, in what W. J. Love has called 'the worst inter-communal incident of the mid nineteenth century in Preston' – the 'Battle of Paddies Rookery'. Shocked contemporary newspaper accounts make it plain that this was a relatively new and unwelcome development in Preston.[29]

The Whitsuntide walks were part of a much-loved and universally popular festival extending over most of Whit Week, and it would be quite wrong to exaggerate their sectarian aspect. The town had a thriving church and chapel life, and members of its congregations took great pride in walking in the Whit Monday processions, as well as watching those of other denominations, in what was really a great carnival – an annual taste of the Preston Guild. The main processions were carefully timed by the authorities to avoid each other in the crowded streets, and on at least one occasion the Town Hall clock was stopped to avoid a collision. The Catholics walked in the morning and the Protestants in the afternoon. On the following days enormous railway excursions were organised; in 1888 for example the Church of England organised trips eight hundred and 3,500-strong to Matlock and Blackpool; the Conservative Working Men's Association took nine hundred to the Isle of Man and the Catholics and Wesleyans respectively took parties of two thousand and nine hundred to Southport.[30]

Laying setts c.1930. Before the development of modern labour-saving machinery much work was done by hand. The marked improvement of Preston's public facilities after 1880 required an enormous labour input.

20266. TOWN HALL, PRESTON. Poulton.

CHAPTER THIRTEEN

Victorian Preston

DURING the first half of the nineteenth century expansion of the cotton industry raced far ahead of Preston's capacity to absorb its greatly swollen population. The pace of technological innovation, the drive for greater production, and the rapid growth of the railway system, were not matched by the improvement of the town's other facilities. After 1850, and particularly in the last decades of the century, however, clear indications of advance became apparent. If conditions were at their worst in 1850, and social relationships pushed to near breaking point by the severe industrial strife of the period, thirty years later despair had begun to be replaced by pride in the progress of the age, and many of the landmarks of modern Preston had appeared.

Charles Dickens used contemporary accounts of the town during the Great Lockout as the background for his novel *Hard Times*. His description of 'Coketown' is thus loosely based on Preston. Dickens' stay in the town was a very short one and he seems to have despaired of obtaining the background material he required: 'I am afraid that I shall not be able to get much here'.[1] Many apparently incidental references to the town are in fact much more reminiscent of the Midlands around Birmingham, an area Dickens knew well. The portrait of 'Coketown', though providing a brilliant impression of a northern manufacturing town of the period, was not intended as a literal description of Preston:

Coketown was a town of red brick, or of brick that would have been red if the smoke and ashes had allowed it: but, as matters stood, it was a town of unnatural red and black like the painted face of a savage. It was a town of machinery and tall chimneys, out of which interminable serpents of smoke trailed themselves for ever and ever, and never got uncoiled. It had a black canal in it, and a river that ran purple with ill-smelling dye, and vast piles of buildings full of windows where there was a rattling and a trembling all day long, and where the piston of the steam-engine worked monotonously up and down, like the head of an elephant in a state of melancholy madness. It contained several large streets all very like one another, and many small streets still more like one another, inhabited by people equally like one another, who all went

The Town Hall c.1880. A fine perspective, showing the buildings to the right subsequently cleared to make way for the Miller Arcade. Badly damaged by fire in 1947, the building was not restored, and was finally demolished in 1962 despite a large petition demanding its preservation.

in and out at the same hours, with the same sound upon the same pavements, to do the same work, and to whom every day was the same as yesterday and tomorrow, and every year the counterpart of the last and next.[2]

Victorian Preston possessed a social vitality and a popular culture strongly at odds with the monotony and poverty of its environment. Crucially there were significant numbers of Prestonians who strove hard to ensure that every day would not be the same as yesterday, and that the next year need not be the counterpart of the last. This stimulus was to have an impact upon the proceedings of the Town Council and its committees, the trade unions, the town's churches, chapels and schools, through the efforts of a myriad of improvers and improvements. By the end of the century the results could be seen across the whole range of Preston's municipal and social life. The town had close links with all the popular political and social movements of the times,[3] and in Joseph Livesey possessed a social reformer of national calibre. Even one of his most bitter political opponents, Thomas Batty Addision, was no less committed to the principle of social improvement.

—— *Joseph Livesey and the seven men of Preston* ——

J oseph Livesey was born in a handloom weaver's cottage in Victoria Road, Walton-le-Dale, in 1794. Orphaned at the age of seven, he was brought up there and educated by his grandfather, accompanying him in the weaving trade until his marriage and move to Preston at the age of 21. These early years were clearly the making of the man:

> I never regretted that poverty was my early lot, and that I was left to make my own way in the world. It was here, I believe, I learned to feel for the poor, to acquire the first lessons of humanity, and to cultivate my own energies as the best means . . . of self-advancement.[4]

Joseph Livesey (1794–1884).

Strongly independent of mind, Livesey found it hard to accept the dogmas of organised religion or of radical politics, although his life's work was characterised by strongly Christian compassion in the search for direct and practical measures for the improvement of the conditions of the poor. His outlook owed more to old-fashioned paternalism and liberality than the class conflict espoused by Marx, or the indifference to social costs manifested by the political economists of the day:

> How pleasant to see the rich and poor mingling together, exhibiting the sympathies of humanity and stirring to strengthen the social bond, [for] no man can visit the poor without being better for it, he learns humility, gratitude and submission, and his benevolent zeal receives a fresh impulse.[5]

Joseph Livesey and the temperance movement. A contemporary illustration at the time of Livesey's death, showing various episodes in the history of the temperance movement.

This philosophy explains Livesey's marked and lifelong personal feud with the town's arch-Tory, T. B. Addison, but it also accounts for his distancing himself from the local Chartist movement and, after the 1840s his position to one side of, rather than at the head of, the move towards political and social emancipation of working people. Unquestionably a man of great influence in Preston particularly during the 1830s and early '40s, when his fame began to spread in association with the temperance movement, he thus became marginalised in later life.

Joseph Livesey combined the genuine social reformer and the great propagandist. The temperance movement was but one avenue of reform; he was closely involved in the town's municipal affairs, was a pioneeer of adult education, a leading agitator on behalf of the Anti-Corn Law League, and a leading opponent of the New Poor Law. During his life he personally assisted many hundreds of townspeople in addition to his organisation of the first seaside trips for the poor, and the various Relief

Committees and the soup kitchens (1830, 1840, 1842, 1858, 1862). As his epitaph in Preston Cemetery states, his was: 'An honoured life of philanthropy and usefulness, as author and worker, as the pioneer of Temperance, the advocate of moral and social reform, and the helpful friend and counsellor of the poor'.[6]

In 1815 Livesey married and settled in Preston. On his travels in the district he quite incidentally became aware of the marked differentials between the farm and market price of cheese, and became a very successful cheese-factor. Clearly a shrewd businessman, he was later credited with saving the Preston Bank from ruin in 1866. He was also a gifted journalist and became a propagandist of great talent. He established, edited and published a range of papers and journals including *The Moral Reformer*, The *Preston Temperance Advocate*, and The *Preston Guardian*. His writings, particularly in the 1830s, are clear, graphic and uncluttered by sentimentality; the journals are genuinely popular and entertaining – all attractive qualities of the early temperance crusade.[7] Livesey believed that indifference among the better-off towards the poor stemmed from genuine ignorance of their conditions. This could only be overcome by visiting the poor in their homes, and so developing 'social bonds'.

Joseph Livesey's death in 1884, at the age of ninety, was marked by an enormous funeral, and testimonials in a huge number of newspapers all over the world. The *Daily News* called him, 'One of the most useful and unobstructively noble men of our time,' whilst the *Manchester Examiner and Times* described him as 'Among the foremost philanthropists of his time . . . A great social reformer'.

Livesey's name is most closely associated with the temperance movement. Alcohol abuse, with its attendant social ills – disruption to employment, consumption of limited wages, violence and resulting domestic hardship – is a timeless social malady. If the extent of drinking could be moderated – so the argument ran – the resulting economic and moral gains would be great for the abstainer, his family and society.

By 1830 temperance societies were already established in many towns. What made the Preston society so prominent was its pledge of total abstinence. This tendency may be traced to a lecture given by James Tearl in the Independent Chapel in Grimshaw Street in June 1832.[8] Shortly afterwards Joseph Livesey and his associates drew up a preliminary total pledge in a room above his cheese shop, and at a meeting of the society on 1st September the pledge was signed by 'The Seven Men of Preston'. In fact a considerable number of members had been abstaining since Tearl's lecture, but were prevented from attending.

In 1833 two thousand people attended the annual meeting of the Preston society, where a total abstinence pledge for one year was introduced. In the next twelve months one thousand people signed it, and the movement began to spread nationally. In July members went on a temperance missionary tour, taking 9,500 tracts and a small silk flag with them, meetings being summoned by handbell or rattle. The society contained a number of notable pioneers. James Tearl was the first public exponent of total abstinence; Henry Anderton of Walton-le-Dale was the movement's 'Poet Genius' and a popular speaker; whilst Edward Grubb was its 'Philosopher'. In a debate with Mr. Bird of the Beer Interest, it was claimed that he proved that a Grubb could master a Bird. John King was another early pioneer from Walton, while Thomas Swindlehurst was the reformed and thus abdicated 'King of the Preston Drunkards'.

The position of the Preston society was therefore an extreme one, which did not find universal acceptance among other societies, who felt that a more moderate attitude was more realistic. Yet under the guidance of Livesey, and with the backing of his press, the Preston society acquired considerable prestige in the growing national movement. The signing of the total pledge by the seven members, and the origins of the word 'Teetotal' itself, became firmly rooted in folklore:

> In the month of September, 1833, Richard, or, as he was more familiarly called, 'Dickey' Turner, was speaking at a meeting in the cockpit at Preston, when, in his own peculiar way, he used these words:
> 'I'll have nowt to do wi this moderation botheration pledge; I'll be reet down out-and-out tee-tee-total for ever and ever.'
> 'Well done!' exclaimed the audience. 'Well done, Dickey!' exclaimed Mr. Livesey; 'that shall be the name of our new pledge.'[9]

Livesey claimed that Turner did not stammer, and had coined a new word for the language, but others have since argued that the word was an old one long in common usage in Ireland and the North.

Preston Workhouse, Watling Street Road c.1909. The workhouse was deliberately made large and forbidding to act as a deterrent against 'idle pauperism'. The foundation stone was layed by T. B. Addison.

To provide its members with entertainment away from the pubs and beer shops the society organised a great array of activities and meetings, which came to provide – like the churches and chapels of the period – a way of life in themselves. Tea parties were particularly successful.

The temperance magazines were similarly attractive, relating horrific stories of drunken excess as well as news and improving lessons:

> VENEER SALE – So dull and stupid are the cabinet makers of Preston, that at a late sale of veneers at the Shelleys Arms, it was found absolutely necessary, in order to put bargains into their hands, to circulate plenty of brandy and other intoxicating liquor. Good order and good bargains were the consequence.[10]

The magazine contained recipes for temperance drinks and the addresses of temperance hotels. Public lectures were also entertaining, and most celebrated was the experiment, or trick, of distilling a quart of beer, and using the spirit to light a lamp. Once a reformed drunkard shouted out, 'I could have lit all the lamps in Manchester.'

There were also temperance poets:

> Drunkards! throw your rags away,
> Feed your children every day,
> From the Beer and Gin Shop stay,
> Stay, oh! stay away.[11]

—— T. B. Addison and the —— workhouse question ——

One of Livesey's most implacable opponents was Thomas Batty Addison (1787-1874).[12] Born into one of the town's ruling families, Addison was educated at Clitheroe Grammar School and Charterhouse. Called to the bar in 1808, and subsequently a practising barrister and chairman of Preston Quarter Sessions, he was appointed Recorder of Preston in 1832. In early life he

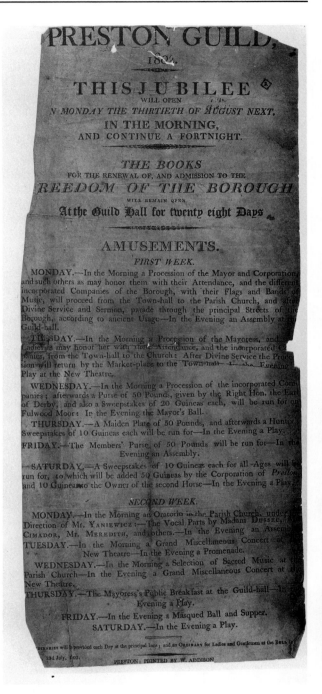

Programme of the Guild, 1802.

Thomas Batty Addison (1787–1874).

was a Whig and chaired the Great Reform Bill meeting in the Corn Exchange on 28th March 1831. He was one of the founders of the Literary and Philosophical Society in 1811, and in 1828 was appointed Chairman of the Mechanics Institute, of which Joseph Livesey was the Secretary. Addison also took a prominent part in the practical improvements of the town: he was a chairman of the town's water company and a director of the Preston and Longridge Railway, whose engine *Addison* was named after him. In later life, however, he became an extreme Tory, often unpopular for his vicious outbursts:

> Many paupers were the slaves of debased habits, clothed in rags, covered in filth, and without funds to provide for the purposes of cleanliness. Their children were uneducated and were thus brought up ignorant of the duties which they owed to Man and God . . . He too well knew that their filthy habits rather drove them to beer shops and gin shops and to the indulgence of a practice he deemed quite as pernicious – the wasting of their limited funds on tobacco.[13]

As a judge he was once in serious trouble for denouncing the jury as 'blockheads' when they came to an agreement not to his liking.[14]

The sea-change in Addison's outlook may be traced to the enormous row which accompanied attempts to introduce the New Poor Law into Preston. For thirty years Livesey and his supporters were able to block the construction of the massive new workhouse which Addison tirelessly advocated. In effect Livesey and Addison kept up a debate on the nature of poverty and its remedy which lasted for a generation.[15]

In 1836 Mr Power, one of the Commissioners of the Poor Law, arrived in Preston to instruct the elected Poor Law officials (the Board of Guardians) how to implement the new law. He got off to a bad start:

> Without in the first place making his mission known, he went with one of the overseers to visit the workhouse, every part of which he minutely examined, and made sundry inquiries respecting the treatment of the inmates. We understand . . . that he appeared dissatisfied with the rule which has always been followed in this place, of allowing the people as much food as they cared to eat at mealtimes![16]

The smaller parishes around the town were to be grouped together as a single Poor Law Union. The Preston Union thus found itself possessed of a number of the former parish workhouses, which were to be replaced by a single enormous workhouse. The system was to be based on deterrence: pauperism was to be stigmatised, and the condition of the pauper was always to be lower than that of the lowest paid section of the workforce. During periods of unemployment relief payments were only to be given for work on public work schemes. Over all loomed the threat of incarceration in the workhouse, and the stigma of being labelled a pauper.

Throughout the various unemployment crises of the early Victorian era, particularly 1836, 1840–2, 1853–4 and 1861–5, Addison was a careful scrutiniser of events, ever willing to uphold the moral fibre of the poor by his blistering attacks on them. In 1864, after renewed promptings by the Poor Law Board in London, moves began once more to establish a single Union Workhouse in the town. Joseph Livesey argued that it was both more humane and cheaper to give relief to the poor in their own homes, rather than split families up in the workhouse. Alternatively, it was pointed out that a new workhouse would be a great 'improvement'; it would be cheaper to run; could be paid for by cheap loans; and:

> . . . one large workhouse would have a more deterrent effect than the honey-suckle fronted places we now have. It would be a bigger and more tremendous embodiment of pauperism – that repulsive idea which we all associate with workhouses would be more tangible.[17]

The crucial Guardians' meeting was deliberately packed with *ex officio* Board members, the magistrates; they were able to outvote the elected members, who opposed the scheme. T. B. Addison laid the foundation stone of the Preston Workhouse in Watling Street Road on 25th July 1869.[18] During the speeches on this occasion the Rev. Brickel explained that, 'Many persons made themselves poor, and it was against that class they had to guard'. Another member was more practical: 'At present they had children in one house and the father in another and the mother in another. The rates could not, under such circumstances, be expended in a satisfactory manner.' Addison, who, Livesey claimed, had stated that a saving of 4d per week on each pauper's food could now be made, reflected on his own reforming path as he laid the foundation stone:

> We cannot expect that all will be persuaded at once on any new doctrine whatsoever. These things come to us one by one . . . until at length that which perhaps was the minority becomes the majority, and what was called heresy gets the name of reformation.

Although losing this battle Livesey's view was ultimately to prevail, as the modern welfare state was not to be built on the foundations of the Victorian Poor Law. For, as Mr. Newsham, one of the Preston Guardians, had remarked in 1864, 'The real question was – could the Union afford to pay for the accommodation it really ought to provide for its poor?'[19]

— *Missions and missionaries* —

For much of the nineteenth century the town's churches were the most important improving influence. The great Victorian religious revival was marked in Preston by much church and chapel building. With their own schools, welfare organisations, societies, self-help groups and social events, these became important community centres.

The process of expansion was most marked in the Church of England which by 1870 accounted for twenty of the Preston district's fifty places of worship. Much was due to the tireless church-building activities of Roger Carus Wilson, Vicar of Preston 1817–39, who established St. Peter's (1825), St. Paul's (1825), Christ Church (1836), St. Mary's (1838) and St. Thomas's (1839).[20]

From the late eighteenth century Preston also had a thriving Methodist community. John Wesley visited the town on a number of occasions. On Thursday 24th May 1781 he recorded in his journal:

> I went to Preston, where the old prejudice seems to be quite forgotten. The little society has fitted up a large and convenient house [in St. John's Place] where I preached to a candid audience. Everyone seemed to be considerably affected: I hope in some the impression will continue.[21]

A frequent visitor to the weaving communities in Walton and Bamber Bridge, Wesley spoke for the last time in Preston in 1790, when he addressed a large audience from the obelisk in the Market Square. A Methodist chapel was established in Back Lane in 1787, moving to Lune Street in 1817, by which time it was the centre of a circuit extending up to twenty miles from Preston.[22]

From the beginning of the nineteenth century Preston's Catholic community underwent a marked revival. Although considerable numbers of Irish people subsequently settled in the town they only accounted for perhaps one fifth of the Catholic congregation. In the years 1868–71 weekly mass attendance reached about 1,400. Church building continued, with the old church of St. Mary's being followed by St. Wilfrid's (1793), St. Ignatius' (1836), St. Augustine's (1840), St. Walburge's (1854) and English Martyrs in 1867. St. Walburge's is the finest of all Preston churches. It was designed by the Preston architect J. A. Hansom, of hansom cab fame, in the Early Gothic style. The roof of the nave alone weighs over one hundred tons and required seven thousand pieces of timber and 18,000 square feet of boarding. The spire, completed in 1866, is the town's most conspicuous landmark; it rises 309 feet 6 inches above the street, reaching 408 feet above sea level. The 'small' cross on top of the spire is in fact fifteen feet high and its arms are five feet across. This impressive building, a cathedral in all but name, cost over £15,000 to build.[23]

On Mothering Sunday, 30th March 1851, a National Religious Census

The Rev. Robert Harris (1764–1862). The Rev. Harris was the father of Edmund Harris, Preston's great Victorian benefactor, and was the incumbent of St. George's Church, Chapel Walks, from 1797 to his death.

Above left: St. Peter's Church on Fylde Road, one of several Preston Anglican churches which has found a new, secular use – as the Polytechnic Arts Centre.

Above right: St. Mary's Church of England on St. Mary's Road, off New Hall Lane.

Left: St. Paul's, built as one of the so-called Waterloo churches in 1825 but now the headquarters of Red Rose Radio.

Above left: The Central Methodist Church on Lune Street.

Above right: St. Mark's Church (1868).

Right: The Moor Park Methodist Church, now an antiques centre.

was taken of the numbers of people attending all churches in England and Wales.[24] Its findings were remarkable: only somewhere between 47 and 54% of the population over ten years of age 'went to church'.

Anthony Hewitson was a keen observer of the town's religious life, and his popular newspaper sketches were published collectively in *Our Churches and Chapels* (1869) and *Our Country Churches and Chapels* (1872). Taking each church in turn, he describes the origin of its dedication, the buildings, their location, and the vicar.[25] He began the series with the Parish Church and Canon Parr: 'Canon Parr is an easy-going, genial, educated man, kindly disposed towards good living, not blessed with over much money, fond of wearing a billycock, and strongly in love with a cloak . . . the smartest man Preston Protestants could have to defend their case'.

Of the parish priest Fr. Cobb, whose weight Hewitson scurrilously estimated to be thirteen stones, he wrote:

> . . . he is shrewd, has a strong intuitive sense: can't be got over: won't be beaten out of the field if you once get him into it, and is sure to either win or make you believe he has . . . We have never heard a more practical preacher: he will tell young women what sort of husbands to get, young men what kind of wives to choose, married folk how to conduct themselves, and old maids and bachelors how to reconcile themselves virtuously to their fate.

Of the Wesleyan Chapel in Lune Street he wrote: 'We know of no place in the town where religious influence has been more actively radiated:

> Mr. Mearns is a calm rather bilious-looking elderly men . . . He is neither fussy, nor conceited, nor fond of brandishing the sword of superiority . . . His words are well chosen: they fit in with cultivated exactitude and polished precision . . . The Rev. Mr. Tindall comes up in a more polished, energetic, and fashionable garb. He is eloquent, argumentative, polemical . . . The Rev. F. B. Swift . . . is a hard worker: but there does not appear to be over much of him at present . . . You can tell 5 minutes off what he is going to say . . . but a beginner.

Having described the missions and their missionaries, Hewitson considered the enormous field for their work which nineteenth-century Preston provided. Around many churches, he wrote, 'You will see enough to convince you that many missionaries, with numerous Bibles and piles of Blankets, are yet wanted at home before being despatched to either farthest Ind or the plains of Timbuctoo'.

In what is perhaps the best piece of descriptive writing relating to Preston, he described the teeming life in one of the town's poorest districts:

> The general scene may be thus condensed and described: Myriads of children, ragged, sore-headed, bare-legged, dirty, and amazingly alive amid all of it; wretched-looking matrons, hugging saucy, screaming

infants to their breasts, and sending senior youngsters for either herring, or beer, or very small loaves; strong, idle young men hanging about street corners with either dogs at their feet, or pigeon-baskets in their hands; little shops driving a brisk 'booking' business with either females wearing shawls over their heads or children wearing nothing at all on their feet; bevies of brazen-faced hussies looking out of grim door-ways for more victims and more drink; stray soldiers struggling about beer or dram shops entrances, with dissolute, brawny-armed females; and wandering old hags with black eyes and dishevelled hair, closing up the career of shame and ruin they have so long and so wretchedly run. Anybody may see the sights we have just described. We mention this not because there is anything pleasing in it, but because it is something which exists daily in the heart of our town.

Around St. Augustine's he found, 'much honest industry, much straightfoward forwardness and everyday kindness, much that smells of gin, and rascality, and heathenism may be seen in the district. There is plenty of room for all kinds of reformers in the district'.

Along Ribbleton Lane the district around St. Joseph's Church was:

full of children, little groceries, public houses and beershops, brick-kilns, smoke, smudge, clanging hammers, puddle-holes, and general bewilderment. When the new gasometer, which looks like the skeleton of some vast colosseum, is finished here, an additional balmyness will be given to the immediate atmosphere, which may be very good for children in the hooping-cough, but anything except pleasant for those who have passed through that lively ordeal.

The Harris Orphanage c.1903. A bequest of £100,000 from the Harris Trustees enabled the town greatly to improve its care of orphans, marking a very real advance in the provision of social services in Preston.

Housing conditions around lower Friargate were particularly bad:

The locality in which the chapel [St. Mary's] is placed is crowded, dark
looking, and pretty ungodly. All kinds of sinister looking alleys, narrow
yards, dirty courts and smoking bad streets surround it: much drinking
is done in each; and a chorus of noise from lounging men in their shirt
sleeves, draggle-tailed women without bonnets, and weird little
youngsters, given up entirely to dirt, treacle, and rags, is constantly kept
up in them.

St. Saviour's was the worst district:

Few district are more thoroughly vitiated, more distinctly poverty-
stricken, more entirely at enmity with soap and water than that in
which the church stands. Physically, mentally, and spiritually it is in a
state of squash and mildew. Heathenism seethes in it . . .

Indeed in 1829 the Vicar of St. Paul's Church had reported, 'The people
are more barbarous and uncivilised than it is possible for anyone to
conceive who has not been amongst them.'[26]

—— The Lancashire Cotton Famine ——

The greatest trial through which Victorian Preston had to pass was
the Great Cotton Panic of 1861-5. At the height of the crisis
perhaps half of the town's population might technically have been
classed as paupers. Its effect was to halt Preston's growth for a decade.

Although generally known today as the 'Lancashire Cotton Famine',
this was in fact a commercial crisis. It arose from excessive over-
production during the great runaway boom of 1860, and the consequent
glutting of the Indian and Chinese export markets. This in turn resulted
in record warehouse stocks of unsold cloth, and as demand fell away
wage cuts, lay-offs and mill closures inevitably began. The fear of likely
raw material shortages arising from the American Civil War produced
manic speculation in the price of raw cotton stocks. Caught between very
high raw material costs, and very low prices for finished goods, the
Lancashire industry closed down. Even if firms had stocks of raw cotton,
it clearly did not pay to manufacture it, since more money could be made
by selling it.

The industry waited for the glut to clear and demand to improve.
Recovery, however, was delayed by fears of a sudden end to the war. Very
large stocks were known to be blockaded in the southern ports of the
United States, and the sudden release of this on to the cotton markets
would flood them and greatly reduce prices. Any firms holding large
stocks, perhaps with a view to re-starting their mills, would be ruined.

In Preston the enormous perils inherent in a society which is based almost entirely on a single industry at once became apparent. During 1861 the Board of Guardians gave outdoor relief to between 2,500 and 3,000. people per week. From October 1861 to March 1862 this total rose steadily to 10,500, and a second surge began in May taking the total to a peak of 22,500 in December 1862. Thereafter numbers fell steadily to reach a plateau of 13–14,000 between August 1863 and March 1864. After this, recovery was fairly rapid despite a sharp setback due to speculation in late 1864 and early 1865.[27] Nevertheless, numbers did not reach their normal levels until August 1865.

This crisis was unlike all earlier depressions and strikes – it dominated Preston society for almost four years. For the unemployed themselves conditions rapidly became extremely harsh, and even those who had managed to save money, such as overlookers and managers, were soon reduced to poverty along with almost everyone else, including the town's shopkeepers. Edwin Waugh, the great dialect writer, visited the town on a number of occasions, and published several graphic accounts of life in Preston at the time:

> I hear on all hands that there is hardly any town in Lancashire suffering so much as Preston . . .

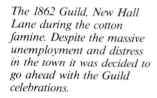

The 1862 Guild, New Hall Lane during the cotton famine. Despite the massive unemployment and distress in the town it was decided to go ahead with the Guild celebrations.

. . . The wail of sorrow is not heard in Preston Market-place; but destitution may be found almost anywhere there just now, cowering in squalid corners, within a few yards of plenty – as I have seen it many a time this week. The courts and alleys behind even some of the main streets swarm with people who have hardly a nail left to scratch themselves with . . .[28]

The Cotton Famine was without question the biggest 'historical event' in most Preston people's lives in the Victorian age. Events in the American Civil War itself were closely followed in the local press, including the career of the Preston-built naval blockade runner, the Confederate *Night Hawk* launched on the Ribble in June 1863.[29] Avenham, Miller and Moor Parks, which were laid out by the unemployed, remain as monuments to the period, along with the Preston Workhouse and perhaps Preston Dock. For there can be little doubt that this collective experience, and the apparent dangers implicit in so narrow an industrial base, were important factors in the widespread support for attempts to diversify the town's economy by means of the Preston Dock Scheme twenty years later. This was to provide some relief from the less dramatic but long-term and final decline of textiles after 1924.

—— *The progress of Preston* ——

Looking back from the Preston Guild of 1882, Anthony Hewitson could point to very real advances in the social and physical fabric of the town made in the previous eighty years.[30] Reflecting the recent

The old post office, Fishergate c.1903. This building stood next to the Preston Gas Company's impressive offices, approximately opposite the present day Woolworth's building.

Preston horse tram c.1900. The horse tramway was established in 1879. The system, electrified after 1904, was to be an important stimulus to the development of the town's outer suburbs.

emergence of the town's cotton industry the Guild of 1802 was dominated by the two great cotton masters, John Watson and John Horrocks. The Guild of 1842 followed shortly after the Chartist agitation and Lune Street shootings, whilst the celebrations of 1862 took place during the Cotton Famine. Yet the appalling social conditions which the cotton industry engendered and which had overwhelmed the former market town and gentry resort, began to be ameliorated after 1850 and the process was gathering pace during the 1880s.

Indeed, by 1882 many of Preston's social and geographical landmarks had been established, reflecting a genuine drive for improvement among many sections of the community. Although piecemeal and *ad hoc*, these developments frequently represented many years of personal and group effort, and were to provide the basis for future progress. Clearly they marked an enormous advance on all that had gone before. At their most practical and necessary in the provision of drains, the aspirations of the improvers could soar to cerebral heights. Around the roof of the Harris Museum and Library are the words, 'May the riches you acquire here abide with you always'. A new town and perhaps a new civilisation were slowly and painfully being engineered.

Many of the town's utilities were first founded as companies, before municipal control was established later in the century. The Preston Waterworks Company was formed in 1832 and began the construction of an extensive series of reservoirs. In 1853 the Corporation purchased the Company, acquiring the reservoirs at Alston, Dilworth, Grimsargh and Fulwood, and began work at Longridge. The Preston Gas Company was established as early as 1815 and in the following year Preston became the first provincial town to be lit by gas.

Expansion of the public services was a much more piecemeal process. The former central police station beside the covered market was begun in 1857, and the force expanded steadily throughout the century, increasing from fifteen men in 1850 (three day-, twelve night-duty staff) to sixty men in 1861 and 98 men in 1882, for a town with a population of about one hundred thousand. In 1810 Preston had just three policemen costing the ratepayers £3 per week, and although the force of six officers established by 1832 had been provided with 'suits', it was only allowed to wear them on Sundays.

In 1805 a public subscription for three engines had been opened, and an Act of Parliament was obtained in 1815 to provide 'Fire Engines and Firemen for the protection of the said Borough'. The Tithebarn Street fire station was built in 1852, and by 1872 boasted a steam fire engine, one serjeant and a force of 25 men.

The provision of medical care, particularly for those least able to pay for it, evolved very slowly. The Dispensary was established in 1809, and the House of Recovery in 1833. The struggle for the foundation and progress of Preston Royal Infirmary was long based on the efforts great and small of a very large number of townspeople from all walks of life. The Preston and County of Lancaster Royal Infirmary was opened in 1870 at a cost of £18,713. Seven years later St. Joseph's Institute for the Sick Poor was established in Mount Street. The Preston Industrial Orphans' Home and School had its origins in a public meeting held in 1863, and the Blind Institute was established in Glovers Court in 1864.

The town's provision for education expanded enormously following

Fire engine outside the Tithebarn Street Fire Station 1896.

Preston Gas Company offices, Fishergate, 1878. By 1900 Preston's main throughfare was dominated by a range of towers and minarets, few of which have survived. Tragically, this notable landmark was demolished to make way for the Fishergate entrance to St. George's shopping centre.

the establishment of the Parish Church National School in 1817, and by the 1870s the district around Winckley Square had emerged as an important centre for the region, with Preston High School for Girls and Preston Catholic College, in addition to the long-established Preston Grammar School which moved into its splendid new building in Cross Street in 1841. Preston Free Library was established in 1879, although there were a number of earlier libraries in the town. The Moor Park Observatory had its origins on the triangle in front of Stephenson Terrace in Deepdale Road, where a fourteen-inch reflecting telescope was acquired by the Corporation in 1881.

The provision of public buildings and parks was a fairly steady process throughout the century. The Theatre Royal in Fishergate was opened in 1802, and improved in 1869 and 1882, when its capacity was 1,700 persons (stalls, one hundred; boxes, three hundred; gallery, seven hundred; pit, six hundred). The Corn Exchange in Lune Street, subsequently Preston's Public Hall, was built in 1822–4 and later extended.

The Miller Arcade c.1895. With its very fashionable shops, the arcade was a clear forerunner of the large purpose-built stores of the twentieth century, as Preston emerged as the premier shopping centre of North Lancashire.

The continued importance of the town as the regional centre of its farming hinterland is well illustrated by the construction of the cattle market (1867) and the remarkable covered market which, after collapsing and bankrupting its builders, was completed in 1875. The splendid Town Hall with its tower and clock was completed on the south side of the market place in 1867, and buildings on the east side were removed to make way for the Harris building. Demolition of adjacent buildings also

The Harris Library and Art Gallery c.1900. The most conspicuous element of Edmund Harris' enormous bequest to the town, the Harris Library, was opened in 1894 and cost over £100,000. Designed by James Hibbert, this stupendous building formed the centrepiece of the town's fine public buildings, which also included the Town Hall, the Miller Arcade, the Sessions House, the Post Office building and the Municipal Building.

The Harris Institute c.1900. A bequest of £40,000 enabled the establishment of the Harris Institute, with its schools of technology, science and art. The forerunner of the Preston (and later Lancashire) Polytechnic, the Harris Institute was thus ultimately to evolve into Preston's University.

made way for the Miller Arcade, so that during the nineteenth century much of the medieval centre of the town was replaced with fine public buildings. As has been seen, the enormous Preston Union Workhouse on Watling Street Road, one of the town's biggest buildings, was completed in 1868.

Preston was in the forefront of the provision of public parks. The Corporation added to the long-established recreation grounds and gardens of Avenham in 1844, when the riverside walk was improved and the park further extended. The area was landscaped as part of the public works programme established during the Cotton Famine. Thomas Miller donated adjoining land in 1864 to form Miller Park. Moor Park, extending over one hundred acres, was enclosed from Preston Moor in 1834, and was similarly laid out during the Cotton Famine and opened in 1867. Over £20,000 was spent on Avenham and Miller Parks, and almost £11,000 on Moor Park. Public recreation grounds were later provided for their adjacent districts at Haslam Park, Ribbleton Park and Ashton Park. Preston Cemetery was opened in 1855.

The town thus benefited enormously from the public works undertaken to provide employment during the Cotton Famine, which provided the formation of Avenham and Moor Parks, construction of the Cattle Market, in addition to land reclamation on the Moor, the laying out of streets, drainage and paving schemes. Social facilities were greatly expanded and developed through the bequest of E. R. Harris to the town. The Harris Trustees provided £100,000 for the Library and Museum, £100,000 for the Harris Orphanage, and £40,000 to establish the Harris Institute with its schools of technology, science and art, allowing long-established schemes finally to come to fruition.

Access to information and rapid personal communication were to be central features of life in the twentieth century. From quite an early date Preston had a good selection of newspapers. The *Preston Journal* was founded in 1807, and merged into the *Preston Chronicle* in 1812. The *Preston Pilot* was formed in 1825, and Joseph Livesey founded the *Preston Guardian* in 1844. In 1840 the town had a single 'letter carrier', who earned 10s. per week. By 1852 24,000 letters were delivered in the Preston and Blackpool postal district, increasing to 128,000 letters in Preston alone in 1882. Before their take-over by the Post Office in 1870, two telegraph companies – the Electric Telegraph Co., and the English and Irish Magnetic Telegraph Co – had Preston offices, both established in 1854. The first telephone exchange

AVENHAM PARK, PRESTON.

The Frenchwood entrance to Avenham Park c.1920.

was opened in September 1881 by G. Sharples, 'Chemist and Electrician', above his shop in Fishergate. Within two years his system using 'Bell's Patent Telephones' operated 118 miles of wire for its one hundred subscribers. A rival firm, the Lancashire and Cheshire Telephonic Exchange Co., established a pioneer 'trunk' link between Preston and Manchester as a special feature of the 1882 Guild celebrations.

—— Success to Preston Docks ——

Preston's access to trade on the River Ribble before the constuction of the Albert Edward Dock in 1884–92 has, rightly, been described as a marginal asset.[31] Below Penwortham the river meandered through a number of channels over the shallow floor of its sandy estuary, fringed by swampy expanses of fen. From the seventeenth century onwards advocates of the development and improvement of the Ribble pointed to the likely benefits which could be expected to accrue to Preston and mid-Lancashire. The cost, it was argued, might be offset not only by the stimulus to the town's trade, and later industry, but also by the sale of reclaimed land along the estuary.

In 1806 the first Ribble Navigation Company was formed, capitalised on forty shares of £50 each. It met with some success, the river was trained into a single course, and the number of ships visiting the port rose from sixty in 1805 to four hundred in 1820. In 1825 the New Quays along the riverside were opened, yet it was still cheaper to import goods through Glasson Dock and the Lancaster Canal than to bring them directly into Preston on the Ribble. Preston Corporation recognised the importance of the enterprise, and acquired its first holding in the company in 1830. When Samuel Horrocks was asked to put money into the scheme, he replied that if he wished to put money into the Ribble he would walk on to Penwortham Bridge and throw it in.[32]

Watery Lane 1892. The Grand Junction Hotel *was suitably adorned for the visit of the Duke of Edinburgh to open the Albert Edward Dock. The Prince sailed around the dock in the steam yacht* Aline *before lunching at the Town Hall. By 2.45pm he was on the train to London.*

The port's custom house was restored in 1843 and duties collected at Preston increased accordingly: 1841 – £6,309; 1843 – £19,375; 1845 – £66,921. In 1845 the New Quay (at the bottom of Marsh Lane) was, 'so thronged that the schooners were obliged to lie two deep . . . We observed 22 vessels occupying their stations'. New trading contacts opened up. In 1848 a large crowd gathered to see the arrival of the port's first three-masted sailing ship, of three hundred tons, 'Direct from New Orleans, full laden with Cotton and Corn'.[33]

Under the third Ribble Company (1853–82) almost four thousand acres of marshland were reclaimed and traffic increased rapidly: 1852 – 64,600 tons; 1861 – 86,501 tons; 1864 – 90,000 tons. The river approaches were further improved, but silting was an ever-present problem. One possible solution put forward as early as 1834 was for a Lytham-Preston ship canal, which in the long run might have been the best solution. By the mid-1860s a wet dock (as distinct from the tidal riverside quays) able to handle larger iron ships appeared increasingly necessary. Nothing practical was done, and by 1882 trade had fallen back to under forty thousand tons.

Following a report by the engineers Bell and Miller (1865) which argued for the construction of a wet dock, the issue became an important one in the town's politics. By 1880 the Preston cotton industry had passed the heyday of its expansion, and contemporary observers pointed to the stagnation in trade, and the absence of the spirit of enterprise which had characterised it fifty years earlier.

In 1882 the Corporation purchased the Company's property for £72,500. Through its Ribble Committee, the Council would construct the docks, borrowing money which would be repaid through the rates. The enterprise was to be a colossal one, the largest construction project in Preston's history, at immense cost. Sir John Goode's plan for the

Sailing ship in Preston Dock c.1900. Sailing ships continued to be frequent visitors to the Port of Preston until the mid 1930s.

scheme was adopted. It required the diversion of the river away from the line of Strand Road into Penwortham Marsh, the construction of a large dock basin, and a system of locks to regulate the water level. It was to cost £558,150, but enthusiasm in the town was such that the dock size was subsequently increased to forty acres, and by 1887 an extra £½m was needed. Alderman Gilbertson cut the first sod of the river diversion on 11th October 1884, and the future Edward VII laid the foundation stone on 17th July the following year. Edward Garlick and his partner Banjamin Sykes, who succeeded him, were resident engineers, and Thomas Walker was the main contractor.

Opposition to the scheme – a revolutionary municipal undertaking for the times, overshadowed only by the Manchester Ship Canal – was led by the railways and coalesced around a 'Party of Caution', of whom John Crook Hamilton was a prominent member. In the Council elections of 1881, however, the party was soundly defeated, and even the ratepayers (who had actually to pay for it) sanctioned the project by a majority of three to one. The dock was clearly seen as a major investment in the

town's future growth.

By 1887 poor management of the enormous scheme, and particularly the enlargement of the original plan, led to the need for a further massive capital injection, and work stopped. The great workings languished for two years. A further Act of Parliament had to be obtained before work could restart in 1889. On Monday 2nd May 1892 the temporary cement dam on the river was carefully breached and water began to enter the enormous basin; by early June the dock was filled. On the 25th the Duke of Edinburgh, having stayed overnight at Darwen Bank, off School Lane, Bamber Bridge, travelled in near-state to the opening. The locals had erected a large banner which read, 'Success to the Preston Docks'.

The 'Albert Edward' was forty acres in extent, three thousand feet long, six hundred feet wide, the entrance basin covered 4¾ acres and was 850 feet long and three hundred feet wide. The entrance locks could form a single basin 550 feet long, or be sub-divided into two smaller ones 325 feet and 225 feet long. It was simply the largest single dock basin in the world – sixteen miles from the open sea! An enormous visionary development,

Unloading timber at Preston Dock c.1910. Timber was a major import through the dock. Here it is being laboriously unloaded by hand onto the quayside, before being carried away by railway.

it was one of which perhaps only the Victorians would be capable. Almost at a stroke a new commercial enterprise (and employer) had been created; a nucleus for the new industries which would grow and later supersede the cotton industry. In 1897 Dick Kerr took up a large site between Strand Road and the dock for an engineering works. It lay directly upon the course of the old river.[34]

Henry Hamer. As Town Clerk, Henry Hamer was closely involved in the Corporation's takeover of the third Ribble Company and its plans for the construction of Preston Dock.

—— *Preston Scientific Society* ——

Throughout much of the nineteenth century Preston had a great array of thriving societies catering for interests of all kinds. The steady reduction of working hours, particularly apparent on Saturday afternoons, resulted in great and enthusiastic development of sporting clubs, and only towards the end of the century did the football interest, for example, become coalesced around just two clubs: Preston Grasshoppers for rugby, and North End under the Association rules.[35] The town also had a rich and varied range of intellectual societies. The Preston Botanic Society existed as early as 1804, and the Literary and Philosophical Society was founded in 1810. Between 1828 and 1834 the Institution for the Diffusion of Knowledge built up a membership of eight hundred, a library of over fifteen hundred books, and had annual subscriptions of £600. Its principal function was the provision of education and instruction to working people. The Preston Literary and

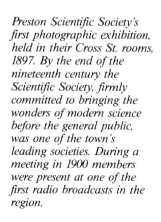

Preston Scientific Society's first photographic exhibition, held in their Cross St. rooms, 1897. By the end of the nineteenth century the Scientific Society, firmly committed to bringing the wonders of modern science before the general public, was one of the town's leading societies. During a meeting in 1900 members were present at one of the first radio broadcasts in the region.

Philosophical Institute and the Avenham Institute were both founded in 1840. The latter, with its elegant building adjacent to Ladies' Walk, built at a cost of £6,000, was transformed into the Harris Institute in 1889.

The Preston Scientific Society is still one of the town's most outstanding societies.[36] A meeting held on 24th February 1876 unanimously agreed, 'That it is desirable to form a society in Preston for the promotion of natural and physical sciences'. The spreading of scientific knowledge and interest through society was a genuine aim of the group. To this end ladies were occasionally admitted (especially for the popular Microscopical Soirees), and in 1880 the Gilchrist Lectures were held in the Guild Hall. Aimed particularly at working people, these were very successful.

Having briefly lapsed, the Society was re-established in 1893, including many former members. By 1898 the society had 710 members, and its sub-committees included an Astro-Physical Section, a Botanical, Natural History and Microscopical Section, and a Photographic Section. Later developments prior to the Second World War included a Literary Section (1900: first chairman Anthony Hewitson), an Art Section (1924), a Cinematography group (1935) and a Psychology group (1935).

The Record and Survey Society (1937) began to record vanishing Preston. A firm commitment to the scientific wonders of the age permeated all proceedings. At the 'Brilliantly Successful' re-launching of the Society in 1893 guests at the Town Hall were able to see and hear 'A 'grammmophone' lent by Mr. Henry Bell, which . . . reproduced songs and instrumental music which could be distinctly heard a *few feet* away'. One society lecture held in the Guild Hall in January 1900, at the height of the Boer War, was a particular harbinger of the future:

> Mr. Cuming spoke of Marconi's marvellous experiment made last year, when he succeeded in transmitting a wireless message from the steamship *Saint Paul*, to the Needles 45 miles away . . . Mr. Cuming, at the conclusion of his lecture, caused a wireless message to be sent through the space from one end of the Guild Hall to the other, which was transcribed as follows – 'Hope for Better Luck in South Africa'.

—— *Preston North End: The Invincibles* ——

On 31st March 1889 Preston North End defeated Wolverhampton Wanderers 3–0 at the Oval, to win the F.A. Cup. Having won the first ever Football League Championship earlier in the year without losing a single game, and the Cup without conceding a goal, North End established a unique record which will probably never be improved upon.[37]

During the height of the Lancashire Cotton Famine in 1862, a cricket club (whose name is lost to history) was set up and played on Preston Marsh, one of the town's few open spaces. In 1867 a section broke away to play on the new Moor Park at what was then the 'North End' of Preston. The phrase seems to have been used for centuries in the town, to designate the edge of the wilderness of Preston Moor, and as the Moor contracted so the 'North End' accordingly moved outwards. About this time William Suddell (1851–1911) joined the club. He was a member of an ancient family which had filled most of the town's civic offices, including that of Guild Mayor in 1682. This cricket team was first known as Preston Nelson, changing its name shortly afterwards to Preston North End. In 1875 they moved on to one of the fields of the adjacent Deepdale Farm.

Venturing into winter sports, a rugby football section was formed in 1876, but perhaps unable to compete with Preston Grasshoppers, two years later Association football was introduced. Accordingly on 5th October 1878 they were beaten 1–0 by Eagley. Right from the start the North-Enders displayed much creativity in the post-match analysis: the players had not mastered the rules properly. On the eve of a match with Blackburn Rovers it was decided to give up cricket and to concentrate on football. The result: Preston North End 0 – Blackburn Rovers 15.

By the early 1880s under Suddell's shrewd and tactical management, Preston North End became one of the top northern sides, attracting large crowds of up to five thousand people to their Deepdale ground, which was steadily improved. Ladies were admitted free of charge, until two thousand turned up for one game. Suddell began to import players rather than concentrating on local talent, particularly the 'Scottish Professors' – the masters of the passing game. Belger in 1882 was thus perhaps the first of the line of these welcome mercenaries, which was to stretch from the 'Invincibles' to Alex James, the 1937-8 and 1954 Wembley sides, to Alex Bruce in the 1970s.

Expelled in 1885 from the F.A. cup for playing 'professionals' Suddell strenuously denied the charge and retaliated by threatening to form a rival British Football Association. The F.A. reinstated Preston. Gradually the 'Invincibles' side was being assembled. The game was 'manly', that is to say extremely rough, if not violent, by modern standards, and behaviour on and off the field left much to be desired. In 1884 Bolton players were attacked by the Deepdale crowd, and on subsequent occasions the Preston players were attacked leaving Queen's Park, Glasgow and most sensationally, Villa Park. The Preston crowd, especially the lady supporters, were extremely direct in their detection of refereeing error, and the team was expected to win every game.

Although at least one heavy defeat was blamed on several team members being drunk, in 1887 Hyde United were swept aside 26-0 in the Cup competition. Defeat in the Cup Final of 1888 by West Bromwich Albion stunned the town – the players had unwisely 'got cold' sightseeing in London. As one of the twelve founder members of the Football League established that year, North End were its first champions. Their record speaks for itself: Played 22, Won 18, Drawn 4, Lost 0, Goals for 74, Goals Against 15, Points 40. Aston Villa trailed in eleven points behind, the first runners-up. Although champions again in 1889-90 and runners-up in 1890, '91, '92, '93 and 1905, the club was unable to hold on to its players and the great side quite quickly broke up.

This first period of the club's greatness has a sad postscript. In 1895 Suddell was found guilty of embezzling £5,000 from his employer, the Preston cotton firm of John Goodair and Co. Though the money had been used, it seems, to further the cause of Preston North End F.C., he was sentenced to three years' imprisonment.

CHAPTER FOURTEEN

Preston
between the wars

THE history of Preston in the twentieth century has been
dominated by the town's struggle to escape from its century old
dependence on the cotton industry, and the attempt to resolve
the appalling social problems which its rapid growth had produced. Yet
the greatest stimulus to social change in Preston came from the two world
wars of 1914–18 and 1939–45. Each was marked by enormous industrial
expansion during wartime and renewed social progress thereafter. The
status of women, in particular, changed markedly, and in Edith Rigby
(1872–1948) Preston had a leading suffragette and social reformer. In
many respects the 'Victorian Age' ended not with the nineteenth century
but with the battlefields of the First World War.

The outbreak of war in August 1914 was greeted by wild enthusiasm in
Preston: 'During the whole of that first day, and indeed for some time
afterwards, great crowds of people thronged the principal streets, everyone evincing a consciousness that we were on the eve of great things'.[1]

As a garrison town and a major railway centre, Preston was an
important base for mobilisation. Cheering crowds followed departing
troops to the railway station. Fulwood Barracks was quickly swamped by
servicemen, reservists and volunteers. The Corn Exchange and even the
tramway power station were used for accommodation, and ammunition
wagons were parked in Lune Street. By the end of August it was estimated
that three thousand men were 'sleeping rough' in outhouses, gardens and
under hedges. Early in September a volunteer party of 250 Tonypandy
coal miners, who had been turned away from the barracks, paraded the
town with a banner which read, 'No food, no shelter, no money'.

It was felt that the chaos at the barracks was deterring respectable
young men from volunteering. Accordingly, on 31st August the following
announcement appeared in the local press:

> It is proposed to form a Company of young businessmen, clerks, etc., to
> be drawn from Preston and the surrounding districts and to be

attached, if practicable, to a Battalion of the L.N.L.R. Will those who would like to join apply here [at the Town Hall] any afternoon or evening this week – the sooner the better.

The men would be allowed to stay together and to go directly to training camp on Salisbury Plain. The condition that they sign on for three years

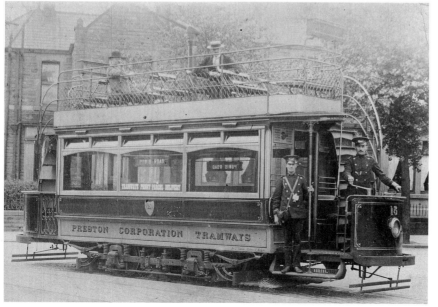

Preston Corporation tram c.1925. The first electric tramcar in Preston was manufactured by Dick Kerr and ran on a system which eventually included 38 double deck and 10 single deck cars. From Lancaster Road the lines extended via North Road to Sharoe Green (2 miles), via Deepdale to Sharoe Green (2 miles), to Farrington Park (1.9 miles), to Ashton (2.2 miles), to Broadgate (1.2 miles) and Ribbleton (2 miles).

was taken as a great joke, for it was widely believed that the war would be over in a matter of weeks. A group of 250 volunteers was quickly formed, and it duly became the 'D' Company of the 7th Battalion L.N.L.R. – the 'Preston Pals'.[2]

The subsequent history of the Preston Pals, like that of their neighbours from Chorley and Accrington, was to be a tragic one:

> Very early in the course of the actual fighting the Company suffered considerable attrition, and vacant places were filled by strangers. The time came when the whole Battalion had fallen so low in numbers that it was broken up and merged into other units. In that way the 'Pals' completely lost their identity.[3]

During an attack on a section of enemy trenches called the Switch Line, on 23rd July 1916, the Pals were almost wiped out, and just fifty men managed to get back to the British lines. The Battalion itself had lost ten officers and 213 men, and by August the Preston Pals had virtually ceased to exist.[4]

The electric carriage works, Strand Road, Preston c.1900. Trams ready for delivery to Sheffield and Carlisle. Subsequently part of the Dick Kerr combine, the Strand Road works were to graduate from the manufacture of tram cars to the most advanced jet aircraft in less than half a century.

In November 1916 the Mayor, Harry Cartmell, addressed the annual Preston Trademen's dinner:

> Have you noticed that as a result of all this we have come to place a much lessened value on human life . . . How otherwise, with the old sensitiveness to pain and sorrow and death, should we be able to contemplate the thought that of whole battalions associated with our own town only a handful of men are now left? How could we bear the knowledge of what has happened to the Preston Pals, that splendid company of fine young fellows, full of fire and life and energy, that left the town in the very early days of the war.

Preston men served in all services and all theatres of the war. When early enthusiasm flagged, as reports of the actual conditions at the front filtered back, a mass rally in the market place addressed by Lord Derby attracted a crowd of twenty thousand, and it was claimed that one thousand men volunteered there and then. By the end of November 1915 the 'Derby Scheme' had identified 9,418 recruits in Preston, in addition to the earlier volunteers. Yet by late 1916 parties of troops from the barracks, marching through the town to the railway station for embarkation to the front, complained that they were no longer cheered and elicited little response from the townspeople.

—— *War work* ——

Preston's contribution to the war effort was prodigious. In January 1915 Dick Kerr's works on Strand Road began to manufacture shells, and by the Armistice had turned out 3¼ million of all sizes (up to

63 inches long for battleships), using one million tons of steel, and in the last eighteen months of the war the works reconstructed over four hundred heavy guns. The manufacture of aircraft began with fairly primitive flying boats capable of carrying four men at just 70 mph. By the end of 1918 one hundred had been supplied and a further 150 were on order. The Dick Kerr workforce of two thousand trebled to include two thousand women, at a weekly wage cost of £22,000. Munitions were also produced in the Corporation's Dock workshops, and at other local firms including Stevensons, Coulthards, Drydens and Fosters.[5]

In addition to men and machines the town also provided capital. In Preston the 'Victory War Loan' was launched at a public meeting in the Palace Theatre on 13th February 1917, raising what was then an unbelievable sum of £2,600,000. To boost the sale of War Bonds, it was found that the public responded to local displays by tanks – then a top secret, revolutionary super weapon. Very large sums were raised by this 'Tank Bank' exercise, and in January 1918 *Egbert*, a 'gigantic toad' arrived in Preston. In what must have been one of the most remarkable scenes ever seen in that historic place, the Mayor attended in state and

Dick Kerr's Foundry c.1925. Between the wars Dick Kerr's and Leyland Motors became major local employers and important international companies.

addressed a crowd of twenty thousand from the top of *Egbert*. In the first day £422,235 was raised, and £1,069,611 during the week, before *Egbert* trundled off to another town. When the issue of War Bonds ended in 1919 Prestonians had invested £2,500,000.[6]

Social work of all types was undertaken. The hospital in Mount Street made fifteen beds available for the wounded, and the Royal Infirmary provided one hundred. The pavilion of the Royal - Lancashire Agricultural Society was brought from Blackburn and erected on the north-east corner of Moor Park. After various extensions, sponsored locally, it provided 174 beds, accommodation for 117 nurses, and treated 1,150 men each year of its existence. When supplies of foodstuffs ran short the Corporation made available 700 allotments on the town's parks, increasing to almost 2,000 by 1919, and a food control office was established in the Harris Museum.

Women played an increasing part in all these efforts. Local members of the Needle Work Guild produced almost 30,000 bandages and dressings. Enormous numbers of food parcels were despatched to local PoWs, and a force of 700 ladies working twelve-hour shifts manned the servicemen's buffet on Preston railway station. During the week before Christmas 1916 a record 12,449 men were served in 36 hours, and throughout the following January 3,250 men were served each day. By the time of its closure in May 1919 no fewer than 3,148,593 men had been served.

More significantly for the future, women found their way into men's jobs from which they had formerly been excluded. Their range of activities broadened as more and more men were called up. They worked as postmen and tramcar attendants, worked on farms, made shells and aircraft, formed a successful football team at Dick Kerr's, and ultimately filled a large proportion of teaching posts at that bastion of male supremacy, Preston Grammar School. These inroads were frequently fiercely opposed by male workers, who saw 'dilution' as a threat to their own – and their families' – livelihoods.

During a routine presentation of medals in front of the Town Hall at 10.45 am on Monday 11th November 1918, the Mayor was able to make the following announcement to a large and expectant crowd:

> Glorious news has arrived. The Kaiser has disappeared for ever. The worst enemy that mankind has known has gone from the stage with those who were behind him. And that is the greatest guarantee for the future peace of the world. I have to announce that the Armistice was signed at five o'clock this morning, and that hostilities cease at eleven o'clock. [At this point the great bell in the Town Hall clock struck eleven.] The clock is striking, the last shot has been fired, and the war is over.

The mill sirens blew, church bells rang, and chapels were packed for hastily organised services of thanksgiving. Yet eye witnesses were struck by the profound seriousness of many people's reaction to the peace, in marked contrast to the outburst with which the war's outbreak had been greeted. The following evening a large audience in the Corn Exchange heard leaders of the town's Anglican, Roman Catholic and Nonconformist communities speak on the theme of 'Peace and the New Opportunities', preceded by the singing of the *Hallelujah Chorus*: all the town's denominations had at last, briefly, found a single voice.[7]

The Cenotaph in the market square remains as a lasting monument to the fallen. The human cost paid by Preston can readily be gauged from the memorial list of names in the foyer of the Harris building, as well as those in villages around the town, but yet another cost had to be paid: thousands of families faced a future without a father, and thousands of women had lost their husbands. The Great War also brought about fundamental shifts in the pattern of world trade, speeding up the decline of the Lancashire cotton industry. Indeed the steady collapse of the industry in Preston was to be the dominant feature of the town's economic and social history for the next half-century.

—— *Preston under the hammer* ——

B efore the end of the nineteenth century it was apparent to at least a section of contemporary observers that the long dominance of world markets by the Lancashire cotton industry was coming to an end. However, continued growth in world demand for cotton goods obscured the early signs of significant changes in the pattern of world trade: the steady erosion of markets in South America and the East as these countries began to industrialise and impose tariffs on British imports to protect their infant industries; and the rising competition from more advanced countries in third world markets.

During the war shortages of raw materials enabled manufacturers to push up the prices of finished cloth, and after 1915 profits advanced accordingly. 1918 was claimed to be the industry's most profitable year ever, but was surpassed in 1919 when dividends of over 20% were paid. When the war ended the demand for 'Lancashire goods' to replenish stocks was enormous, and the industry embarked on a frenzy of speculation in mill shares. But, although the general post-war boom continued into the mid-1920s, the boom in textiles was over by 1921.[8]

As Lancashire men waited for a recovery, the underlying trends became apparent. The supply of Lancashire textiles was simply larger than the demand for them. Firms resorted to short-time running, but once it became clear that this was no short-term setback they began to close. Mills producing low-quality coarse fabrics were most at risk, since it was in these 'counts' that competition came first and was most acutely felt, particularly from Japan. The finer quality end of the trade, usually using finer Egyptian cotton, fared better, however, and Preston, with Horrockses and a relatively high proportion of 'fine' firms, was not

One of Fosters' Lancashire boilers c.1930. Drawn by a steam engine, the boiler is navigated below Preston's tramway wires. As early as 1885 Preston had fifteen firms of engineers and millwrights, four firms of boiler makers, and three foundries in addition to Fosters.

An engine fly-wheel manufactured in the Soho Foundry, Preston, by Fosters for the Sao Paulo Railway, 1931. Graphic and impressive evidence of the scale of Preston's heavy engineering sector between the wars. From the 1860s onwards the town's economy had begun to diversify away from cotton.

hit as badly as other towns. Unemployment in Blackburn at one stage approached 50%.

By 1930 58% of the industry's spinning capacity and 54% of its weaving were not being utilised.[9] At this point any lingering hopes of recovery were dashed by the world economic crisis of 1931. Caught between a

A section of Joseph Foster and Sons' Soho Foundry, c.1920. Established in 1835 in Avenham Lane, Joseph Foster and Sons came to specialise in the manufacture of heavy industrial plant. The Soho works produced large mill engines and boilers, whilst the firm's Bow Lane works claimed to produce some of the largest rotary printing machines in the world.

contracting market share of a contracting market, and, starved of investment, the industry was drawn into a spiral of closure and retreat which, though slowing between 1937 and 1951, was virtually continuous. Preston, though better placed than many of its neighbouring towns, was very badly hit. As J. H. Spencer recalled in 1941:

> Competition in the foreign markets made itself felt towards the end of 1900, especially in the plain and coarser sections, and the war of 1914 gave the death blow to our vast Chinese and Indian trade . . . We all know how this affected Preston: all the mills serving the Indian and Chinese markets have closed down, and it may be said that the Lancashire cotton trade of today, and especially our local trade, is confined to the finer counts and specialised fabrics.[10]

The path of the slump is clearly apparent in the decline of the dividends declared by Preston firms:[11]

Cliff Spinning Mill, Dundonald Street
320 employees, 94,108 mill and ring spindles
spinning high quality Egyptian cotton

1924/5	1925/6	1926/7	1927/8	1928/9	1929/30	1930/1	1931–5	1935/6	1936/7
22½%	12½%	15⅝%	15$^{5}/_{12}$%	18$^{5}/_{6}$%	10$^{5}/_{12}$%	5¾%	<3¾%	5%	10%

The pace of company closures can be seen by comparing the listings of the Preston firms in the various cotton trade yearbooks. This provides only a general guide to closures for some mills were subsequently taken over by other manufacturers:[12]

To 1926: Southgate Mill, Kirkham Street Shed, Pole Street Mill, Phoenix Mill.

1926–32: Bushell Street Mill, Marsh Lane Mill, Frenchwood Mill, Astleyfield Mill, Moor Park Mill, Isherwood Street Mill.

1932–36: Broomfield Mill, Albert Mill, Springfield Mill, Moor Hall Mill, Alliance Works, Ashton Kinder & Co., Wellfield Mills, Park Lane Mills.

1936–40: Deepdale Mill, Steam Mill, Parker Street Mill, Bold Street Mill.

In 1929 50% of the adult insured population of the Preston Employment Area (Preston and Fulwood Urban Districts, and Preston, Garstang and Fylde Rural Districts) were employed in textiles, representing almost 25,000 people. By 1939 this figure had fallen to 25% and by 1946 stood at just 13%.

The contraction of textiles, in a town where almost every street had a cotton mill, dominated the inter-war years. Unemployment over-shadowed all other issues, and slowed the drive towards the improvement of the social fabric of the town, in particular slum clearance and the provision of better social services.

—— *The depression and recovery* ——

Life in Britain between the wars was dominated by the trade cycle.[13] Preston's economic difficulties were well advanced by the late 1920s, even before the plunge into the Depression of the early 1930s. During the '20s and '30s unemployment in the town generally hovered between five and ten thousand, and it would be difficult to exaggerate the local impact of these changing economic patterns.

Yet by 1920 Preston's economy was no longer that of the typical mill town. It had considerable importance as the administrative centre of many organisations, notably the County Council. It was an important route centre, with its dock, railway yards and roads, and was an important base for the distribution sector (including timber, fish, coal and petrol). Preston remained an important market and service centre for its agricultural hinterland, and a centre for agricultural planning highlighted by the Milk Marketing Board, established in 1933, with its drive to 'Drink More Milk!'. Many of the 'new' engineering and electrical industries were well established, notably English Electric, Siemens and Ensign Lamps, and, to the south, Leyland Motors. The town was also an

The main entrance to the Yard Works c.1920. Once the entrance to one of the best known industrial sites in the world, by 1992 only the offices to the left of the gateway survive. A century earlier the 30 acre Yard Works had employed 3,500 people and consumed 3–400 bales of cotton per week to weave a roll of cloth 13,000 miles long each year. The Yard Works closed in 1962.

Moveo Engineering, De Lacy Street. One of the town's several forays into the field of motor engineering. Large numbers of Prestonians found employment between the wars at Leyland Motors, as the base of the district's economy began to shift from cotton to engineering.

important banking, insurance, legal, educational and military centre, and a natural location for the headquarters of the expanding service industries of gas, electricity and telephones. Over and above these considerations, however, the Town Council was strongly committed to the attraction of new industries (most successful in the case of the enormous Courtauld's plant) and the development of new housing.

The inter-war years saw the emergence of the consumer and service industries to feed increasing home demand, which eventually replaced the great nineteenth-century exporting industries, which were so vulnerable to changing patterns of world trade. By the late 1930s these new industries were well established in Preston, and were to provide the basis for the town's lasting economic recovery – virtually a second Industrial

Revolution – up to the 1980s. By the late 1930s, they employed a third of the manufacturing workforce and a fifth of all people in work. On 1st February 1938 employment in the town was as follows: cotton 16,800; distributive trades 7,300; transport 4,200; building 4,180 (an increase of nine hundred over the previous year); engineering 2,000 (increase of two hundred); and coach building 1,700.[14] In 1935 the dock handled over one million tons of trade for the first time, and in the same year work began on the Courtauld's rayon plant. In 1938 work started on the R.O.F. at Euxton and the development of Samlesbury aerodrome. The town thus fared much better than its neighbours, particularly the East Lancashire towns. By December 1937 the comparable figures for unemployment were: Preston 6,578; Black-burn 14,000; Burnley 8,000; Oldham 11,000.[15] By June 1939 the Preston figure had fallen to six thousand, and a year later stood at just over three thousand.[16]

The new industries

The partnership of two Glasgow merchants, W. B. Dick and John Kerr, was formed in Kilmarnock in 1875.[17] Though Dick left the firm, his name was retained by the company, Dick Kerr. In 1898 a subsidiary, the Electric Railway and Tramway Carriage Works Ltd., took over premises formerly occupied by the North of England Carriage and Iron Co. (1867–78). This, the east works on Strand Road, at that time faced the open river and occupied five acres of a thirteen-acre site. The works grew to a capacity of eight hundred vehicles per year and employed six to eight hundred men. It represented a shrewd expansion into the developing world market for electric urban tramway systems, and fitted in well with Dick Kerr's Scottish interests.

Drive machinery for the vehicles had to be imported from the United States, and shortly after the move to Preston a second company was established along the west side of Strand Road. This, the English Electric Manufacturing Co., also had close links with Dick Kerr's and in 1905 changed its name to the United Electric Car Co. Thus by 1903 two complementary factories had been established along Strand Road under the control of Dick Kerr and their associates. In 1918 the English Electric Company was formed through the merger of Dick Kerr's with a number of related interests, to form a company with a capital of £5m. In 1969 the firm was taken over by GEC.

Already considerable by 1914, the Preston works expanded enormously during the First World War, and by 1918 employed eight thousand people. In addition to munitions the firm, with its experience of producing light wooden tramway bodies, began the manufacture of aircraft with the Felixstowe F3 flying boat. Towards the end of the war land was acquired on the Ribble at Lytham for flying boat hangars and a slipway. This survived until 1926 when the works closed, causing much unemployment in the Lytham area. In 1932 it was largely demolished to make way for Cookson's bakery.

With the formation of English Electric, the Preston works reverted to the manufacture of traction and ancillary equipment, but in 1922 aircraft production was resumed: the Wren made its first flight from Ashton Park on 5th April 1923, and construction of the Kingston flying boat began. During the Depression the west works was closed, but the firm supplied Blackpool's famous trams between 1933 and 1939, and the last trams produced at Preston were despatched to Aberdeen in 1940.

Dick Kerr's benefited enormously from re-armament in the late 1930s, providing a tremendous boost to the Preston economy. The west works was re-opened and, in 1938/9, the east works was re-constructed for war production. In October 1938 representatives from Vickers-Armstrong visited Samlesbury 'to inspect the site for the central aircraft factory, for the assembly of RAF bombers and fighters'.[18] After the German invasion of Czechoslovakia the project was urgently pushed on. By 1942 Dick Kerr's workforce (1,000 in 1938) had increased to 13,000. Manufacturing at the east works thus evolved from tramcars to flying boats and ultimately to jet aircraft. In 1964 it was taken over by BAC. Similarly the west works was to progress to the manufacture of heavy electric locomotives. Both developments owed much to defence spending during the two world wars.

Many Prestonians also found employment at Leyland Motors.[19] By the 1860s Richard Sumner was the owner of a small metalworking workshop in Water Street, Leyland. As early as 1880 the workshop produced a five-ton steam wagon for John Stanning's bleachworks, a steam tricycle was completed for the biscuit manufacturer Theodore Carr, and steam-powered lawnmowers were an early success. James Sumner took over the business in 1892 and in partnership with Coulthards of Preston formed the company of James Sumner Ltd. This Preston link was to have very important consequences. When Coulthards was taken over by a Manchester firm their representative, George Spurrier, became closely involved in developments at Leyland. In 1896 his father, Henry Spurrier I, was persuaded to invest in the firm, George's brother, Henry II, joined it, and the Leyland Steam Wagon Company was founded.

The firm grew rapidly and gained a reputation for its steam-powered vehicles, or 'traction engines', manufactured at its Herbert Street works. By 1903 it had a workforce of 160, a working capital of £50,000, and had begun to export vehicles. In 1904 work began on petrol driven vehicles; in 1905 the first petrol driven bus appeared; and in 1907 the firm changed its name to Leyland Motors. By 1914, with its north and south works on Hough Lane and premises at Farington, the company employed fifteen hundred people, had a share capital of £400,000 and had already produced over two thousand petrol driven vehicles.

Expansion during the First World War was rapid, and six thousand petrol vehicles were produced. James Sumner died in 1924, but under the leadership of Henry Spurrier II it survived the post-war slump in demand, buying back from the government its surplus vehicles which otherwise would have flooded the market. The famous Lion and Titan buses, and Hippo trucks, went into service all over the world, and the company emerged as a leading British manufacturer of commercial vehicles. By 1929 orders for fourteen hundred buses had been received, and Leyland Motors had become a major source of employment throughout the Preston district. With re-armament employment had risen to six thousand by 1939, and further expansion was to follow during the war.

Trade through Preston Dock had been dislocated badly by the Great War: the tonnage handled fell from 743,580 tons in 1914 to just 371,807 tons in 1917.[20] By 1919 it had more than halved again to 150,492 tons. To make matters worse, the river channel had not been maintained properly, and had silted. The Ribble Rate paid by the town's ratepayers to subsidise the dock had fallen steadily before 1914, when it stood at 1s 6¼d, but by 1919 it had risen to a peak of 3s 0¼d. These were thus the hardest years for the dock, which only returned to an operating profit in 1921.

By the 1930s the dock had recovered from these setbacks. Annual trade rose again – to 843,340 tons in 1935 and 963,773 tons by 1940 – while in 1935, it exceeded the psychologically important one million tons for the first time.[21] Exports of coal and coke, which had been below twenty thousand tons in 1893, had risen to almost 300,000 tons in 1938, in which year the Port of Preston handled, among other things, forty thousand Irish cattle, 25,000 tons of china clay and 176,758 tons of woodpulp. The national economic recovery is reflected in the burgeoning imports of

Preston Dock's twenty ton coal hoist c.1921. The dock hoist was built in 1921, the year that the dock returned to profitability following the post-war crisis. By the early thirties trade was expanding satisfactorily and over one million tons were handled in 1935. Coal became a particularly important component of the dock's trade with the opening in 1924 of the town's Penwortham 'A' power plant.

timber for industry and house building and the growth of petrol imports for motor vehicles. The first oil and petrol storage tanks were built in 1915, and between 1933 and 1936 200,000 tons of fuel per year were imported. In April 1939 the 8,417-ton Norwegian oil tanker *Osthav*, 465 feet long, nudged its way up the Ribble with a cargo of Persian oil.[22] To handle this new trade both railway and road distribution were expanded, benefiting the district as a whole. By 1938 the dock had 28 miles of railway lines, and the Ribble Branch Railway moved 500,000 tons of goods per year, with a further 300,000 tons being moved by road.

In 1924 Preston Corporation embarked on a further large-scale project, opening the town's first large power station opposite the dock at Penwortham. This was supplied with fuel from the docks by an overhead gantry system. Subsequently known as Preston 'A', the station had an output of 40,000Kw. In August 1940 the C.E.G.B. began work on Preston 'B' and three other generators were later added and ran to maximum output during the winter of 1947. By the 25th anniversary of Preston 'B' it was estimated that the station had burned six million tons of coal to generate ten thousand million units of electricity.[23] The huge power station buildings, a familiar part of the dock skyline, were completely removed in the early 1980s. Preston developed a sizeable electrical manufacturing sector as early as 1903 when Dick Kerr founded a lamp works in Strand Road: the Britannia Lamp Works. In 1919 the firm was merged with Siemens and became their main factory in 1923. Further expansion followed during the 1930s when the plant was doubled in size. With rivals Ensign Lamps (which by the mid-1950s employed 850), this sector thus became a very important employer in the town.[24]

The town's greatest success in industrial development was undoubtedly the attracting of Courtaulds to the Red Scar estate. Land was acquired as early as 1929, but in 1933 Courtaulds decided to cancel plans for a huge rayon factory. Within two months, however, the decision was reversed and it was decided to go ahead. The plant's enormous chimneys became a local landmark, and by April 1938 £2 million had been spent. Production began early in 1939 when 4.3 million pounds of viscose yarn were manufactured, rising to 10.2 million in 1940.[25] Employment quickly rose to two thousand, stimulating housing development along the Longridge Road axis and in Ribbleton. By 1970 the plant employed 3,500 and was the largest rayon factory in the world.[26]

The housing boom: the new suburbia

T he inter-war years witnessed a remarkable boom in house building. Throughout much of the previous century investment in this sector had lagged far behind that in industry, and new and improved housing became an important political issue at the end of the Great War.

In 1920 the majority of the town's 120,000 inhabitants still lived in badly overcrowded districts, even though extensive building land was available within the borough. The development of the town's tramways, the suburban railway lines and stations, and the availability of motor bus, motor car and bicycle transport enabled people to live at ever greater distances from their work. These factors meant that when successive inter-war governments continued a policy of slum clearance, many of the new housing estates were built further out, along the great arterial roads within the town, resulting in the migration of Prestonians out to the town's suburbs, especially Fulwood and Penwortham.

The largest road building project completed before 1939 was the northern by-pass, Blackpool Road.[27] Between Pedders Lane in the west and New Hall Lane in the east this closely followed the edge of town and country as it was in 1930, and to the west of Pedders Lane it ran through open fields. Cadley, to the west of Garstang Road and north of Lytham Road, was largely agricultural land. To the east, Fulwood comprised only a ribbon of development along Garstang Road and Watling Street Road, at the northern limit of the tramway system. The 'Canary Islands' (between Penguin Street and Dove Street) stood on the edge of open fields.

Between the wars 4,347 houses were built within the borough, including forty new dwellings erected on the sites of 335 cleared slum houses. Of these, 2,847 were owned by the Borough Council, whilst 1,500 had been built privately.[28] Houses were constructed to a much improved standard, usually on the semi-detached plan, in relatively low-density estates with good access to the town's new by-pass road. By the early 1930s work had begun on estates at Ashton; between Blackpool Road and Lytham Road in the vicinity of Tulketh Mill; on both sides of Blackpool Road between Lowthorpe Road and Manor House Lane; to the west of Blackpool Road between Ribbleton Avenue and Farringdon Lane; and to the south of New Hall Lane in the great arc formed by Fishwick Parade and Downing Street. These formed the basis of subsequent developments at the Larches, Holme Slack, Ribbleton and Farringdon Park.

Between 1918 and 1948, twenty housing estates were constructed in Preston Borough and Fulwood Urban District, representing 5,981 dwellings for 21,143 people. At the peak of this effort over four hundred houses per year were completed. Twelve new schools were built, over seventeen thousand yards of new sewers were laid, and the present Town Hall was constructed, along with Saul Street Baths and the Maternity Hospital.[29]

Beyond the borough large areas of Fulwood and Penwortham were also developed and migration into these areas accelerated. During the 1930s the borough's population fell by eight thousand, and those of the rural district (including Penwortham) and Fulwood rose by 6,250 and three thousand respectively. In the half-century between 1900 and 1950 Preston's population remained stable at just below 120,000, by 1961 it had fallen to 113,000, and by 1971 to below 100,000.[30]

Although the development of the consumer society was halted by the war, many of its characteristics had begun to emerge in the 1920s and 1930s. The great popularity of the motor car is reflected in the proliferation of garages and car sales rooms, and Preston's emergence as a major traffic bottleneck. The vehicles for sale at Loxham's showroom in Fishergate during January 1938 included: '1932 Hillman Minx Saloon – £45; 1937 Austin Riley, Saloon-de-Luxe, as new – £89; 1934 Daimler Saloon, fitted pre-selector gears – £155'.[31]

The motorist's 'fastest friend', Rocket Motor Spirit, was available at 1s. 3½d. per gallon, but Rocket Benzole Mixture cost 1s. 6d. Motorbikes were very popular, and Stan Marks Ltd. on Lancaster Road offered a 1935 Enfield 250 Sports at 10 gns, a 1937 Triumph Tiger 80, '4 speeds, £39 10s. 0d.', and a 1931 BSA 3-wheeler, 2-seater 'excellent £25'. To cater for the cyclist, Manchester House on Friargate had shorts at 3s. 11d. and stockings at 1s. per pair.

Fashions were seasonal. In winter 1937-38 Owen and Owen of Fishergate had rayon and cotton vests for 9½d., whilst jumpers and cardigans usually 2s. 9d. were reduced to 1s. 9d. 'while stocks last'. The store had a 'Clearance of Gowns . . . A thrilling collection of coats, frocks, afternoon and evening gowns. Smart styles and delightful colours . . . 5s. 9d.' Men's hats were offered at Manchester House at two prices – 4s. 9d. and 6s. 9d. each; grey flannel trousers were 4s. 11d. a pair, and fashionable silk-lined gabardine raincoats were available at 15s. 11d. each.

Consumer items connected with the ideal home, the dream 'new house', were much in evidence. The Cavendish Furniture Co. had 250 folding table mangles at 79s. 6d. each, gas refrigerators were on offer at 1s. 3d. a week, and 10-inch blade lawnmowers could be had for 15s. 9d.

By the late 1930s a very good selection of new houses was on the market: 'The Gammul Lane Estate Ribbleton (near Messrs. Courtauld's New Works) Freehold houses at £499, £560 and £720 each; The Clifton Park Estate: Healthy, Sunshine, Semi-Detached houses for sale, Price £355'. At Easter 1939 fifteen types of house were offered for sale around the town. Modern dwellings in Ashton and Deepdale were available at £582 18s. 0d., houses in Winmarleigh Road, Tulketh were £695 – or by weekly payments of 18s. 2d. – and at Ribbleton homes on the Sulby Park estate ranged from £500. In the suburbs houses at Cadley Causeway, Fulwood, were priced from £355, and in Penwortham and Howick house prices ranged from £460 to £1,000 with a deposit of £25 and repayments from 12s. weekly. The first tenants moved into the Corporation's Ribbleton estate in January 1939.

However, to put these prices into a proper perspective, it is important to consider contemporary incomes and the cost of living. A clerk might earn 37s. 6d. per week, a railwayman 80s., a weaver 37s. (rising to 60s. in a 'good' mill), but the old age pension was just 10s., and an unemployed couple might be allowed 26s. with an additional 3½d. per day for each child.[32]

These years also witnessed a considerable expansion of recreational activities; hiking, cycling and motoring, and sports and entertainments of all kinds. Preston's town centre and its suburbs rapidly acquired cinemas. By 1913 the town had twelve picture houses, increasing to over twenty by the 1930s.[33] The first local film shows were simple features of the live entertainments in the town's theatres – the Theatre Royal by 1911 and the Princes Theatre by 1913. The Empire, which opened in 1911 at a cost of £65,000, concentrated on films after 1930. Both the Kings Palace (capacity three thousand, 2550 seated, 450 standing) and the Hippodrome (capacity 2,500) showed films but continued to be important 'live' venues. The Hippodrome occupied the site of the present C&A store in Friargate, and many famous celebrities appeared on its stage, including Marie Lloyd, Gracie Fields, George Formby, Harry Lauder and Richard Tauber. Variety survived up to 1946 when a short run by the Salberg Players, a repertory company, was ultimately extended to 1953. The centre of Preston's theatre land was Tithebarn Street, with the Empire, the Palace and the Princes theatres.

The town's first talking picture was *The Singing Fool* seen at the New Victoria (now the Odeon) in June 1929. Several of the cinemas had orchestras and cinema organs, most notably the Theatre Royal and the New Victoria – where Reginald Dixon began his career in the 1930s. Many of the early cinemas had been converted from other uses; some had been chapels, and the Plaza on New Hall Lane had formerly been part of the warehouse of Calvert's India Mill and was subsequently to become a garage. Stylish purpose-built cinemas included the New Victoria (1928) and the Carlton on Blackpool Road (1932). In 1940 the *Wizard of Oz* came to the Theatre Royal (subsequently the ABC) and *Gone With the Wind* opened in Southport. The town's leading theatre/ cinema personalities of these years included Will Onda, Claude Talbot, and the Leyland Music Hall artiste Max Erard with his wife.

North End between the wars

The inter-war years were a strangely mixed period at Deepdale.[34] Though promoted in 1915, the club struggled in the first division, once league football restarted after the war, and was relegated in 1925. Beaten cup semi-finalists in 1921, North End lost to Huddersfield Town by a hotly-disputed penalty in the final of the following year. This match was played at Stamford Bridge and was the last non-Wembley cup final.

Improvements continued to be made at the Deepdale ground following the opening of the west stand in 1906 (one of the finest surviving examples of its type, and a listed building), the Spion Kop (so-called from the crescent shaped hill of that name, scene of a major British reverse during the Boer War) was improved, and during 1934-6 the south pavilion stand was constructed. The latter did not run along the full length of the pitch because plans existed to turn the pitch through ninety degrees in a reconstructed Deepdale, so that the pavilion would overlook one of the goal ends.

Between 1912 and 1950 J. I. Taylor directed affairs from the boardroom at Deepdale. Taylor was an extremely influential figure. The Football League headquarters were conveniently located off Winckley Square, and during the 1930s Preston's supremo was described as the

Dick Kerr's Ladies' F.C. c.1930. Preston's most successful football team? Seated in the centre of this group is J. I. Taylor, mastermind of Preston North End's greatness in the second quarter of the twentieth century.

St. Andrews Boys Football Club 1907–8. Generally reduced working hours in the second half of the nineteenth century provided increased leisure time. Sports of all kinds became enormously popular. This boys' football team poses proudly in front of Deepdale's new West Stand.

'Joseph Stalin of English football'.

By 1924 the club had a large overdraft and in the early 1. likely to be relegated to the third division. The bottom of the s. reached in 1932 when just three thousand people attended a home . against Bury. Taylor was responsible for bringing many fine playe. Deepdale. Amongst them was the legendary Alex James, signed fro.. Raith Rovers in 1925 for £3,250. His subsequent sale to Arsenal in 1929 was never really forgiven, and the period was a harbinger of events in the post-Finney era. In the event it was the eve of North End's golden age. Taylor signed Ted Harper who, in 1932–3, established the club's record for the most goals scored in a season – 37 – and the following year North End returned to the first division.

By the mid 1930s a truly great team was in the making, and in the finest traditions of the Old Invincibles it was a Preston-Scottish side. Many of the players are still local household names. Bill Shankly was to become not only a great player and manager, but one of the country's best-loved figures, and Jimmy Milne was to be the last North End manager (up to the present time) to lead his side out at Wembley. Shankly played well in the 1937 cup final against Sunderland, but though leading 1–0 at half-time, Preston were beaten 3–1. This was the first televised cup final. The season 1937–8 saw the side come close to emulating the Invincibles, and right up to the end of the season a repeat of the 'double' was very much on the cards. A crowd of 42,684 witnessed the crucial game at Deepdale on 23rd April 1938, which Arsenal won 3–1; a defeat made worse by an injury to Milne which meant he would miss the cup final against Huddersfield Town.

Saturday 30th April 1938 dawned to find North End at Wembley. Mr. Radcliffe led the singing of *Abide With Me* by the 93,000 spectators, and North End's Wembley anthem *Keep Right On To The End Of The Road*. For the first time at Wembley the game went to extra time.

In Preston the town was deserted as people crowded around their wirelesses:

> It's a penalty . . . Mutch has scored . . . Then the streets filled. Radios were left blaring in empty rooms, from which people rushed into the streets to shake hands with neighbours and tell each other how happy they were.[35]

The cup final ball, subsequently displayed in a Preston shop window, bore the unmistakable signs of the whitewash it had gathered from the crossbar on its way into the net.

The club's further progress was interrupted by the war, and the league was reorganised on a regional basis. In 1941 North End completed a second double, winning the Northern Section Championship and the War Cup, against old enemies Arsenal. This was the first Wembley cup final to be replayed, at Ewood Park – one of the most important matches played at that place. At the end of the 1941 season Deepdale was taken over by the War Department for use as a store – to the evident disgust of the local sports writer 'Perseus'.

The pre-war years saw the club's establishment of a pioneering youth policy scheme: it will be no surprise that an early hopeful to be turned away was one Tom Finney.

—— *Wartime Preston* ——

New Year 1938 was greeted with much optimism in Preston, and there were high hopes that the town's economic revival would accelerate. This confidence was not misplaced, with new sources of mass employment being created at Courtaulds and the Royal Ordnance Factory at Euxton. Investment in housing was also beginning to make significant improvements to the town's housing list. Preston was generally regarded as having withstood the Depression better than the other mill towns, and was the first to emerge from it. In the spring of 1938, however, attention switched to events in Central Europe.

As each European crisis followed the other, war began to appear the only outcome. During the Czechoslovak crisis the town's lack of preparedness became starkly apparent. By 20th September 1938 air raid warning sirens had only been located at the English Electric Works, the Dock, Horrockses Mill and the new council offices, and large residential areas in Deepdale and Ribbleton were not served. As late as June 1940 many people claimed to be unable to hear the warnings. It was planned to use cellars as makeshift air raid shelters. By August 118,000 gas masks had been stored in Preston gaol, and on the day of the Munich Agreement, 30th September 1938, 61,964 masks were hurriedly issued in Preston.

After Munich re-armament surged ahead. In October the Samlesbury site was inspected by representatives of Vickers-Armstrong, and just two weeks later was confirmed as the site of a new aircraft assembly plant. By the end of November employment at Leyland Motors had increased to six thousand, and in January 1939 the first section of Courtaulds factory opened. This pace of development contrasts starkly with the decaying regional economy of the late 1920s and early 1930s. On 16th March Hitler invaded Slovakia. On 27th April detailed plans for the blackout in Preston were announced, and in June the first seven hundred Preston men in the 20/21 age group were called up under the Military Training Act.

In July, as Len Hutton scored his two thousandth run of the season, the construction of air raid shelters and work at Samlesbury was pushed on urgently. As the Polish crisis reached its climax Blackpool, Morecambe and Southport were reported to be crowded with holidaymakers, and Sir Malcolm Campbell, at Coniston Water with his son Donald, broke the world water speed record in *Bluebird II*. On 23rd August the Russo-

German pact was signed leaving Hitler free to invade Poland and attack the west. By the end of the month paintings in the Harris Museum had been stored away for the duration of the war, the railway station and public buildings had been sandbagged, two hundred thousand evacuees were expected in Lancashire, and the Mayor urged townspeople to stay calm: 'Preston is fully prepared'. On 1st September, as the Germans attacked Poland and seized Danzig, fifty thousand evacuees changed trains at Preston and four thousand of them, many in their Sunday best, were taken in by local people. Air raid personnel and all services were mobilised. At 11.15am on Sunday 3rd September, as many Prestonians were in church, Neville Chamberlain made his historic broadcast.

The first casualties came at sea. On 16th September the Fleetwood trawler *Davara* was sunk by submarine, and on the 20th the sinking of HMS *Courageous* resulted in the deaths of a number of Preston men. Able Seaman J. Smith was killed just one week before his 21st birthday. On 14th October it was announced that *HMS Royal Oak* had been sunk, and Preston men were on the lists of both casualties and survivors. On the home front during the black-out there was a spate of vicious attacks on passers-by, and large numbers of people were killed or injured in road accidents. John McCormack sang at the New Victoria, and skiers were seen in Avenham Park during severe winter weather. By May 1940 £500,000 worth of National Savings Certificates, Defence Bonds and Savings had been invested by the townspeople, and three hundred Belgian refugees had arrived.

On 9th April 1940 German forces attacked Denmark and began the occupation of allied Scandinavia. Chamberlain was forced to resign, and Attlee assured the King of Labour's support for Winston Churchill, who became Prime Minister on 10th May. The same day Hitler put 'Case Yellow' into effect and 136 divisions were thrown into the western offensive. General Guderian broke through the French defences at Sedan, and on 24th May were ordered to advance towards Calais and Dunkirk. Between 26th May and 4th June 338,226 men were evacuated from Dunkirk. On 3rd June parties of exhausted troops were photographed by the *Daily Post* at a railway station 'somewhere in the north-west', presumably at Preston.[36]

With the airfields along the European coast in German hands, much of Britain – including Preston – was now within range of the Luftwaffe. On 19th June the first bombs fell on Lancashire, at Altham, near Accrington.

—— *Bombs and rockets* ——

Although no-one in the borough was killed by bombing, Preston and district was attacked during both the blitz of 1940–41 and the flying bomb offensive of Christmas 1944. An 'official' list of enemy action in the district was published in 1944, although it is vague in its account of attacks on strategic industries, notably Leyland Motors, and may thus be incomplete. Although Preston itself was very fortunate, in the wider district over a hundred 'incidents' were reported.[37]

With the German attack on Russia the frequency of raids on the North-West reduced and appeared to have ended. During the summer of 1944, as the Russians reached Poland and the allies followed up the D-Day landings in the west, the indiscriminate V-1 flying bomb attacks on London and the South-East began. In October 1944 intelligence reports suggested that an attack on the north, where anti-aircraft batteries had been reduced, was being planned.[38] During the early hours of the morning of Christmas Eve 1944, fifty Heinkel 111 bombers launched their missiles over the North Sea. Each carried 1870lb of high explosive, the attack lasted one hour, and the target was Manchester. The V-1s reached England successfully but fell over a wide area. Only one reached the city, but in Oldham 28 people were killed, 35 houses were destroyed and over a thousand were damaged.

At 5.50 a.m. one of the rockets made a direct hit on a hen house opposite Hewn Gate Farm at Gregson Lane, Brindle. It created a crater 32' x 20', damaged cottages and farm buildings, the local mills and 112 houses, but fortunately casualties were slight.

—— *Little America* ——

Throughout 1942 the number of American soldiers and airmen built up steadily in Britain, to support the extensive bombing of enemy targets and, later, in preparation for the invasion of Europe. Large American camps were established in the Preston district and the area around Warton and Freckleton became known as 'Little America'. The soldiers became a familiar element in Preston's wartime life, and after 1945 many local war brides went to make their homes in America.

The greatest local tragedy of the war years occurred on the day that Paris was liberated, 23rd August 1944. At 10.30 a.m. a four-engined Liberator aircraft approaching Warton aerodrome was struck by lightning during a freak storm and fell on to the centre of Freckleton, striking the school and falling, blazing, across the road.[39] Sixty-one people were killed, 38 of them young children from the new infants' class. Much of the recovery work was undertaken by shocked American servicemen stationed locally, many of whom had known the children well, and a mass funeral was attended by between two and three thousand people.[40]

The 'mutiny' or 'battle' at Bamber Bridge during the evening of 24th June 1943 was largely an all-American affair, when a series of incidents highlighted the problem of racial tension within the American forces.[41]

The trouble started at the Hob Inn, when two white military police attempted to arrest a black soldier who was out without a pass. After an argument during which both locals and British servicemen sided with the soldier and his companions, the MPs left to seek reinforcements and intercepted the soldiers as they returned to their barracks. A general fight broke out, guns were drawn and several men were shot. A minor incident had grown into a full-scale armed riot in just thirty minutes.

At the hastily roused camp rumour was rife that the MPs were going to shoot the men, and a large crowd gathered at the gates. A party of armed men drove out, and renewed shooting began in the village; white Americans were chased along the streets and passing army vehicles were fired upon. Military reinforcements were brought into the village and a machine-gun ambush was set up along Station Road. Local police were kept out of the area, and the locally based soldiers warned the villagers to stay out of the way.

At midnight a large force of MPs arrived at the camp armed with machine-guns. This caused further panic and most of the men armed themselves from the camp gunroom. For some hours chaos reigned as armed groups stalked each other in the fields and lanes around the village. At 3 or 4 a.m. an American general arrived to take control of the camp and once the only coloured officer had been placed in charge the rifles were handed in. One man had been killed and three injured, and 35 were arrested.

How are things in Preston?

On 8th May 1945 it was announced that the European war was to end at midnight. Relief was tempered by the fact that the war against Japan was reaching its climax, with many local men involved, and it was estimated that about 150 Prestonians had been captured at the fall of Singapore in 1942. But Preston celebrated, as the local press reported:

> After waiting hours, spent mostly within reach of their wireless sets, Preston people realised the horrors of war in Europe were at an end . . . Preston was ablaze with flags and bunting for VE-Day. Public buildings and business premises displayed a great variety of patriotic emblems. A striking feature was the colourful show made in the side streets, particularly in the Plungington, and Ribbleton Lane, and New Hall Lane districts.[42]

By July Hermann Göring was in the North West, a prisoner at Windermere.

With the bombings of Hiroshima and Nagasaki on the 7th and 9th August, the Pacific war, which had been expected to enter its bloodiest phase with landings on the Japanese coast, was suddenly over. This coincided with Preston Holidays, and Blackpool was said to be Preston-on-Sea. On 15th August the Mayor announced the termination of hostilities from the Town Hall steps:

> With ships' hooters, church bells and railway whistles sounding a welcome to peace, it did not take Preston people long to get the victory spirit and to start their own unofficial celebrations. Soon after the midnight radio news a large crowd gathered in the Market Square . . . But it was not all fun and frivolity. When they heard the news many Preston women with relatives in the Far East wept unashamedly. The lone figure of a woman in the front room of a riverside street, holding a handkerchief to her eyes while the revellers swept past, cheery, symbolises the grief of hundreds of mothers, wives and sweethearts who are still awaiting news of a loved one.[43]

On 5th September 1945 a British force liberated PoWs held in Singapore, and the BBC Far Eastern correspondent reported that the first question the survivors had asked was, 'How are things in Preston?'[44]

CHAPTER FIFTEEN

The Brave New World

THE long-term difficulties faced by Preston in the post-war years mirrored those of the country as a whole. Housing, industrial development and economic re-structuring – neglected during the war – required urgent attention, while resources were very restricted. That progress often appeared painfully slow was a reflection, in part, of the continued intractability of the problems remaining from the rapid growth of the mid-nineteenth century. The struggle to overcome these problems has continued to form the central theme of Preston's late-twentieth-century history. Fortunately the long period of post-war economic growth which extended into the 1970s provided both a buffer to the eclipse of the local cotton industry and the funds with which to undertake redevelopment on a scale previously unknown.

Preston weaves out

At the outbreak of war in September 1939 cotton cloth prices advanced 30% as demand for military stores soared. By December every mill was running to capacity, and by March 1940 there was a shortage of hands. The cotton industry was closely regulated by the state, and in 1941 it was decided to close surplus mills for the duration of the war in order to release labour for war work. The 'Utility' scheme was devised to enable continued production of key consumer items such as sheets and pillowslips, and this survived until 1952. At the end of the war the 'concentrated' mills were re-opened, much foreign competition had been destroyed, and for a time markets demanded all that the Lancashire mills could supply.

The profits and dividends of Preston's companies reflect the post-war recovery of the industry, which lasted only until 1951 and was followed by a rapid rise in unemployment. Further contraction came in the late 1950s, and in July 1956 the closure of Queen's Mill was announced, the company having decided, like many others, to operate a shift-working system and concentrate production in its more modern mills.[1] In 1958 there was a stampede of mill closures, and in August Bute Mill became the sixth local mill to 'weave out' during that year. Cyril Lord sent every MP a photograph of the interior of the recently-closed Embroidery Mill showing its rows of smashed machinery. In Preston the proportion of the workforce still employed in textiles fell to 15%, while nationally 344 mills had closed and 55,000 people had left the industry since 1955. The *Lancashire Evening Post* reported that 'The slump in the cotton industry – blamed on imports of cheap cloth from abroad – has forced thousands of mill operatives in the Preston area to continue working on a short time basis. The system of working a week and playing a week is now widespread at local mills and many others have adopted a four-day week while the struggle to maintain a minimum level of production goes on'.[2] Horrockses was taken over in 1960, and both the Yard Works and Cliff Mill closed in 1962.

By 1966 just a handful of local firms remained. Early in the New Year came the shocking news of the closure of Tulketh Mill. Built in 1905, the mill had been re-equipped in 1963 in a £1 million modernisation scheme, making it one of the most up-to-date mills in the country. Eighty thousand new ring frames had been installed, and yarn output rose from 40,000lbs to over 100,000lbs per week. The mill's 550 employees worked on multi-shifts to operate the plant at full capacity in order to meet demand.[3] After the closure of Tulketh, textiles no longer played a major part in the town's economy, and further closures in the 1970s and '80s eliminated all but a tiny remnant of the industry. Just two hundred years after John Horrocks first began trading in the town, Preston no longer had a textiles sector, and its era as a mill town was over. The Horrockses link with Preston finally came to an end in 1988, and little remains to indicate that the town was once the home of the world-famous company whose 1950s publicity jingle claimed:

> *For yarn we spin and fabrics make,*
> *With cotton wares great pains we take,*
> *And modern woman ever wise,*
> *Will cherish all our goods she buys,*
> *Our name, it cannot be forgotten,*
> *HORROCKSES, THE GREATEST NAME IN COTTON.*[4]

—— *The technological revolution* ——

I n the Second World War, as in the First, Dick Kerr's Strand Road works was at the forefront of Preston's war effort. Aircraft production once again made a principal contribution, but whereas lack of orders after 1920 had discouraged inter-war development, the years following 1945 saw the remarkable rise of Preston as a major centre for the design and manufacture of advanced aircraft. Taken in conjunction with the post-war development of a nuclear technology at the Springfields site, Preston and district had, by the 1970s, evolved an economy strongly rooted in the 'new technology'.

The government's rapid re-armament policy in the late 1930s soon made its impact on Preston. Between the wars English Electric had concentrated on its traditional electrical and heavy engineering business, but was quickly able to develop efficient systems for the mass production of aircraft. Since further expansion at the Strand Road site was precluded by lack of space, the Company decided to develop the large aerodrome at Samlesbury, where there was plenty of space for final assembly and testing.[5] The aerodrome at Warton was built by the government in 1940-42, and from 1942 until the end of the war it was run by the American Army Airforce as an aircraft assembly plant. Thus between 1938 and 1942 two very large centres emerged which were to be key elements in the post-war aircraft business and which were eventually to replace the parent Strand Road works.

By December 1939 the first hangar for the assembly of Hampden bombers was operational at Samlesbury, and the first 'plane was delivered to the RAF in March 1940. On the eve of the Battle of Britain a second hangar was completed for the Handley-Page Halifax bomber, and by the end of 1941 714 Hampdens and seven Halifaxes had been handed over. Thereafter production raced ahead, further hangars were built, and in February 1944 alone 81 Halifax bombers were built.

Amidst the greatest secrecy a prototype jet fighter – subsequently to become the Vampire – made its test flight in September 1943, and the following year Preston received an order for the first 120 aircraft. The first Vampire flew from Samlesbury on 20th April 1945, and 1,366 were ultimately built. The Preston works thus gained unrivalled expertise in the design and manufacture of the most advanced aircraft of the time; experience which was to make a crucial contribution to the company's success after the war. Warton similarly developed very rapidly, and at its peak of production in 1944–5 employed some twenty thousand American technical servicemen, assembling a great range of aircraft including Flying Fortresses, Liberators and Mustangs.

At the end of the war the company identified the production of jet aircraft as a major future market, and in 1947, in the unlikely surroundings of an art deco car showroom on Corporation Street, beside the old canal basin, work began on the world's first jet bomber, the Canberra. The prototype flew from Warton on Friday 13th May 1949. Further experiments undertaken at Warton subsequently led to the development of Britain's first supersonic fighter, the Lightning, and a prototype took to the air in April 1957.

From their very inception, plans for a general service replacement for the Canberra were beset by conflicts between inter-government departments and the aircraft makers.[6] The TSR-2 (Tactical, Strike and Reconnaisance) was to be built by Vickers with English Electric as the sub-contractor. In the face of rising costs the cancellation of the aeroplane in 1965 and the decision to buy the American Phantom in its place caused a major political storm and came as a bombshell to Preston. However, widespread fears for the virtual end of the Preston-based operation, and the resulting high local unemployment, were not realised. In 1966 work began in co-operation with Bregeut of France on the development of the Jaguar, and the prototype flew in 1969. Preston was also a contractor on the Anglo-French Concorde, and in 1974 production began on the Tornado swing-wing aircraft, which made its maiden flight from Warton in July 1979.

Subject to such a range of external factors and pressures, especially in peacetime, the production of high-performance military aircraft will always be an uncertain business. During these years the organisational structure of the three Preston plants evolved considerably. By the late 1980s, as the military division of the privatised and restructured British Aerospace, the Preston plants had to face both the challenge of the changing international situation and the drive to greater commercial efficiency. The RAF cancelled an order for 33 Tornado combat 'planes in July 1990, and in November of that year the company announced significant job cuts. British Aerospace was to reduce its workforce in the military division from 27,000 to 22,000 in 2½ years, and Preston's enormous Strand Road works was to close with the loss of three thousand of its 4,700 jobs, the remainder being redeployed at Samlesbury and Warton.

Salwick, between Kirkham and Preston, became the location for a similarly bold post-war march into the field of advanced technology, with the development of the Springfields nuclear fuels complex on a site that had formerly housed a wartime poison gas factory. Providing fuel elements for the world's first commercial-scale nuclear power station at Calder Hall which opened in 1956, the plant subsequently became the fuel supplier to all Britain's stations, and a major employer in the district. By 1979, when the three-millionth Magnox fuel element was produced, the two-hundred-acre site employed 3,500 workers, with a further six hundred employed there by the United Kingdom Atomic Energy Authority. Employee numbers have fallen since the mid-1980s when four thousand people were employed on the site, but still exceeded 3,500 in the late 'eighties.

By contrast, new technology, and related methods of transit, were to be important factors in the decision to close Preston Dock. The improving performance of Preston Dock in the late 1930s was marked in 1936 by the opening of the attractive building housing the new dock offices in Watery Lane.[7] Trade was severely disrupted by the war and the dock was twice closed by mines. From the late 1940s the port recovered and developed steadily to a peak of activity in the late 1960s. Between 1955 and 1972 it was sufficiently viable no longer to be a charge on the rates, and was a net contributor in the years 1962–9. As Jack Dakres points out, however, this £120,000 'profit' represented virtually the only return that the Corporation had in a hundred years.

Important post-war developments included the inauguration of the first roll-on roll-off service, which was the brainchild of Col. Frank Bustard and based on his wartime experience with tank-landing craft. Fittingly, the first service between Preston and Larne in May 1947 used a former tank-landing ship reborn as the *S.S. Empire Cedric*, and dock equipment from the *Mulberry Harbour* of Normandy landings fame.

The 'banana run' began in 1954 with a cargo for Geest Industries, and in all some six hundred cargoes of bananas and other tropical fruits were landed from the Windward and Leeward Islands. In October 1954 the *Lancashire Evening Post* reported that 'The whole citrus crop of two islands in the West Indies . . . will be handled at Preston Dock during the next six months. The crops include limes, lemons, grapefruit, pears, tangerines, oranges, apples and coconuts. They are this year's harvest from the sun-drenched islands of Dominica and St. Lucia . . .'[8]

These years of relative success could never overcome the intrinisic natural problems which had always dogged the project: the silting of the channel, the problem of access into the tidal river, and the impossibility of handling large ships. During the 1970s these factors rapidly brought about a deterioration in the port's trading position. As the successful Preston operations developed they simply outgrew the port's capacity to handle them. The cost of maintaining the waterway also accelerated alarmingly. Dredging became very expensive; in 1947/8 it had accounted for 17% of the income, and by 1976/7 this had risen to 45%. With the development of ever larger ships and the need for rapid turnround and access, the port's position became more and more precarious.

During the early 1970s structural changes in the shipping industry began to become apparent, and trade began to decline steeply. In 1969 the china clay trade ended, followed by the banana boats in 1971 and the Irish coal and coke trade in 1972. In June 1973 the Larne service was moved to the quicker crossing at Cairnryan, and other Irish services were lost in 1975/6.

In October 1976 the Borough Council came to the conclusion that the port would have to close, with the loss of 350 jobs. In 1977 a report on the operation gave hope of recovery, but in November the Sealand service, attracted to the port in 1973, was lost. However, the government stepped in to underwrite a two-year 'test period' for the port's viability, management was restructured and facilities were improved.[9] Despite these efforts 1978/9 saw a further decline in trade, and on 8th November 1979 the decision was taken to close the dock as a commercial undertaking. On 31st October 1981 the closure became formally effective, just a few days after the port's last commercial visitor the *Hoveringham V* had slipped down the Ribble. The dock had cost £4½ million to close.

Closure of the operation threw open an enormous 450-acre site for redevelopment. After a hesitant start the work of site clearance and redevelopment began and, with the help of a multi-million pound Derelict Land Grant, the project began to make significant headway in

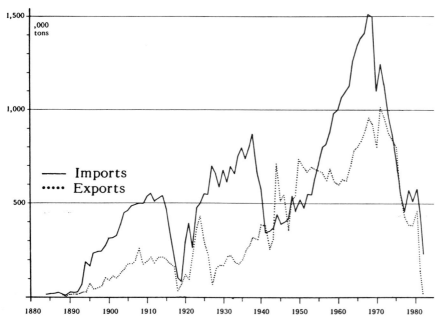

Left: graph showing Preston Dock's total volume of imports and exports by thousands of tons from 1884 to 1981. Particularly noticeable are the slumps caused by both World Wars and the fact that, in terms of tonnage at least, the 1960s were the most successful years of the Dock's operation.

Below: The new Control House for the locks at Preston Dock.

the mid-1980s. By the early 1990s the dock estate had emerged as a major nucleus of commercial, industrial, recreational and residential development, reminiscent of dockland redevelopments elsewhere, and to the fore of the 'Preston Means Business' campaign. By the end of 1990 the dock complex was providing jobs in a wide variety of businesses from finance to leisure, and the number employed on the site was more than six times what it had been under the old Port of Preston.[10]

The long post-war 'boom' shuddered to a halt somewhere in the 1970s, and recessions at both ends of the 1980s cut great swathes through British manufacturing industry. The period 1979-80 was an extremely harsh one in Preston, perhaps the worst in fifty years. In 1979 the final decision was taken to close the docks, and Carrington-Viyella's modern mill at Bamber Bridge (formerly A.S. Orr) was closed with the loss of eight hundred jobs. In September Courtaulds announced 370 redundancies at Preston, and two months later closed their Red Scar works with the loss of 2,700 jobs, one third of which were held by people from the Asian community.[11] Almost four thousand jobs had been wiped out in a few months, excluding those lost by the local suppliers of the firms concerned. The sudden closure of the Courtaulds plant was, and remains, highly controversial.

In 1979 British Leyland announced plans to lose 25,000 jobs, 4,000 of them at Leyland. Thereafter the decline of the Leyland-based enterprise has been more or less continuous, despite eventual takeovers of the bus division by Volvo in 1988 and Leyland trucks by DAF in 1989. An appeal in the Commons that the area be granted Development Area Status was turned down,[12] and many Prestonians faced a gloomy Christmas:

> The majority of the 2,600 Courtauld workers at Preston – who have now accepted the closedown of the giant Red Scar plant – are likely to face spring on the dole. For in spite of Industry Secretary Sir Keith Joseph's claim at a meeting with Courtauld's workers that there were 4,000 to 5,000 jobs in the Preston area, only 500 unfilled jobs were available in Preston last month'.[13]

Recovery from these disasters was to be a difficult process. Both the Red Scar Estate and the Dock complex were transformed into development sites and the Industrial Censuses of 1984 and 1987 revealed that employment in the Borough had risen from 66,574 (51,133 full-time) to 71,464 jobs (53,566 full-time). Between 1979 and 1989 growth was most marked in the services sector, especially business services and retailing, and between September 1985 and November 1990 unemployment fell from 15.6% to 7.2%.[14] By the end of 1990, however, the decline in unemployment was sharply reversed, as the slack in the national economy was taken up and the North West began to reel under the impact of the acute recession in the South East. As in 1979 a major local employer was severely affected, with plans by British Aerospace to close its Strand Road works.

Amidst these signs and portents one central trend does clearly emerge.

In the last quarter of the twentieth century Preston's ancient role as the natural business and administrative centre of Lancashire – its principal services capital – was re-asserting itself as the dominant theme of its future; a future which cannot be divorced from the town's importance at the hub of an emerging urban and suburban metropolis – a city in all but name.

—— *Towards a prouder Preston: housing* ——

R edevelopment and town planning policy over the last forty years falls into two broad phases. During the 1950s and 1960s the emphasis in Preston, as elsewhere, was on large solutions; the clearance of whole districts of sub-standard housing, the development of estates of multi-storey flats and the construction of large town-centre shopping complexes. These radical and intrinsically expensive developments also had a high social cost, as the wishes of local people were often ignored and long-established communities broken up.

The war had severely disrupted Preston's house-building programme. By the end of 1944 it was reported to have fallen two thousand houses behind pre-war targets, and 'factory-made homes' (or 'prefabs') appeared to be the Council's only hope of making up lost ground. The scale of the task facing the town was made clear in *Towards a Prouder Preston*, produced by the Council in 1946: half of the town's 32,000 houses had been built between 1840 and 1890, and one sixth of these would, it was thought, have to be demolished, whilst almost 70% of the five thousand people waiting to be re-housed were living in overcrowded conditions. To overcome these problems the Council would need to build 750 houses a year for the next twenty years.

Demolition site, Oxford Street, November 1963. During the house clearance programme whole districts were razed to the ground and removed from the landscape, notably in the Queen Street and Adelphi districts.

Towards a Prouder Preston envisaged extensive redevelopment of the town centre, 'There [being] much in the central area of the town that is old and obsolete and which has today no right to occupy some of the most valuable sites in the town'. The main feature of this plan was to be a great processional way along Lancaster Road, dominated by a new civic hall. With new housing was to come a real attempt to improve the quality of life: 'Housing between the two wars failed because most of the estates were not planned as small communities within the town, and provided only for one class of tenant and lacked many of the amenities that were available in the centre of the town'.[15]

The *Development Plan for the County Borough of Preston* was published in

The Oxford Street flats, Avenham, December 1960. In the late 1950s and early 1960s strenuous efforts were made to overcome the town's housing problems.

1951, at the end of the immediate post-war recovery. It provided a clear analysis of the town's planning and development problems in the context of long-term economic and social trends. The survey's conclusions were stark. Over sixteen thousand new houses were needed, double the pre-war effort, and 'it appears inescapable that for at least another generation many citizens will have to continue to live and bring up families in undesirable surroundings'.[16]

The Preston plan and the County Council's Development Plan were to provide the framework for subsequent developments. Both envisaged a continued drift of population out of the centre of the town into its suburbs, whilst the County plan identified Leyland as a major area of potential urban growth – a forerunner of the New Town concept. Within Preston itself great efforts were to be made. Existing housing development programmes at Ribbleton and Brookfield were to be extended to include a new scheme at Larches, and road improvements were to include a by-pass and a town-centre ring road with an integral central bus station.

Progress during the 1950s was steady if unspectacular, though in 1955 it was claimed that at the then current rate of demolition it would take two hundred years to clear the worst of the town's housing. In that year Preston's first large-scale slum clearance scheme since the war began, with the compulsory purchase of 209 properties in the Pleasant Street and Brunswick Street districts.

In 1956 a second programme was announced for 350 houses within the triangle formed by Lancaster Road North, Moor Lane and Walker Street, and clearance orders for parts of Bow Lane, Carlisle Street, Dover Street,

Markland Street, Marsh Lane and Nile Street followed in 1958 as the planned demolition of over six thousand pre-1850s' houses gathered momentum. Gradually the core residential areas of the early Industrial Revolution were removed from the Preston townscape. Compulsory Purchase Orders were served, residents moved out and entire districts were razed.[17] By 1967 only a handful of shops and houses remained in the Adelphi district, for example, and the *Lancashire Evening Post* commented, 'It is only a roadway running through a landscape that looks more like the other side of the moon than a place where hundreds of people once lived and worked'.[18]

The Council's first large-scale post-war development was the Larches estate at Ashton. This was to be a self-contained community of six hundred houses and flats, with 'bungalows and a hostel for old people, a community centre, health clinic, library and a church' and a children's play park. The cost of the houses, roads and sewers, without any of these additional amenities, was estimated at £220,000.[19] Rents were to range from 3s. 6d. for a one-bedroomed bungalow to 7s. 3d. for 'the dearer type of brick house'.

Building outside the Borough boundaries also continued. In 1951 and 1953 large housing schemes of 113 and 1,076 dwellings respectively were announced for Middleforth Green and Kingsfold in Penwortham. In 1950 work began on the Brookfield estate, which was to have 1,200 houses and to accommodate five thousand residents; this was to increase by 1963 to 2,500 'luxury dwellings' housing 7,500 people. The first review of the 1951 Borough Plan in 1960 envisaged the development by 1974 of 'a new little town' of more than two thousand houses at Ingol, and early in 1964 it was announced that the 'new Ingol housing is a dream come true'.

The town's first block of multi-storey flats was opened in Samuel Street in 1957 and the Council agreed in principle to the plan for flats in Avenham in 1958. By 1962 high-rise flats had begun to tower over the Craggs Row windmill. The new residents' reactions to the revolutionary multi-storey flats were mixed, and a development of maisonettes which 'made Prestonians boggle with amazement and disgust' was awarded an architectural prize.[20]

Between 1921 and 1968 Preston built ten thousand council dwellings ranging from bungalows to flats in tower blocks, and during the late 1960s new housing was being completed rapidly. In one district 'Quickbuild Homes' were building at the rate of 180 homes per year, needing only four men, a crane, a lorry and a constant supply of factory parts. This drew comparisons with the celebrated achievement of William Price who, for a £5 bet, built No. 41 Fylde Street in just 24 hours!

By the mid-1970s government policy had shifted towards a much more conservative approach. It was decided that funds might now be expended more economically through gradual renewal, and by making relatively small grants available locally for improving existing dwellings. Since the worst of the housing had been removed in earlier years, whole districts could be upgraded to a satisfactory level in this way. Similarly the vast funds expended on overspill schemes and the New Towns could, it was felt, be used more efficiently by targetting them directly on deprived and inner-city areas. The success of this more modest approach can be seen in Borough Council and New Town schemes in Plungington, Broadgate, Fishwick, Tulketh and the 'Saints' area of Deepdale, where selective demolition and rebuilding, combined with the modernisation of existing well-built terraced housing, have provided varied accommodation in pleasant surroundings.

—— Town-centre developments ——

As part of the zoning of the town into distinct industrial and residential areas came plans to redevelop the town centre – the business, shopping and administrative district that covered the site of the entire eighteenth-century town. These developments had an inauspicious start in March 1947 when fire extensively damaged the Guild Hall and the clock tower of the Town Hall. The structure was made safe, rather than restored, though the Council received the then enormous sum of £140,000 insurance compensation. Local opinion was generally adamant that the building should be restored, but the debate over the building's future dragged on.

In 1962, despite a petition signed by eight thousand people, it was decided to demolish the surviving building and to lease the site to the Calgary and Edmonton Land Company for one hundred years at a

The Tithebarn Street Bus Station 1967. Tucked in behind Lancaster Road, and later replaced by one of the town's most remarkable buildings – the enormous town centre bus station – the Tithebarn St. station was nevertheless spacious for its day. The Ribble Bus Company was founded at Gregson Lane near Hoghton, and rapidly became a major local employer, with its head office at Frenchwood.

The Tithebarn Street Fire Station, c.1938. The fire service had progressed markedly by the 1930s. In 1936 'the station . . . is at present equipped with two "Merryweather" pumps 5–600 gallons, one "Leyland" 3–500 gallons, one "Ford" emergency tender, one "Leyland" trailer pump and two "Daimler" ambulances . . . the present permanent staff consists of three officers, twelve men and eight auxiliaries.'

ground rent of £36,750 per year. Broadly coinciding with the closure of Horrockses, the height of the house clearance and relocation programme and other extensive town centre developments, the demolition of the Town Hall has come to be symbolic of the negative aspects of the period as a whole. Crystal House, erected on the site, met with much local scorn, was found to be difficult to let, and was subsequently blamed for a slump in the land company's profits.[21]

By the mid-1950s plans were well advanced for the developments which came to dominate the town centre: a ring road and central bus station, a new market hall, the replacement of the Public Hall with the new Guild Hall, the St. John's and St. George's shopping centres, and a number of large new stores.

The St. George's Shopping Centre was an enormous development overlaying and obliterating the centre of the medieval town plan to produce two floors of shops and parking for six hundred cars.[22] Work began on the £3 million project in June 1963 and the centre was opened on 20th November 1964 with 44,000 people visiting it on the first day. According to the *Sunday Times*, 'a 4½-acre tangle of mean alleys and sagging warehouses' had been transformed into a shopping centre of the future, 'with its half-mile of shop windows, its circular, 2-tier central piazza, its winter warmed escalators and its Venetian tesselated pavements'.[23]

In 1965 plans were announced for another new centre on Tithebarn Street, adjacent to the bus station site. This was to have 35 shops, a supermarket and a bowling alley. Though plans had been unveiled in 1955, the go-ahead for the bus station was delayed, but early in 1968

The Guild Hall, completed just too late for the 1972 Guild celebrations, now hosts a wide range of leisure events, from bowls and snooker championships to concerts and plays.

Right: Preston Bus Station and car park, one of the most controversial architectural legacies of the 1970s.

artists' impressions of the spectacular £2 million building, six hundred feet long and a hundred feet high, appeared in the local press. At the adjacent Ward's End redevelopment between Lancaster Road and Tithebarn Street, a site was reserved for the new Civic Hall. According to the 1967 plans, this was to cost £600,000 and provide both a 2000-seater concert hall and a smaller hall or theatre.

Thus by the late 1960s an enormous area of the old town had undergone, or was undergoing, redevelopment. Occasional traces of old buildings come to light. In 1959 work on the Maypole Dairy premises in Cheapside exposed an early seventeenth-century mud and straw wall, while demolition of the town's tithebarn dating from 1680 revealed its structure of enormous oak beams and handmade bricks resting on a stone plinth.[24]

—— *The Preston by-pass and the new roads* ——

The perceived need to adapt the ancient town to the requirements of the motor car was also central to the town planning of the post-war years, and the solutions adopted were to have particularly profound implications for the town's environment.

The 1951 Borough Plan proposed remedies for the town's acute traffic problem, which was largely caused by the need for through traffic to thread its way in and out of the medieval town centre. An entirely new

The Grand Junction, Watery Lane Roundabouts 1953. Before the development of the town's ringroad in the 1970s, a number of less spectacular measures were taken in an attempt to remedy Preston's serious traffic problem. A good view of 1950s Preston: Tulketh and Shelley Road Mills can be seen on the skyline, and television aerials are still marked by their absence.

A model of the Preston By-pass at Longridge Road c.1955. Preston boasted the first length of British Motorway when Prime Minister Harold MacMillan opened the Preston By-pass on 5th December 1958. As the Lancashire Evening Post *reported, 'It was one of those events – like Preston Guild – where future generations will be told by their elders – "I was there!"'.*

north-south highway between Lancaster and Warrington and passing east of the town, had been proposed as early as 1936, and this by-pass ultimately became Britain's first length of motorway – the M6. To ease congestion in the west a Liverpool-Blackpool by-pass was recommended. In order to take through traffic away from the central area, and to connect the east and west approaches, an inner ring road was also proposed, with an integral central bus station and adequate car parking.

In December 1953 plans to construct the Lancaster and Preston by-passes as part of the £13 million Warrington–Lancaster trunk road were announced by the Ministry of Transport. The Preston road would take two million cars a year away from Preston, and in June 1956 work began; the *Manchester Guardian* explained to its readers the novel concept of the motorway: 'a road designed exclusively for the use of motor traffic'.[25] Although by later standards a very modest two-lane affair, at the time it was as revolutionary an undertaking as construction of the railways had been a century earlier, and was followed just as avidly by the press. The giant girders of the Samlesbury bridge, weighing 1,100 tons, were lowered into place in March 1958, and on 5th December 1958 Prime Minister Harold Macmillan opened the new road and drove along it in style. At £3,750,000, the final cost was almost double the original estimate.

The following month the new road had to be closed following heavy rain and, amidst much official secrecy, 34 miles of drains were laid in six days. The road was subsequently widened and by December 1964 the Preston-Lancaster section, with its spectacular flyover at Broughton, was almost complete. The new M6 quickly became the principal route into Scotland. The new route to Manchester – the M61 – followed, while the M55 took Blackpool-bound traffic away from the town's bottlenecks.

Preston's ring road, linking its eastern and western approaches but by-passing the centre, was to be a source of great controversy, and profoundly altered the geography of the town centre, sweeping away Starchhouse Square, cutting Friargate in half and eventually demolishing part of the Corn Exchange (the Public Hall). By 1957 plans were well advanced, but almost ten years of delays followed and the first work on the project did not begin until the end of September 1966. As the work progressed a successful local campaign thwarted plans to demolish the Public Hall, which for a further twenty years sat astride the thoroughfare. But the building was not used and was allowed to fall into decay, and this period of neglect eventually culminated in the demolition of the main body of the hall, and the restoration of the ornamental Corn Exchange frontage. The Ringway could thus be linked directly to the western approach roads.

Investment in new roads was a major feature of the Central Lancashire New Town. Primary roads and new throughways were to be the key to further housing and industrial development in much the same way that Blackpool Road had been associated with the inter-war housing schemes. Although the box of motorways around the town envisaged in the mid-1970s has not yet transpired, the western primary route from south of Leyland to Penwortham, and the new route from Ashton to Longsands (Tom Benson Way-Lightfoot Lane-Eastway) has been the basis of a great deal of development. This is particularly marked in the Ingol district and to the south of the Broughton roundabout, where the built-up area of the town extended northward nearly two miles beyond the 1930s' perimeter formed by Blackpool Road.

——— *The new city* ———

Schemes for the development of a new city in central Lancashire, based on the expansion of Leyland, can be traced to the County Council's Development plan of 1951. The district's locational advantages were further strengthened with the construction of the motorway network, and in 1965 Richard Crossman, Minister of Housing, designated the Preston-Chorley belt as the site of a new town. It was to be a means of helping Manchester and Merseyside deal with their housing problems. Central Lancashire was destined to be the last of the second-generation new towns typified by Milton Keynes.

The Central Lancashire Development Corporation (CLDC) came into operation in March 1972 and its outline plan was published in 1974, only two years before a change in government policy re-directed support towards inner-city areas. The Corporation was wound up in 1985, its remaining functions being taken over by the Commission for New Towns.[26]

A disconcerting insight into 'official thinking' is revealed by Richard Crossman's diary, in which he recorded his visit to the area in 1965:

> I arrived in Preston and spent the morning in a bus, taking a look at that dreary Lancashire Plain, quite nice country but appallingly built over and its villages totally undistinguished. I found that I had designated the new town in an area with at one end a really ghastly town called Chorley and at the other a slightly less ghastly expanded village called Leyland.[27]

Although the role of the CLDC was widely perceived as the developing of a great metropolis, this was not strictly the case. A 'new town' might emerge from its work but its primary function was to be economic and social development. Government funds were to be injected into the Preston-Leyland-Chorley belt in the hope of stimulating continued and related growth to combat economic decline in East Lancashire and urban decay in and around Manchester. The CLDC thus worked in conjunction with the seven local councils and the County Council, providing additional capital for the development of the urban and industrial infrastructure.

Central Lancashire: Study for a City [28] was produced in 1967, outlining plans which focused on Preston as the administrative, retail and service centre. By 1970 little had been achieved, and developments proposed for the centre of Preston were being held in abeyance until a decision was made on the new town scheme.

The official go-ahead was given in March 1970 and the decision was welcomed by the participating local authorities, though civic leaders in Liverpool and Manchester declared that the scheme was not relevant to their needs. Even before the outline plan had been published in March 1974, the original scheme had suffered a 20% cut-back, though the estimated cost was still £900 million.

The older parts of Preston had much to gain from urban regeneration, and the population of the pre-1974 Preston Borough was in fact planned to decrease by 23,000 within thirty years. The 'new town' area as a whole, however, was set to reach the rather unrealistic population target of 430,000 by 1990, an increase which meant that several of the surrounding rural townships would be overwhelmed by urban development.[29] For example, Haighton, a quiet hamlet with a population of 240, was to develop into a town of almost thirty thousand people by the end of the century.

Local attention was distracted initially by much talk in the media of the benefits likely to accrue from the development, and by efforts to find a suitable name for the conurbation (none was ever found), but the planners soon had to face a rising tide of popular revolt and many of the affected districts formed local campaigns to fight the proposals. When in November 1971 the public enquiry into the outline plan was opened in the Guild Hall, 'the massive main hall . . . was just, but only just, large enough to accommodate the objectors to various aspects of the proposals, and their representatives.'[30] The local farming interest was particularly irate at plans to acquire a huge 'land bank' by Compulsory Purchase, to be released for future development, while Manchester City Council denounced the entire scheme as a 'wildly extravagant way of spending limited public resources'.

Nevertheless, CLDC became operational in March 1972, and by October 1974 had a staff of two hundred and had purchased over four thousand acres of land at a cost of £17 million. By 1974/5 it claimed to be spending £1 million per month, and by the end of 1976, when Peter Shore announced that government aid was to be switched instead to inner-city areas, over eight thousand acres had been purchased and both residential and industrial developments were well under way.[31]

In April 1977, when £100 million had been spent, plans were again cut back – this time very significantly. The land bank was frozen, and areas to the east of the M6 were entirely removed from the scheme. The target population was considerably reduced, and the plans to develop Haighton, Grimsargh, Ulnes Walton and Runshaw were all dropped.[32] Local campaigners celebrated the defeat of the 'concrete invaders' and Ray Johnson, a leader of the Grimsargh protest group, believed that 'we have won because we refused to accept that it was impossible to keep them out'.

As the Mayor of Preston, Harold Parker, pointed out in 1977, much of the investment up to that time had been focused on projects to the south of the river, but developments in Preston now assumed a higher profile and the new road system began to emerge. Many projects did not come to fruition, though, until after Secretary of State Michael Heseltine's announcement in 1981 that the Corporation would be wound up at the end of 1985, and as late as 1992 work was being started on houses

Fishergate has changed markedly during the 1980s. The Evening Post building has gone; the Fishergate Centre has shifted the focus of retailing towards the railway station; and several older buildings, like the new M & S store, have been renovated.

authorised by the Commission for New Towns.

The CLDC will long remain a highly controversial subject, but its impact and importance cannot be denied. Almost £200 million of central government funds was pumped into the district, providing additional housing for the continued outflow of Preston's population and, especially important, for the improvement of many of the older areas of the town. By 1982 3,200 jobs were located on CLDC developments, 237 factories had been built and the 150-acre former Courtauld works was being redeveloped as an industrial park. Almost ten thousand houses had been built, and the population of the area had actually increased from 235,000 to 255,000 during the fiteen years of the Corporation's existence. The system of new roads, though coming into use after the CLDC's winding-up provided considerable relief to the existing network. In short, CLDC made available enormous resources for long-term investment in infrastructure and housing, far exceeding anything that the post-war planners could have envisaged.[33]

⸺ *A cosmopolitan society* ⸺

U p to the late eighteenth century Preston's population remained relatively homogeneous and inward-looking, but the great social upheaval of the Industrial Revolution, the coming of the railways and the steady demand for new labour which had to come from outside the town began to break down the town's insularity. By the end of the nineteenth century Preston's mills provided employment for a large number of immigrants, and a significant proportion of Prestonians could claim Irish descent. The trend towards a more cosmopolitan society was considerably accelerated at the end of the Second World War with the arrival of ex-servicemen, displaced persons, and immigrants from Poland, the Ukraine, White Russia and Italy. Many of these people readily found work in the local textile and engineering industries.

From the mid-1950s, and especially in 1960–62, British industry faced acute labour shortages, particularly in the transport and health sectors. In Lancashire the shortage hampered the textile industry in its drive to maximise capital investment by running the mills 24 hours a day on multiple shifts. This labour shortage was met in part by migrants from the New Commonwealth countries of India, Pakistan and the British West Indies.

The 1981 census showed that 10,999 people out of Preston's population of 122,082 had New Commonwealth or Pakistan origins, forming at least seventeen religious, national or ethnic groups. From the mid-1950s Hong Kong Chinese families began to establish themselves; East African Asians, largely from Kenya and Uganda, arrived between 1968 and 1972; and during the 1980s the town welcomed a small number of refugees from Vietnam. Preston's population has thus developed into one which is highly diverse and culturally rich.[34]

—— Keep right on to the end of the road . . . ——

I n the midst of the enormous geographical, economic and social changes to have overwhelmed Preston in the second half of the twentieth century, one name among all others became associated with the town – that of Tom Finney, the Preston plumber.

Throughout much of the early twentieth century successive Preston North End teams laboured under the lingering shadow of the Old Invincibles. Revival began in the early 1930s, and although the 'Double' narrowly escaped the great Preston-Scottish side in 1937–8 the club had clearly regained its former heights. North End under the leadership of J. I. Taylor was one of the top clubs in the country. Although this position was confirmed by the team's exploits in the early part of the war, in 1949 the club returned to the second division.[35]

As in the late 1920s Taylor responded decisively to relegation by signing players. Charlie Wayman came from Southampton, and having established a pioneer youth policy before the war as a safeguard against the high transfer fees paid by the city sides, North End smashed the transfer record themselves by paying Sheffield Wednesday £26,500 for Eddie Quigley. Having tried to re-sign Finney after the war on part-timer's wages of £5 per week, Taylor now took pains to reassure him that the club's sojourn in the second division would be a short one: 'You should never leave Preston, Tom. Preston needs you'.[36]

The results were almost instantaneous: the season 1950–51 was among the most successful in the club's history. Average gates of over thirty thousand saw the Invincibles' record of thirteen successive wins exceeded by one, in a run of twenty matches without defeat. These were Tom Finney's, and North End's, golden years: second division champions in 1951, seventh in the league in 1952, whilst 1953 saw the most remarkable end of a league campaign ever. Despite a 2–0 defeat at Deepdale in the 'run-in' Arsenal hung on to take the League Championship on a technicality – by 0.1 of a goal under the 'goal-average' system.

In 1954 North End returned to Wembley for their fourth Cup Final there in seventeen years, but as in 1888 West Bromwich Albion (themselves runners-up in the league) achieved a memorable victory. The late 1950s saw a second peak of achievement. Narrowly avoiding relegation in 1955–56 and starting the 1956–57 season badly, Jimmy Milne shrewdly perceived the endless possibilities of playing Finney not as a winger but as a centre forward.[37] North End finished that season third, nudged out of second spot by Spurs on goal average, with the championship going to the 'Busby Babes'. The season 1957–58 saw North End runners-up again, this time behind Wolverhampton Wanderers.

As a player and leading sporting personality Tom Finney has been the subject of a number of studies, most recently and successfully in a major book by Paul Agnew, *Finney – A Football Legend*. Despite the offer of a large transfer fee from Palermo in 1952 North End refused to release him, and the town was thus remarkably fortunate to share only with England the services of a player who in Bill Shankly's judgement was the greatest footballer of all time. Although the statistics of his career are well-known – his 210 goals in 473 games for the club and thirty goals in 76 games for England – these are but a pale reflection of his immense skill and presence on the field, something which is perhaps best captured in the two famous studies of him, *The Splash* and *The Magnet*. Tom Finney is thus a significant figure in Preston's history, as an ambassador of the town, of sport, and of his country. The most distinguished Prestonian of the twentieth century, he ranks alongside Sir Richard Arkwright in the select band of townspeople whose names have become famous throughout the world.

Though relegated to the second division in 1961, North End had a number of talented young players on the edge of the team and in Peter Thompson many felt that they had the second Finney. These hopes were fulfilled in 1963–64 when under Jimmy Milne's leadership the club came close to achieving a remarkable double of promotion from the second division and winning the FA Cup. Once Wembley came in sight however, league form slipped away, but the 1964 Cup Final was to be one of the best seen since the war. Though very much the underdogs to first division West Ham United, who in Hurst and Moore had the architects of England's World Cup triumph two years later, North End were twice ahead through goals by Doug Holden and Alex Dawson, only to lose 3–2 in the last minutes of the game. The team, and particularly Howard Kendall, then the youngest player to appear in a final, were given a tremendous welcome on their return to Preston.

By the mid-1960s the balance of power within the English game had shifted decisively in favour of the wealthy city clubs. North End's position was aggravated by the magnitude of their former success, abolition of the maximum wage, the retirement of Finney at a crucial stage of the team's evolution, and the fact that the club did not own its own ground – an enormous financial asset for funding a club's overdraft. Later changes in the Scottish League's regulations for the signing of players by English

Arsenal v. Preston North End, Highbury, March 4 1949. The war robbed many of the Preston players of the best years of their careers, including Bill Shankly, seen in action here at the close of his playing career. Though relegated in 1949, J. I. Taylor assured Tom Finney that the club would soon be back in the first division. During the next decade the club was to become Second Division Champion, twice runner-up in the League and Cup finalist, whilst Finney was twice to be nominated 'Player of the Year'.

clubs obstructed the club's access to its traditional source of talent.

Indeed, seen against this harsh new order, the club has not been without at least a measure of success. As so often in the past it bounced back from relegation in 1969–1970 to secure the third division championship, and the great Bobby Charlton managed and played for the club in the mid-1970s. Under the guidance of Nobby Stiles the team won promotion in 1978, and enjoyed their most successful spell in the second division since the mid-1960s. Although unlucky to be relegated on the last match of the season in 1983, the rather unfortunate dismissal of Stiles heralded the club's darkest days for half a century. The club's first and disastrous season in the fourth division was followed by immediate promotion in 1986/7 when North End narrowly failed to become the only club to have won all the league championship titles.

In 1986 an artificial playing surface, the celebrated 'plastic pitch', enabled Deepdale – the oldest professional football ground in the world – to be used for community sports. The first major game played upon it was historically apt, a memorable cricket match between Ian Botham's 11 and the great West Indies tourist side led by Viv Richards.

Thus in recent years the club has been at the forefront of the community-based approach to the game, inspired by a former player Mick Baxter, whose tragic early death was deeply mourned by both the town and district, and was a massive loss to the club.

Despite the anti-climax of the post Taylor-Finney era, the town has consistently shown itself able to support a higher level of football. Throughout the century North End have been the town's most widely publicised ambassadors, and one of the most distinguished clubs in the history of the game. Their many friends throughout the world might join with the town to echo the sentiments of the club's president: 'I still cling to the hope that one day I will walk down Lowthorpe Road on a Saturday afternoon, take my seat in the stand and witness the return of First Division football at Deepdale'.[38]

Notes on the text

Chapter One

1. B. Barnes, *Man and the Changing Landscape: A Study of Occupation and Palaeo-Environment in the Central Pennines* (1982).
2. F. A. Hibbert, V. R. Switsur and R. G. West, 'Radio-Carbon Dating of Flandrian Pollen Zones at Red Moss, Lancashire', *Proceedings of the Royal Society of London*, series B, vol. clxxvii (1971), pp. 161–176.
3. J. S. Hallam, B. J. N. Edwards and A. J. Stuart, 'A Late-glacial Elk with associated Barbed Points from High Furlong, Lancashire', *Proceedings of the Prehistoric Society*, xxxix (1973), pp. 100–128; B. J. N. Edwards, *The Story of the High Furlong Elk* (1972). For recent C14 dates, see *Lancashire Archaeological Bulletin*, xi, no. 5.
4. J. D. Bu'lock, 'The Pikestones: a Chambered Long Cairn of Neolithic Type on Anglezarke Moor, Lancashire', *Transactions of the Lancashire and Cheshire Antiquarian Society* (hereafter *T.L.C.A.S.*), vol. lxviii (1958), pp. 143–5; F. Lynch, 'The Pikestones, Anglezarke, Lancashire', *Proceedings of the Prehistoric Society* (hereafter *P.P.S.*), xxxii (1966), pp. 347–8.
5. S. Piggott, *Neolithic Cultures of the British Isles* (1954), p. 295. Local finds refer to items in the collection of the Harris Museum, Preston.
6. For the Astley Site, see J. S. Hallam, *The Surviving Past* (1985), pp. 33–38. For the Bleasdale Circle, see W. J. Varley, 'Excavations at Bleasdale', *Antiquities Journal*, xviii (1938), p. 154. I am grateful to Mr. Ben Edwards for details of recent analysis of the finds.
7. For Kate's Pad, see S. J. Sobee, *A History of Pilling* (1953), pp. 9–25; for the Pilling burial, see B. J. N. Edwards 'Archaeological Note', *Transactions of the Historic Society of Lancashire and Cheshire* (hereafter *T.H.S.L.C.*), cxxiii (1969), p100.
8. R. F. Taylor, 'The Archaeology of Preston Dock and the Ribble Flood Plain', unpublished notes, Harris Museum (1965); W. H. Heathcote, 'Upon Recent Discoveries in the Ribble Valley', *T.L.C.A.S.*, v (1887), pp. 342–5; W. H. Heathcote, 'A Second Communication . . . ', *T.L.C.A.S.*, vi (1888), pp. 188–9; E. Dickson, 'Notes on the Excavations for the Preston Docks', *Liverpool Geology Society Proceedings*, v (1887), pp. 249–256; E. Dickson, 'Geological Notes on the Preston Docks Works and the Ribble Development Scheme', *Liverpool Geology Society Proceedings*, v (1888), pp. 369–376.
9. B. Barnes, op. cit., pp. 72–83; J. D. Blundell and I. H. Longworth, 'A Bronze Age Hoard from Portfield Farm, Whalley, Lancashire', *British Museum Quarterly*, xxxii (1968), pp. 8–14.
10. D. Shotter, *Romans in Lancashire* (1973); D. Shotter, *Roman North-West England* (1984).
11. C. Hardwick, *History of Preston* (1857) (hereafter, Hardwick, *History of Preston*). For local folklore and finds see p. 47. J. S. Hallam, *The Surviving Past* (1985), pp. 48–54.
12. For general descriptions of the Ribchester site, see J. H. Hopkinson, *The Roman Fort of Ribchester* (1928); A. L. F. Rivet and C. Smith, *Place-Names of Roman Britain* (1979); J. Garstang, *Roman Ribchester* (1898); B. J. N. Edwards, *Ribchester* (1972).
13. The account of recent work at Ribchester is based upon: B. J. N. Edwards and P. V. Webster, *Ribchester Excavations Part 1: Excavations within the Roman Fort* (1985), *Ribchester Excavations Part 2: Excavations in the Civil Settlement: The Structures* (1987); *Ribchester Excavations Part 3: Excavations in the Civil Settlement: Pottery and Coins* (1988).
14. Hardwick, *History of Preston*, pp. 37–47. See especially Plate 2. E. E. Pickering, 'Roman Walton-le-Dale 1947–1957', *T.H.S.L.C.*, cix (1957), pp. 1–46. See fig. 1, showing the presumed course of the River Darwen.
15. The account of recent work at Walton is based on provisional reports in the *Lancashire Archaeological Bulletin*, viii (1982), pp. 4–5.
16. Harris Museum, Preston; D. Shotter, *Roman North-West England* (1984), p. 26.
17. Quoted in Hardwick, *History of Preston*, p. 51 and p. 52.
18. E. Ekwall, *Place-Names of Lancashire* (1922, reprinted 1972); H. H. Wyld and T. O. Hirst, 'Addenda and Corrigenda to Ekwall's Place-Names of Lancashire', *English Place-Names Society Journal*, xvii

(1985). The writer stresses that historians 'need a cautious approach to Ekwall'. Place-name lists are based on these three sources. D. Kenyon, *Archaeology, Place-Names and Settlement in Lancashire and Cheshire c. 400–1066* (unpublished Ph.D Thesis, University of Manchester, 1984). For the Wale-tun place-name, see M. Gelling, *Signposts to the Past* (1988).

19. R. Millward, *Lancashire – An Illustrated Essay on the History of the Landscape* (1955), p. 71.
20. F. T. Wainwright, 'Scandinavians in Lancashire', *T.L.C.A.S.*, lviii (1947).
21. Ekwall, op. cit.
22. Harris Museum, Preston.
23. F. Coupe, *Walton-le-Dale: A History of the Village* (1954), ch. 3. This account is based on F. A. Philpott, *A Silver Saga: Viking Treasure from the North-West* (1990), a guide produced for the exhibition of Viking artefacts and a large selection of the Cuerdale Hoard held at Liverpool Museum in 1990 to commemorate the 150th anniversary of its discovery.
24. P. Morgan, *Domesday Book: Cheshire including Lancashire, Cumbria and North Wales* (1978). This account is also based on *Victoria County History* (hereafter *V.C.H.*), i, 'Domesday Survey'.

Chapter Two

1. M. R. G. Conzen, 'The Use of Town Plans in the Study of Urban History' in H. J. Dyos (ed.), *The Study of Urban History* (1968). See also M. Morris *The Archaeology of Greater Manchester Volume One: Medieval Manchester* (1983), pp. 31–2, fig. 18. The map series attributed to Dr. Kuerden and produced in the 1680s may be found in L.R.O., DDX 194/1–9.
2. A. Hewitson, *History of Preston* (Preston, 1883) (hereafter Hewitson, *History of Preston*), p. 55. For details of the early charters see pp. 47–56. Fishwick, *The History of the Parish of Preston* (1900), ch. 3, pp. 83–102.
3. See transcription in Fishwick, ibid, pp. 14–17.
4. *V.C.H.*, vii (1912), p. 92.
5. On the occasions when the King did grant the manor out to subjects the Burgesses did not, however, fare so well, notably between 1194–1205 when the Hundred of Amounderness with its capital manor of Preston was granted to Theobald Walter. See R. Cunliffe-Shaw, *The Royal Forest of Lancaster* (1956), p. 96.
6. Hewitson, *History of Preston*, pp. 92–97.

Quote on p. 92.
7. W. A. Abram, *Memorials of the Preston Guilds* (1882) (hereafter Abram, *Memorials*); W. A. Abram, 'The Rolls of the Burgesses of the Guild Merchant of the Borough of Preston 1397–1682', *Record Society of Lancashire and Cheshire*, ix (1884) (hereafter *Guild Rolls*), p. 37.
8. Hewitson, *History of Preston*, p. 297.
9. J. H. Lumby, 'De Hoghton Deeds and Papers', *Records Society of Lancashire and Cheshire*, xcviii, (hereafter *D.H.D.P.*), deed 310.
10. M. Morris, op.cit., p. 21.
11. For contemporary accounts of the church lands see, A. N. Webb, 'An Edition of the Cartulary of Burscough Priory', *Chetham Society*, xviii (1970), series 3; W. H. Hulton, 'The Coucher Book or Chartulary of Whalley Abbey', *Chetham Society*, x, xi and xvi; W. Farrer, 'The Cockersand Chartulary', *Chetham Society*, xxxviii–xl. For a list of the Chantries, see, F. R. Raines, 'A History of the Chantries', *Chetham Society*, lix–lx (1862).
12. Hewitson, *History of Preston*, p. 62.
13. *V.C.H.*, vii (1912), p. 82.
14. Hardwick, *History of Preston*, p. 462.
15. Hewitson, *Our Churches and Chapels* (1869), p. 7.
16. *V.C.H.*, ii (1908), pp. 163–4.
17. W. Farrer, *Lancashire Pipe Rolls and Early Lancashire Charters* (1902), pp. 333-5; 'Walter de Ingol's Grant', ibid., series vii, charter no. 2, p. 335.
18. Fishwick, op. cit., pp. 193–7.
19. T. C. Smith, *Records of the Parish Church of Preston* (1892) (Hereafter Smith, *Records of the Parish Church*), p. 243.
20. Raines, op. cit., p. 205; *V.C.H.*, ii (1908), pp. 163–4.
21. *V.C.H.*, ii (1908), p. 162; Fishwick, op. cit., pp. 198–207.
22. R. Kuerden, *A Brief Description of the Burrough and Town of Preston, and its Government and Guild* (c. 1682, published with additional notes by J. Taylor, Preston, 1818) (hereafter Kuerden, *A Brief Description of Preston*), p. 15.
23. P. Whittle, *History of the Parish of Preston* (1837), i, p. 126.
24. E. Baines, *The History of the County Palatine and Duchy of Lancashire* (1836), iv, p. 305.
25. Ibid.
26. Morris, op. cit., p. 27.
27. Fishwick, op. cit., pp. 34–35.
28. Morris, op. cit., p. 30.
29. Fishwick, op. cit., p. 24.
30. Smith, *Records of the Parish Church*, p. 8.
31. *V.C.H.*, ii (1908), pp. 29–31, quote p. 29.
32. Ibid., iv, p. 73, footnote 17.

33. Abram, *Guild Rolls*, p. 20.

Chapter Three

1. D.H.D.P., no. 225.
2. D.H.D.P., no. 233.
3. Respectively: L.R.O., DDPd 11/2; L.R.O., DDPd 11/4; L.R.O., DDPd 11/15.
4. D.H.D.P., no. 296.
5. *V.C.H.*, vii (1912), p. 79, footnote 98. Towneley Manuscripts.
6. D.H.D.P., no. 257.
7. L.R.O., DDLn 61/41.
8. D.H.D.P., no. 350.
9. D.H.D.P., no. 354.
10. A. Hewitson (ed.), *Preston Court Leet Records: Extracts and Notes* (Preston, 1905) (hereafter Hewitson, *Court Leet Records*), p. 83.
11. Ibid., p. 68.
12. L.R.O., DDX 9/2.
13. L.R.O., DDX 900/113.
14. L.R.O., DDK 805/10 and 11.
15. L.R.O., DDPD 11/33.
16. *V.C.H.*, vii (1912), p. 79, footnote 98.
17. W. Farrer, 'The Cockersand Chartulary', *Chetham Society* vol. xxxix (1898), ch. 3, p. 219.
18. *V.C.H.*, vii (1912), p. 79, footnote 98; Hewitson, *Court Leet Records*, p. 76, footnote 3.
19. Farrer, op. cit., xxxix, ch. 11, p. 224.
20. D.H.D.P., no. 234.
21. D.H.D.P., nos. 241 and 244.
22. D.H.D.P., no. 319.
23. The classic work on this subject is R. Cunliffe-Shaw, *The Royal Forest of Lancaster* (1956). This account is extensively based on it.
24. Ibid., quoted p. 69.
25. Ibid., quoted pp. 142-3.
26. Ibid., quoted p. 65.
27. W. Farrer, 'Lancashire Pipe Rolls and Early Lancashire Charters' (1902), p. 423.
28. Cunliffe-Shaw, op. cit., quoted p. 68.
29. Ibid., p. 443.
30. Ibid., quoted p. 447-8.
31. Ibid., p. 450-1.
32. Ibid., quoted p. 451.
33. Ibid., p. 451-3. See also Fulwood Enclosure Award, L.R.O. AE/1/4; papers of the Enclosure Commissioners, L.R.O. DDX/103/12-13. Maps of Award are in Cunliffe-Shaw, op. cit., p. 432 (Cadley) and p. 433 (Fulwood). For subsequent Land use see the Fulwood Tithe Map L.R.O. DRB 1/83. For the enclosure of Preston Moor see L.R.O. DDPr 141/3, 'Plan of Moor Park and Adjacent Streets, 1833', and L.R.O. DDHe 98/1, 'Explanation of Phillip Parks Plan for the Enclosure of Preston Moor'. For subsequent land use see the Preston Tithe Map, L.R.O. DRB 1/157.

Chapter Four

1. Baines, op. cit., i, p. 494.
2. Fishwick, op. cit., pp. 47-8.
3. *V.C.H.*, vii (1912), p. 74.
4. Hardwick, *History of Preston*, pp. 142-4.
5. Fishwick, op. cit., p. 48.
6. Hardwick, *History of Preston*, p. 138.
7. Fishwick, op. cit., pp. 38-42.
8. Ibid., p. 45; *V.C.H.*, ii (1908), p. 39, footnote 16.
9. Coupe, op. cit., pp. 90-1.
10. C. Haigh, *Reformation and Resistance in Tudor Lancashire* (1975), p. 109; *V.C.H.*, ii (1908), p. 39, f. 275. Much of this account of Preston is based on Haigh.
11. Baines, op. cit., i, p. 480.
12. Haigh, op. cit., p. 84.
13. *V.C.H.*, ii (1908), p. 40.
14. Smith, *Records of the Parish Church*, pp. 252-3.
15. Haigh, op. cit., p. 240.
16. *V.C.H.*, ii (1908), p. 224, f. 28.
17. Haigh, op. cit.
18. *V.C.H.*, ii (1908), p. 225.
19. *V.C.H.*, vii (1912), p. 87.
20. Raines, op. cit., i, p. 206; see also Smith, *Records of the Parish Church*, pp. 41-3 for the full letter.
21. Smith, *Records of the Parish Church*, pp. 44-5.
22. *V.C.H.*, vii (1912), p. 85, f. 196.
23. *V.C.H.*, ii (1908), p. 55, f. 359.
24. M. Mullett and L. Warren, *Martyrs of the Diocese of Lancaster* (1987), p. 15.
25. Haigh, op. cit., p. 289.
26. F. O. Blundell, *Old Catholic Lancashire*, ii (1938), pp. 128-9.
27. C. Talbot (ed.), 'Recusant Records', *Catholic Record Society* (hereafter *C.R.S.*), liii (1960), p. 104; H. Bowler 'Recusant Roll no. 2 (1593-4)', *C.R.S.*, lvii (1965), pp. 55, 69, 76 and 78.
28. J. S. Leatherbarrow, 'The Lancashire Elizabethan Recusants', *Chetham Society*, cxi (1947), p. 149.
29. Leatherbarrow, op. cit., p. 41.
30. *V.C.H.*, ii, (1908), p. 227, f. 57.
31. Leatherbarrow, op. cit., pp. 103-5.
32. F. R. Raines, 'The State, Civil and Ecclesiastical, of the County of Lancashire, about the year 1590', *Chetham Society*, xcvi (1875), pp. 1-48 and pp. 2-3.
33. Haigh, op. cit., pp. 327-9.

34. W. E. Waring, 'Two Old Halls of Leyland: their Origin and People', *Lailand Chronicle*, xxxvi (1990), pp. 23–30; L.R.O., DDF 2438/92; see also F. Edwards *The Gunpowder Plot* (1951).
35. *V.C.H.*, vii (1912), p. 75.
36. Haigh, op. cit., p. 302.
37. Smith, *Records of the Parish Church*, p. 47.
38. *V.C.H.*, vii (1912), p. 88, f. 224.
39. Leatherbarrow, op. cit., p. 149.
40. Fishwick, op. cit., p. 180.
41. Smith, *Records of the Parish Church*, pp. 57–8.
42. Ibid., p. 61.
43. Haigh, op. cit., p. 240.

Chapter Five

1. Preston Parish Registers, L.R.O. PR 1432-79.
2. Smith, *Records of the Parish Church*, p. 270.
3. R. Sharpe France, 'A History of Plague in Lancashire', *T.H.S.L.C.*, xc (1938), pp. 1–175 and p. 85.
4. Ibid., pp. 61 and 69.
5. Ibid., p. 70.
6. Ibid., p. 70.
7. Ibid., pp. 80 and 63.
8. Abram, *Memorials*, p. 42.
9. L.R.O., DP 353, 'Sermons Preached by Christopher Hudson, Preacher of Gods Word at Preston' (1643).
10. Preston Hearth Tax in Fishwick, op. cit., pp. 432–7; Preston Protestation Return in Fishwick, op. cit., pp. 424–31.
11. F. C. Markwell and P. Saul, *Facsimiles of Documents of Use to Family Historians* (1987), p. 75.
12. J. Paler in Smith, *Records of the Parish Church*, pp. 47–8.
13. A. Hewitson, *Diary of Thomas Bellingham* (1908).
14. H. W. Clemesha, *Diary of Lawrence Rawstorne of Hutton 1687–9* (L.R.O. Library transcript).
15. The diary is quoted in G. Miller, *Hoghton Tower* (1948), pp. 82–3.
16. Ibid.
17. C. Morris (ed.), *The Illustrated Journeys of Celia Fiennes* (1982), p. 162.
18. Kuerden's maps of Preston: L.R.O. DDX 194/1–9. G. L. Bolton, 'Leyland's First Local Historian', *Lailand Chronicle*, xvi (1976), pp. 8–12.
19. Abram, *Memorials*, p. 61.
20. Kuerden, *A Brief Description of Preston*.

Chapter Six

1. Abram, *Memorials*, p. 21: 1562 Guild Order.
2. Ibid., p. 34: 1598 Interim Guild Order.
3. Ibid., p. 57.
4. Ibid., p. 32: 1582 Guild Order.
5. Ibid., p. 37: Council Book, 26 August 1612. Hardwick, *History of Preston*, p. 281.
6. Abram, *Memorials*, p. 53: 'The Manner of holding a Councell for makeing of any Law or Order, for the welfare of this Towne'.
7. Ibid., p. 51. For Kuerden's account see ibid., p. 55.
8. Ibid., p. 57: Council Book October 1666. Ibid., p. 70: Council Book 25 June 1685.
9. Kuerden, *A Brief Description of Preston*.
10. Extracts have been published in: Hardwick, *History of Preston*, pp. 272–284; in the late local nineteenth century press by Hewitson and Abram; but most cohesively in Abram, *Memorials*, pp. 37–8, 57–8, 69–70, 75–6, 81–3, 87–9 and 101–2.
11. Ibid., p. 37: Thomas Wall, Council Book 21 January 1609. Ibid., p. 69: Fairs, Council Book 20 August 1683.
12. Ibid., p. 48.
13. Ibid., p. 70: William Worden, Council Book 11 July 1698. Ibid., p. 75: Thomas Gradwell, Council Book 14 April 1712. Ibid., p. 58: John Kellett, Council Book 23 October 1676.
14. Ibid., p. 37: Council Book 26 August 1612.
15. Ibid., pp. 73–4: 1702 Guild Order.
16. Smith, *Records of the Parish Church*, p. 248.
17. Ibid, pp. 248–9.
18. Ibid, pp. 265–6.
19. A. Hewitson (ed.), *Preston Court Leet Records: Extracts and Notes* (1905) (hereafter Hewitson, *Court Leet Records*), p. 105: Great Court Leet, 15 October 1666.
20. Smith, *Records of the Parish Church*, p. 266.
21. Clemesha in Hewitson, *Court Leet Records*, p. 14.
22. Hewitson, *Court Leet Records*, p. 1: Great Court Leet, 20 October 1653.
23. Ibid., p. 168: Thomas Parr, Great Court Leet, 20 October 1720.
24. Ibid., pp. 66–7, f. 2.
25. Ibid., pp. 136–7, f. 2: Shambles, Great Court Leet 23 October 1657.
26. Ibid., p. 157: Ladder for the Ducking Stool. Ibid., p. 53, f. 3: Ducking Stool. Ibid., p. 93, f. 3: Pillory. Ibid., p. 68, ff. 1–2: Stocks and Rogue's Post. Ibid., p. 204, f. 4: Lock-up or 'Prison'.
27. Ibid., p. 24: George Worden, Inquisition 30 January 1654. Ibid., pp. 64–5: Great Court Leet 25 April 1656.

28. Ibid., pp. 27–8: Pinders Inquisition, 30 January 1654.
29. Ibid., p. 168: William Gradwell, Great Court Leet, 20 Feb. 1720 and 20 October 1720. Ibid., pp. 97–8: Guild Expenses, Great Court Leet, 16 April 1663.
30. Ibid., p. 144: William Jolly, Inquisition, February 8 1691.
31. Ibid., p. 126: Repair of Highways, Great Court Leet, 5 April 1675.
32. Ibid., p. 48: William Bannaster, Great Court Leet, 4 May 1655. Ibid., p. 110: John Cottam, Inquisition, 18 February 1668.
33. Ibid., p. 34: Great Court Leet, 18 April 1654.
34. Ibid., p. 97: Great Court Leet, 16 April 1663.
35. Ibid., pp. 65–6, f. 1 and pp. 187–8, f. 3.
36. Ibid., p. 105: Hugh Rimmer, Great Court Leet, 15 October 1666. Ibid., p. 97: Robert Brindle, Great Court Leet, 19 October 1660. Ibid., p. 117: Ellis Makeinge, Great Court Leet, 19 April 1669. Ibid., p. 129: Thomas Hoghton, Great Court Leet, 5 April 1677. Ibid., p. 113: Thomas Holme, Great Court Leet, 19 April 1669. Ibid., p. 113: Thomas Cooper, Great Court Leet, 19 April 1669. Ibid., p. 85: William Threlfall, Great Court Leet, 7 May 1658.
37. Ibid., p. 94: John Greenwood, Great Court Leet, 4 October 1662. Ibid., p. 52: Thomas Abbott, Great Court Leet, 4 May 1655.
38. Ibid., p. 139: Great Court Leet, 14 May 1685.
39. Ibid., p. 139: Size of bricks, Great Court Leet, 20 October 1685. Ibid., p. 12: Roger Woodroofe, Great Court Leet, 20 October 1653.
40. Ibid., p. 96: Henry Blackburne, Great Court Leet, 16 April 1663. Ibid., p. 96: Henry Wildinge, Great Court Leet, 16 April 1663. Ibid., p. 112: Richard Brookfield, Great Court Leet, 19 April 1669. Ibid., p. 116: John Mosse, Great Court Leet, 8 April 1670.
41. Ibid., p. 109: William Blacoe, Great Court Leet, 14 October 1667. Ibid., p. 134: Richard Woods, Inquisition, 16 February 1682.
42. Ibid., p. 9: Millers dishes, Great Court Leet, 20 October 1653. Ibid., p. 125: Transgressors, Great Court Leet, 23 October 1674.
43. Ibid., p. 145: John Hatch, Great Court Leet, 26 October 1691. Ibid., p. 83: Pinders, Inquisition, 10 February 1658. Ibid., p. 131: John Baly, Great Court Leet, 27 March 1679.
44. Ibid., p. 27: Moor Gate, Inquisition, 30 January 1654. Ibid., p. 44: Herdsmen for March, Inquisition, 12 February 1655. Ibid., p. 117: Geese, Great Court Leet, 8 April 1670.
45. Ibid., p. 46: Swineherd, Great Court Leet, 4 May 1655.
46. Ibid., p. 26: Clay Pits, Inquisition, 30 January 1654. Ibid., p. 76: Swillbrook Bridge, Great Court Leet, 22 October 1656.
47. Ibid., p. 58, f. 2: Moor Brooke, 12 February 1656.
48. Ibid., p. 130: Ashes on Marsh, Inquisition, 13 February 1679.
49. Ibid., p. 9: Henry Bullow's wife, Great Court Leet, 20 October 1653. Ibid., p. 20: Middens, Inquisition, 30 January 1654. Ibid., p. 8: Anne Ingham, Great Court Leet, 20 October 1653.
50. Ibid., p. 46: Cleaning Streets, Great Court Leet, 4 May 1655.
51. Ibid., p. 35: Carryon, Great Court Leet, 18 April 1699. Ibid., p. 150: Dead Horse, Great Court Leet, 26 April 1699. Ibid., p. 138: James Cowp, Great Court Leet, 14 May 1685. Ibid., p. 69: Hanging dogs, Great Court Leet, 25 April 1656.
52. Ibid., p. 35: Garbage in streets, Great Court Leet, 18 April 1654. Ibid., p. 29: Butchers, Great Court Leet, 18 April 1654. Ibid., p. 177: Burning Hoofs, Great Court Leet, 24 October 1735. Ibid., p. 158: Rotten meat, Great Court Leet, 25 October 1705.
53. Ibid., p. 87: Barrel of Beef, Great Court Leet, 22 October 1658.
54. Ibid., p. 101: Joseph Boulton, Great Court Leet, 6 April 1665. Ibid., p. 113: John Singleton, Great Court Leet, 19 April 1669.
55. Ibid., p. 27: Market Day, Inquisition, 1 November 1653. Ibid., p. 111: George Gregson, Great Court Leet, 20 October 1668. Ibid., p. 111: Luke Greenfield, Great Court Leet, 20 October 1668.
56. Ibid., p. 101: Elizabeth Woodhouse, Great Court Leet, 6 April 1665. Ibid., p. 111: Nicholas Watson, Great Court Leet, 20 October 1668.
57. Ibid., p. 193: Penwortham Bridge, Great Court Leet, 22 October 1760. Ibid., p. 53: Hedges, Great Court Leet, 4 May 1655. Ibid., p. 148: Fire, Inquisition, 7 March 1697.
58. Ibid., p. 110: Wells, Great Court Leet, 3 April 1668. Ibid., p. 54: Almshouses, Great Court Leet, 4 May 1655.
59. Ibid., p. 69: Friargate, Great Court Leet, 25 April 1656.
60. Ibid., p. 37: Cleaning wells, Great Court Leet, 20 October 1654. Ibid., p. 120: Ellis Makin, Great Court Leet, 11 April 1672. Ibid., p. 144: James Clayton, Great Court Leet, 20 October 1690. Ibid., p. 165: John Threlfall, Great Court Leet, 15 May 1717.
61. Ibid., p. 175, f. 1: Water works. Ibid., p.

175: Robert Abbott, Great Court Leet, 4 May 1732. Ibid., p. 196: Thomas Addison, Great Court Leet, 12 October 1771. Ibid., p. 92: Thomas Silcoke, Great Court Leet, 10 April 1661.

62. Ibid., p. 129: Tildesley Atkinson, Great Court Leet, 14 October 1678. Ibid., p. 39: William Dobson, Great Court Leet, 20 October 1654.

63. Ibid., p. 114: Elizabeth Woodhouse, Great Court Leet, 14 October 1669. Ibid., p. 138: Roger Bannester, Great Court Leet, 4 April 1684. Ibid., p. 113: John Preston, Great Court Leet, 19 April 1669. Ibid., p. 93: Henry Graddell, Great Court Leet, 10 April 1661.

64. Ibid., p. 149: John Shaw, Great Court Leet, 19 October 1697. Ibid., p. 142: Henry Graystocke, Great Court Leet, 10 May 1688.

65. Ibid., p. 45: William Walmesley's wife, Inquisition of Office, 12 February 1655. Ibid., p. 89: Ellen Haworth, Great Court Leet, 19 April 1659. Ibid., p. 90: Anne Dickson, Great Court Leet, 12 October 1659.

66. Ibid., p. 90: John Salter and John Bolton, Great Court Leet, 4 May 1655. Ibid., p. 80: James Parcevall, Great Court Leet, 30 March 1657.

67. Ibid., p. 50: Mary Shakshaft, Great Court Leet, 4 May 1655. Ibid., p. 80: Margaret Watson, Great Court Leet, 30 March 1657. Ibid., p. 118: Robert Loxam, Great Court Leet, 3 May 1671. Ibid., p. 110: John Smith, Great Court Leet, 3 April 1668.

68. Ibid., p. 6: Evan Rogerson, Great Court Leet, 21 October 1653.

69. Ibid., p. 117: William Charnocke, Great Court Leet, 14 October 1670.

70. Ibid., pp. 5–6: Seth Morte and Richard Morte, Great Court Leet, 21 October 1653. Ibid., pp. 29–31: Seth Morte and Edward Morte, Great Court Leet, 18 April 1651. Ibid., p. 31: Alexander Breres.

Chapter Seven

1. This account draws extensively on the following works: E. Broxap, *The Great Civil War in Lancashire 1642–51* (1910, republished with additional notes 1973); W. Beamont (ed.), 'A Discourse of the Warr in Lancashire', *Chetham Society*, lxii (1864) (hereafter Discourse of War); G. Ormerod (ed.), 'Tracts Relating to the Military Proceedings in Lancashire during the Great Civil War', *Chetham Society*, ii (1844) (hereafter Civil War

Tracts). Much original material is available in the two celebrated *Chetham Society* volumes. Discourse of War is believed to have been written by Edward Robinson of Buckshaw Hall near Leyland. The Preston campaign of 1648 I have based upon R. Holmes, *Preston 1648* (1985).

2. Civil War Tracts, pp. 327–8; 'Rigby's Letter to the Speaker' in Broxap, op. cit., pp. 12–13.

3. Discourse of War, p. 16.

4. Civil War Tracts, pp. 22–4: 'Diurnall of Occurrences'.

5. Abram, *Memorials*, p. 47.

6. Civil War Tracts, p. 22; Abram, *Memorials*, p. 46.

7. Ibid., pp. 46–7: White Book, 10 October 1642.

8. Miller, op cit., p. 55.

9. Ibid., p. 55; Broxap, op. cit., p. 59.

10. Discourse of War, p. 23.

11. Civil War Tracts, p. 127: 'Lancashire's Valley of Achor'.

12. Ibid, pp. 71–3: 'The True Relation of the Taking of the Town of Preston'.

13. Discourse of War, p. 24.

14. Civil War Tracts, p. 81: 'Taking of Hoghton Tower'.

15. Ibid., p. 128: 'Lancashire's Valley of Achor'.

16. Discourse of War, p. 30.

17. Civil War Tracts, p. 86: 'Storming of Preston by Lord Derby'.

18. Fishwick, op. cit., p. 52.

19. Discourse of War, p. 32.

20. Ibid., p. 34.

21. Ibid., p. 60; Broxap, op. cit., p. 137.

22. Discourse of War, p. 54.

23. Ibid., p. 56.

24. Ibid., p. 57.

25. Ibid., p. 58.

26. Civil War Tracts, pp. 255–8: 'Leiutenant Cromwell's letter concerning the total routing of the Scots' Army'.

27. Ibid., p. 263: 'Lt. General Cromwell's letter to the Hon. William Lenthall'.

28. Discourse of War, p. 67.

29. Civil War Tracts, p. 288: 'Mercurius Politicus'.

30. Discourse of War, p. 74.

31. The Composition Papers have been published by *The Record Society of Lancashire and Cheshire* (hereafter *R.S.L.C.*). Individual persons are listed alphabetically in the volumes. J. H. Stanning (ed.), *R.S.L.C.*, xxiv (1891), xxvi (1892), xxix (1894), xxxvi (1898). J. Brownbill (ed.), *R.S.L.C.*, lxxii (1916), vc (1941), vci (1942).

32. *R.S.L.C.*, xcvi (1942), p. 372.

33. *R.S.L.C.*, vc (1941), pp. 21–2.

34. Civil War Tracts, pp. 277–8: 'Pestilence in Lancashire.

Chapter Eight

1. Fishwick, op. cit., p. 56.
2. Ibid., p. 57; *V.C.H.*, vii (1912), p. 76, f. 51.
3. M. Mullett, 'To Dwell Together in Unity: The Search for Agreement in Preston Politics 1660–1690', *T.H.S.L.C.*, cxxv (1974), p. 70; J. M. Gratton, 'The Origins of Political Parties in Late Seventeenth Century Lancashire', *T.H.S.L.C.*, cxxxvi (1987), pp. 39–58; S. Hibbert Ware, *Lancashire Memorials of the Rebellion: 1715* (1844), pp. 1–2.
4. Mullett, op. cit., pp. 74–5.
5. Mullett and Warren, op cit., p. 6.
6. J. M. Gratton, 'The Origins of Political Parties in Late Seventeenth Century Lancashire', *T.H.S.L.C.*, cxxxvi (1987), pp. 48–49; H. W. Clemesha, *A History of Preston in Amounderness* (Preston, 1912) (hereafter Clemesha, *A History of Preston*), p. 159.
7. Hardwick, *History of Preston*, pp. 251–2.
8. L.R.O. DDH 475/1–7; Miller, op cit., ch. 10 and appendix 4; ibid., p. 113.
9. Ibid., p. 112.
10. S. Hibbert Ware, *Lancashire Memorials of the Rebellion: 1715* (1844), p. 96, 'Peter Clarke's Journal'. This volume contains two eye-witness accounts: those of Peter Clarke and the 'Merse Officer'. Peter Clarke, 'Clerk to Mr. Crockenthorpe of Kendal', and the 'Merse Officer', a professional soldier who was able to follow proceedings from the Parish Church tower. An account by Robert Patten, Forster's chaplain, is quoted extensively in Hardwick, *History of Preston*.
11. Ibid., p. 98, 'Peter Clarke's Journal'.
12. Ibid., p. 107, 'Peter Clarke's Journal'.
13. Ibid., p. 108–9, 'The Merse Officer's Account'.
14. Ibid., p. 125, 'Peter Clarke's Journal'.
15. Ibid., p. 127, 'Peter Clarke's Journal'.
16. Ibid., p. 128, 'The Merse Officer's Account'.
17. Ibid., p. 132, 'Peter Clarke's Journal'.
18. Ibid., p. 133, 'The Merse Officer's Account'.
19. Patten, quoted by Hardwick, *History of Preston*, pp. 231–2.
20. R. C. Jarvis, *The Jacobite Risings of 1715 and 1745* (1954), p. 186; Patten, quoted by Hardwick, *History of Preston*, p. 219; Hibbert Ware, op. cit., p. 100; Clemesha, *A History of Preston*, p. 188.
21. Patten, quoted by Hardwick, *History of Preston*, p. 219.
22. Hibbert Ware, op. cit., p. 110.
23. Ibid., p. 190.
24. Ibid., p. 190.
25. Ibid., p. 140.
26. R. C. Jarvis, *Collected Papers on the Jacobite Risings*, ii, p. 7; J. Byrom, quoted in ibid., p. 25; W. Dobson, *History of the Parliamentary Representation of Preston* (1868).
27. Chambers in Hardwick, *History of Preston*, p. 242.
28. Ibid., pp. 249–50.
29. J. Ray in ibid., p. 243.

Chapter Nine

1. D. Defoe, *A Tour through England and Wales* (1928), p. 268; R. S. Fitton, *The Arkwrights Spinners of Fortune* (1989), p. 5.
2. Marchant in Hardwick, *History of Preston*, p. 248. Ray in ibid., p. 247.
3. Pococke in *V.C.H.*, vii (1912), p. 78.
4. M. M. Schofield, 'The Statutory Registers of British Merchant Ships for North Lancashire in 1786', *T.H.S.L.C.*, cx (1958), pp. 107–129; M. M. Schofield, 'The Virginia Trade of the Firm of Sparling and Bolden of Liverpool 1788–99', *T.H.S.L.C.*, cxvi (1964), pp. 117–165; M. M. Schofield, 'The Slave Trade from Lancashire and Cheshire Ports outside Liverpool 1750–1790', *T.H.S.L.C.*, cxxvi (1976), pp. 30–72; M. M. Schofield, 'Shoes and Ships and Sealing Wax: Eighteenth Century Lancashire Exports to the Colonies', *T.H.S.L.C.*, cxxxv (1986), pp. 61–82; F. E. Sanderson, 'Biographical Essay: Lancashire and the Slave Trade: A Guide to Sources', *T.H.S.L.C.*, cxxiv (1972), pp. 154–176. I am most grateful to Jack Humble for drawing my attention to this aspect of the town's history.
5. Skippool: see M. M. Schofield, 'The Slave Trade from Lancashire and Cheshire Ports outside Liverpool 1750–1790', *T.H.S.L.C.*, cxxvi (1976), p. 43. Freckleton: see F. J. Singleton, 'The Flax Merchants of Kirkham', *T.H.S.L.C.*, cxxvi (1977), pp. 73–101 and p. 90.
6. Abrams, Harris Reference Library Cuttings Book no. 1, p. 77, f. 242.
7. Abrams, Harris Reference Library Cuttings Book no. 1, p. 57, f. 110.
8. M. M. Schofield, 'Shoes and Ships and Sealing Wax: Eighteenth Century Lancashire Exports to the Colonies', *T.H.S.L.C.*, cxxxv (1986), p. 79.
9. M. M. Schofield, 'The Slave Trade from Lancashire and Cheshire Ports outside Liverpool 1750–1790', *T.H.S.L.C.*, cxxvi (1976), p. 30ff., Table 4, p. 44.
10. M. M. Schofield, 'Shoes and Ships and Sealing Wax: Eighteenth Century Lanca-

11. shire Exports to the Colonies', *T.H.S.L.C.*, cxxxv (1986), p. 66 and p. 69.
11. Ibid., p. 73.
12. L.R.O. DDK 1549/1, 4a, 5.
13. M. M. Swarbrick, 'Preston: a Study of the Growth and Development of a Lancashire Market Centre and its Hinterland' (Thesis, Harris Reference Library, 1975), p. 30.
14. Will at Richmond 1763: see L.R.O. DDPd 25/13; Brown Channell: see Hewitson, *Court Leet Records*, p. 123.
15. L.R.O. DDK 1549/1.
16. Thoresby Diary in Abram, *Memorials*, p. 74. 1722 Guild in Abram, *Memorials*, p. 93.
17. *Preston Journal* (Harris Reference Library): 7 June 1745, 13 October 1752, 13 October 1752, 12 August 1750, 8 February 1751, 24 September 1742, 22 March 1745, 24 September 1742, 17 September 1742.
18. Abram, *Memorials*, p. 94.
19. Abram, *Memorials*, pp. 105–6.
20. S. H. Paviare, *The Devis Family of Painters* (1950).
21. S. W. Urbanski, *Parliamentary Politics 1792–1832 in an Industrial Borough: Preston* (Ph.D, Atlanta, U.S.A., copy in L.R.O.)
22. L.R.O., DDK 2/6.
23. L.R.O., DDK 7/1; see also surveys of 1514 and 1521 respectively in L.R.O., DDK 3/6 and L.R.O., DDK 3/14.
24. Hewitson, *Court Leet Records*, pp. 54–56.
25. J. J. Bagley, *The Earls of Derby 1485–1985* (1985), pp. 131–3.
26. L.R.O., DDK 1981 (Preston Estate Rentals). The Derby records for the Preston Estate fall into two categories, as follows. 1. Papers relating to the Preston Estate Office, including: rental books DDK 1807; the Preston surveys L.R.O., DDK 1549/1–6 and L.R.O., DDK 1549/7–10. 2. Records compiled centrally at Knowsley. Daily cash books DDK 1901–, the cash journal DDK 1942–, and the mster books to the estate, The ledger DDK 1981. Only the latter contain the full picture of finances, the Preston Sources relate closely to the housing aspect of the estate, but much larger rentals are only recorded in the Knowsley books. Annual revenues fluctuate greatly from year to year in proportion to the extent of arrears and short term economic conditions.
27. L.R.O., DDK 1549/10.
28. Hewitson, *History of Preston*, pp. 119–20.
29. Ibid., p. 120; Hewitson, *Court Leet Records*, p. 194, f. 2.
30. Hewitson, *History of Preston*, p. 118.
31. Abrams, Harris Reference Library Cuttings Book, no. 1, p. 21.
32. Ibid., p. 25.
33. Hardwick, *History of Preston*, p. 331.
34. 'Poll Book', L.R.O., DDPd 11/51. See also: 'Tally Register', L.R.O., DDPd 11/50; 'Foreign Voters', L.R.O., DDPr 138/7; 'Canvas Return', L.R.O., DDPr 131/a.
35. L.R.O. DDPd 11/51.

Chapter Ten

1. Clemesha, *A History of Preston*, p. 100. Hewitson, *Court Leet Records*, pp. 187–8, f. 3.
2. R. S. Fitton, *The Arkwrights Spinners of Fortune* (1989), ch. 1.
3. Ibid., p. 219.
4. Ibid., p. 1.
5. S. D. Chapman and S. Chassagne, *European Textile Printers in the Eighteenth Century* (1981), p. 20; W. A. Abram, *History of Blackburn* (1887), pp. 224–7.
6. Hewitson, *Court Leet Records*, p. 200.
7. Information courtesy of Chris Aspin, Sun Insurance: Sun Fire Office Policy Registers 'Old Series', MS 11,936, cccxc, policy number 609294, Guildhall Library, London.
8. J. Livesey, *The Autobiography of Joseph Livesey* (1881), pp. 1–3.
9. L.R.O., DDK 808/22; L.R.O., DDK 808/24–5.
10. L.R.O., DDK 808/70.
11. L.R.O., DDK 1901.
12. C. H. Lee, *A Cotton Enterprise 1795–1840: A History of McConnel and Kennedy Fine Cotton Spinners* (1977), p. 7 and p. 78.
13. L.R.O., DDK 1942; see also DDK 803/31.
14. L.R.O., DDK 1982, pp. 261–2.
15. L.R.O., DDP (uncatalogued), 'John Watson Cotton Mill Papers'.
16. Hewitson, *Court Leet Records*, p. 200; *Preston Journal*, 7 November 1807.
17. *Preston Journal*: 7 November 1807; 28 November 1807; 12 December 1807.
18. *Preston Journal*, 7 May 1808.
19. Information courtesy of Chris Aspin: *London Gazette*, 7 May 1808; *Blackburn Mail*, 11 May 1808.
20. *Preston Journal*, 8 February 1808.
21. Information courtesy of Chris Aspin.
22. L.R.O., WCW, 1824, J. Watson.
23. Anon, 'Horrockses, Miller and Co.', *Fortunes Made in Business*, iii (1887), ch. 1, p. 6. This account appears to be based on W. Dobson, *Parliamentary Representation of Preston* (1868), pp. 52–65.
24. R. Boyson, *The Ashworth Cotton Enterprise: The Rise and Fall of a Family Firm 1818–1880* (1970), p. 5.
25. *Fortunes Made in Business*, iii (1887), p. 9.
26. L.R.O. DDHs 1/1.

27. *Blackburn Mail*, 20 February 1796.
28. S. Birtles, *Horrockses – The Development of a Cotton Enterprise* (unpublished dissertation, 1980).
29. *The Story of Horrockses* (1950). An account produced for visitors to the Yard Works.
30. H. I. Dutton and J. E. King, *Ten Per Cent and No Surrender* (1981), p. 10.
31. L. Rawstorne, *Some Remarks on Lancashire Farming and on Various Subjects* (1843), p. 22.
32. J. Holt, *General View of the Agriculture of the County of Lancaster* (1795), p. 179.
33. D. A. Hunt, *A History of Leyland and District* (1990), pp. 74–88; G. Timmins, *Handloom Weavers Cottages in Central Lancashire* (1977).
34. Hewitson, *History of Preston*, p. 170.
35. W. Dobson, *Parliamentary Representation of Preston* (1868), p. 63.
36. *Fortunes Made in Business*, iii (1887), p. 35.
37. H. N. B. Morgan, *Vanished Dwellings: Early Industrial Housing in a Lancashire Cotton Town – Preston* (Preston, 1990), hereafter Morgan, *Vanished Dwellings*.
38. Dobson, op. cit., p. 59.
39. R. Crawford and J. Lennon, *Report of the Parliamentary Select Committee on Handloom Weavers* (1834).
40. R. Brickel, *Our Relationship and our Work* (1875). I am most grateful to Jacqueline Izat for bringing this work to my attention.

Chapter Eleven

1. H. N. B. Morgan, *An Introduction to the Social History of Housing in Victorian Preston* (Preston, 1982), hereafter Morgan, *Housing in Victorian Preston*. This is a classic work on the subject.
2. *Preston Guardian*, 30 November 1844. Quoted in Morgan, *Vanished Dwellings*, p. 20.
3. J. Clay, *Report on the Sanitary Condition of Preston* (1842).
4. Quoted in Morgan, *Vanished Dwellings*, pp. 19–20.
5. See also Morgan, *Housing in Victorian Preston*, pp. 6–32. The process and implications of growth have been the subject of a very detailed study by Nigel Morgan.
6. M. Roberts, *The Story of Winckley Square* (1988).
7. Hardwick, *History of Preston*, p. 431.
8. Morgan, *Housing in Victorian Preston*, pp. 44–7.
9. Ibid., pp. 64–101, and especially maps 1–3, pp. 4–5.
10. Ibid., pp. 34–39 and 64–73.
11. Council proceedings June 1874, quoted by Morgan, ibid., p. 71.
12. Ibid., p. 87.
13. Quoted by Hardwick, *History of Preston*, p. 383.
14. Hewitson, *History of Preston*, pp. 195–7.
15. G. Biddle and C. Hadfield, *Canals of North West England* (1970).
16. G. Biddle, *The Railways Around Preston* (1989); J. Marshall, *The Lancashire and Yorkshire Railway* (1969). The development of the railway system in and around Preston may be briefly summarised:
    1838 Preston and Wigan Railway (links to Manchester and Liverpool).
    1839 Preston and Bolton line.
    1840 Preston and Longridge line (station behind Stephenson terrace; 1846 extended by tunnel under Preston to Maudlands; 1886 linked to Whittingham Hospital).
    1840 Preston and Lancaster Railway.
    1840 Preston and Fleetwood Railway.
    1846 Preston, Lytham and Blackpool line.
    1846 Preston and Blackburn Railway (link to Preston Quay constructed).
    1849 Preston and Liverpool via Ormskirk line.
    1855 Preston and Southport via Liverpool line.
    1880 North-south lines quadrupled by construction of a second Avenham Bridge.
    1882 Preston to Southport direct (West Lancashire line).
17. C. Aspin, *The First Industrial Society* (1969), p. 25.
18. D. A. Hunt, *A History of Leyland and District* (1990), pp. 97–100.
19. *Preston Chronicle*, 3 November 1838.
20. J. E. King, *Richard Marsden and Preston Chartists* (1981), p. 32.
21. *Preston Chronicle*, 19 March 1862; see also Morgan, *Vanished Dwellings*, p. 8.
22. H. I. Dutton and J. E. King, *Ten Per Cent and No Surrender* (1981), p. 11. For the best general account of the development of the Preston industry at this time see pp. 6–12.
23. Hewitson, *History of Preston*, pp. 185–6.
24. Dutton and King, op. cit., p. 14.
25. T. C. Dickinson, *Lancashire Under Steam* (1984). See especially pp. 33–43. For a map of the Preston mills, see pp. 42–3.

Chapter Twelve

1. L.R.O., DDPr 138/87 B.

2. *Preston Chronicle,* 1 July 1865.
3. Ibid., 10 February 1855. John Paley junior in ibid., 18 July 1857.
4. Ibid., 29 March 1862.
5. Ibid., 28 April 1866.
6. Ibid., 30 March 1895.
7. Ibid., 18 October 1873.
8. *Preston Guardian,* 16 June 1880.
9. *Report of the Royal Commission on the Employment of Children in Factories* (1833), p. 269. Ibid., supplementary report, pp. 266–268.
10. Hewitson, *History of Preston,* p. 189 and p. 175.
11. *Preston Chronicle,* 6 May 1826.
12. Hewitson, *History of Preston,* pp. 282–3.
13. Dutton and King, op. cit., p. 21.
14. Hardwick, *History of Preston,* p. 415.
15. J. E. King, *Richard Marsden and the Preston Chartists* (1981).
16. This account is based upon, *Preston Chronicle,* 13 August 1842.
17. T. Banks, *A Short Sketch of the Preston Cotton Trade in the Last 60 Years* (1888).
18. *Northern Star,* 10 September 1842; quoted by King, op. cit., p. 31.
19. *Preston Chronicle,* 29 October 1842.
20. Dutton and King, op. cit., p. 222, f. 74.
21. L.R.O., DDPr 138/87 B.
22. W. Dobson, op. cit., p. 71.
23. S. M. Hunt, *The Radical Party in Preston 1815–32* (unpublished thesis, 1950), p. 28.
24. W. Proctor, 'Orator Hunt: M.P. for Preston', *T.L.C.H.S.,* cxiv (1962), pp. 129–154 and p. 143.
25. W. Proctor, op. cit., p. 144.
26. Clemesha, *A History of Preston,* p. 280.
27. Ibid., p. 286.
28. Ibid., p. 274.
29. W. J. Lowe, *The Irish in Lancashire 1846–71: A Social History* (Ph.D Thesis, Dublin 1974), vol. ii, pp. 271–2 and pp. 443–8.
30. *Preston Chronicle,* 26 May 1888; see also L.R.O., DDX 433/17.

Chapter Thirteen

1. Dutton and King, op. cit., p. 198.
2. C. Dickens, *Hard Times* (1854).
3. H. N. B. Morgan, *Social and Political Leadership in Preston 1820–60* (unpublished M. Litt Thesis, University of Lancaster, 1980).
4. J. Pearce, *The Life and Teachings of Joseph Livesey* (1887), p. 3.
5. *The Moral Reformer* (1831), i, p. 51 and p. 366. Quoted in D. A. Hunt, *Social Attitudes towards Poverty in Preston 1861–4* (unpublished dissertation, 1977) (hereafter Hunt, *Social Attitudes towards Poverty in Preston*), p. 13. See also D. A. Hunt, 'The Silent Mills: Preston and the Lancashire Cotton Famine', *Leyland Historical Society Occasional Papers Series* (1991), hereafter Hunt, *The Silent Mills.*
6. A. Blackhurst, *Joseph Livesey 1794–1884* (1979). Obituary in *Preston Chronicle,* 6 September 1884. *Dictionary of National Biography,* xxxiii, pp. 380–1. J. Livesey, *The Autobiography of Joseph Livesey* (1881).
7. Nationally important collections of these works are held by the Harris Reference Library and the Lancashire Polytechnic Library.
8. This account is based on P. T. Winskill, *The Temperance Reformation* (1881), pp. 42–57.
9. Ibid., p. 54.
10. *Preston Temperance Advocate,* x, October 1835.
11. Ibid., xxii, December 1835.
12. Obituary in *Preston Chronicle,* 13 June 1874.
13. Quoted by W. Proctor, 'Poor Law Administration in Preston Union', *T.H.S.L.C.,* cxvii (1965) (hereafter Proctor, 'Poor Law Administration'), pp. 145–165 and p. 153.
14. Information courtesy of Marian Roberts.
15. For an account of the later years of the Workhouse debate see Hunt, *Social Attitudes towards Poverty in Preston,* pp. 43–59.
16. Proctor, 'Poor Law Administration', p. 146.
17. *Preston Chronicle,* 7 May 1864.
18. *Preston Guardian,* 28 July 1865; *Preston Chronicle,* 29 July 1865; L.R.O., PUT 1/29.
19. *Preston Chronicle,* 13 August 1864.
20. T. C. Smith, *Records of the Parish Church of Preston* (1892), p. 78. For full details of the enormous literature which is available on the history of the Preston churches see the local studies index of the Harris Reference Library. Described in detail in Hewitson, *History of Preston,* the major developments may be briefly summarised:
    1853–5 Rebuilding of the ancient parish church at a cost of £9,500.
    1725 St. George's, St. George's Road, enlarged 1799, clad in stone 1843–4. Both Samuel Horrocks and Dr. Shepherd are buried here.
    1815 Trinity Church, Trinity Square, cost £9,080.9.3d.
    1825 St. Peter's, St. Peter's Square. Tower and spire added 1852. Dickey Turner is buried here.
    1826 St. Paul's, St. Paul's Road.
    1836 St. Andrew's, Ashton.
    1836 Christ Church, off Bow Lane.

Enlarged 1851.
1838 St. Mary's, off New Hall Lane. Enlarged 1855.
1839 St. Thomas, St. Thomas Street.
1841 St. James, Avenham Lane. Building opened 1837, taken over by the Church of England, rebuilt 1841. Cost £11,800.
1846 All Saints, Elizabeth Street.
1859 St. Luke's, Fletcher Road.
1858 St. Saviour's, Leeming Street. New church 1868.
1870 Emmanuel, Brook Street.
1883 St. Matthew's, Derby Square, New Hall Lane.

21. T. C. Smith, *A Popular History of Preston Guild* (1902), p. 32.

22. W. Pilkington, *The Makers of Wesleyan Methodism in Preston* (1890); W. F. Richardson, *Preston Methodism's 200 Fascinating Years* (1973).

23. Visitor's Information Sheet (1990), St. Walburges, Preston.

24. Census of Religious Observation 1851 (1854).

25. Extracts are taken from A. Hewitson, *Our Churches and Chapels* (1869), as follows. Rev. Parr, p. 11; Fr. Cobb, pp. 17–18; Wesleyan, pp. 27–8; poorest district, p. 142; St. Augustines, p. 39; St. Josephs, p. 185; St. Marys, p. 183; St. Saviours, p. 142–3. For a similarly candid description of the contemporary town council see A. Hewitson, *Preston Town Council, or Portraits of Local Legislators* (1870).

26. Quoted by Morgan, *Vanished Dwellings*, p. 39.

27. R. A. Arnold, *The History of the Cotton Famine from the Fall of Fort Sumpter to the Passing of the Public Works Act* (1865); Hunt, *The Silent Mills*.

28. E. Waugh, *Home Life of the Lancashire Factory Folk* (1867), pp. 24–5.

29. Hewitson, *History of Preston*, p. 187.

30. This account is based on Hewitson's extensive and contemporary description of the town during the 1882 Guild. For subsequent historical studies see the local history catalogue, Harris Reference Library. Important subsequent works are given below. E. C. Oakes, *Water Supplies through 3 Centuries* (1953); J. Wilkinson and J. Mullaniff, *History of Preston County Borough Fire Brigade 1702–1952* (1952); G. Timmins et. al., *Preston Polytechnic: The Emergence of an Institution* (1979); J. Wilkinson, *Preston Royal Infirmary. A History of Health Care in Preston 1809–1986* (1987); B. G. Awty, 'The Introduction of Gaslighting in Preston', *T.H.S.L.C.*, cxxv (1974), pp. 82–118; J. E. Plank, *The Free Public Library Movement in Preston 1854–*

1900 (dissertation, 1977).

31. H. N. B. Morgan, *The Port of Preston: A Victorian Community and the Perils of a Marginal Natural Asset* (1977, Typescript in Harris Reference Library), hereafter Morgan, *The Port of Preston*; E. Johnson, *The River Ribble and Preston – A Study in Public Ownership* (1951); J. Dakres, *The Last Tide: A History of the Port of Preston 1806–1981* (1986).

32. Morgan, *The Port of Preston*, p. 42, quoting *Preston Chronicle*, 30 October 1867.

33. Morgan, *The Port of Preston*, p. 41, quoting *Preston Chronicle*, 29 March 1845, and *Preston Guardian*, 6 May 1848.

34. The Lancashire Record Office has a large collection of related documents: L.R.O., DDPp 34/1: Dock-opening ceremony press cuttings. L.R.O., DDPp 21/1: Plan of the Dock Estate. L.R.O., DDPp 5/1–58: Dock Construction Papers. L.R.O., DDPp 14/1–38: Plans of the Ribble Estuary. L.R.O., DDPp 12/1–9: Reports.

35. A. Marsden, *The Preston Grasshoppers Centenary Brochure 1869–1969* (1969).

36. This account is based on materials kindly loaned to me by Harry Shorrock on behalf of the society: *The first Society Minute Book*, and, Dilworth Abbatt, *Records of the Preston Scientific Society 1893–1937*.

37. D. Russell, *Preston North End: 100 Years in the Football League* (1989); H. Berry and G. Allman, *One Hundred Years of Football at Deepdale 1881–1981* (1981).

Chapter Fourteen

1. H. Cartmell, *For Remembrance: An Account of some Fateful Years* (1919), p. 23. The following account is based on Cartmell's history of Preston's part in the First World War. I am most grateful for the advice of Michael Quigley on all matters pertaining to the First World War.

2. Ibid., p. 36.

3. Ibid., p. 37.

4. I. Birtwistle, *The Life of the Preston Pals* (dissertation, Tuson College, Preston, 1987).

5. Cartmell, op. cit., pp. 116–9.

6. Ibid., pp. 144–9.

7. Ibid., p. 204.

8. B. Bowker, *Lancashire Under the Hammer* (1928), pp. 31–43.

9. L. G. Sandberg *Lancashire in Decline* (Ohio, 1974), p. 121.

10. *Preston Herald*, 18 April 1941.

11. This analysis is based on figures pub-

lished in the *Cotton Trade Yearbooks* for the relevant years.

12. Directories of Preston: 1913, 1926, 1932, 1940.

13. National economic trends and statistics are based on R. S. Sayers, *A History of Economic Change in England 1880–1939* (1978), and C. L. Mowat, *Britain Between the Wars 1918–1940* (1968).

14. *Lancashire Daily Post* (hereafter *L.D.P.*), 1 February 1938.

15. Ibid.

16. Ibid., 11 June 1940.

17. This account is based on: W. G. S. Hyde and F. K. Pearson, *The Dick Kerr Album* (1972), and, S. Ranson and R. Fairclough, *English Electric Aircraft and their Predecessors* (1987).

18. *L.D.P.*, 24 October 1938.

19. This account is based on D. A. Hunt, *A History of Leyland and District* (1990), pp. 129–139.

20. E. Johnson *The River Ribble and Preston: A Study in Public Ownership* (Dissertation, 1951, Harris Reference Library), p. 24ff.

21. Ibid., p. 42.

22. *L.D.P.*, 17 April 1939.

23. *Lancashire Evening Post* (hereafter *L.E.P.*), 21 December 1967.

24. *Preston Guardian*, 15 August 1958.

25. D. C. Coleman, *Courtaulds: An Economic and Social History*, ii, pp. 349–50; *L.D.P.*, 1 January 1938; *L.D.P.*, 21 November 1938.

26. D. M. Smith, *The North West* (1969), p. 207.

27. This section is based on *The Development Plan for the County Borough of Preston* (1951) (hereafter *The Preston Plan*), diag. 1; and the Harris Reference Library's collection of contemporary maps.

28. *The Preston Plan*, p. 88; *L.E.P.*, 19 April 1960.

29. *The Preston Plan*, p. 88 and p. 12.

30. Ibid., table 2.

31. Preston prices (including houses) are taken from *L.D.P.*, 1938–1939.

32. Wages are based on figures provided in W. Greenwood, *How the Other Man Lives* (1938). Since these are largely based on wages in the S.E. of England they are perhaps in advance of those in Preston.

33. This account is based on J. Cotterall, *Preston's Palaces of Pleasure* (1988).

34. This account is based on D. Russell, *Preston North End* (1989); and H. Berry and G. Allman, *One Hundred Years of Football at Deepdale 1881–1981* (1981), with many anonymous contributors.

35. *L.D.P.*, 2 May 1938.

36. *L.D.P.*, 3 June 1940. The account of wartime Preston is based on a survey of the *L.D.P.* 1938–1946, Harris Reference Library.

37. *L.D.P.*, 7 October 1944.

38. D. Upton, 'Flying Bombs Over Lancashire', *Lancashire Magazine*, November–December 1987, pp. 15–17.

39. *L.D.P.*, 23 August 1945.

40. N. Garfield, 'Lancashire's Aberfan', *Lancashire Magazine*, September 1976, pp. 50–53.

41. K. Werrell, 'The Mutiny at Bamber Bridge', *After the Battle*, xxii (1978), pp. 1–11; *L.D.P.*, 25 June 1943.

42. *L.D.P.*, 8 May 1945.

43. *L.D.P.*, 15 August 1945.

44. *L.D.P.*, 7 September 1945.

Chapter Fifteen

1. *L.E.P.*, 9 July 1956.

2. Ibid., 4 January 1958 and 6 June 1958.

3. Ibid., 4 June 1963 and 11 January 1968.

4. *We'll Spin you a Yarn* (1955), Horrockses publicity book. I am most grateful to Derek Edmondson for loaning me his collection of Horrocks' publications.

5. This account is based on G. Green, *British Aerospace: A Proud Heritage* (1988). There is an enormous literature on the history of specific aeroplanes. See: R. Beamont and A. Reed, *English Electric Canberra* (1984); B. Philpott, *English Electric/B.A.C. Lightning* (1984); B. Barrymore Halfpenny, *English Electric/B.A.C. Lightning* (1984); W. Gunston, *Panavia Tornado* (1980).

6. For the references to this crisis, see Harris Reference Library Newspaper Cuttings, 1963–66, p. 170ff.

7. This account is based on J. Dakres, *The Last Tide*.

8. *L.E.P.*, 25 October 1954.

9. *Lloyds List*, 31 May 1977.

10. Information supplied by Preston Borough Council Development Department. I am most grateful for the assistance of Keith Launchbury, in clarifying current economic trends in the town.

11. *L.E.P.*, 20 September 1979 and 16 November 1979.

12. *Hansard*, 28 November 1979; see Courtaulds file in the Harris Reference Library Newspaper Cuttings Collection.

13. *L.E.P.*, 17 December 1979.

14. *Preston Borough Council Economic Development Plan* (1991).

15. Preston Borough Council, *Towards a Prouder Preston* (1946).

16. *The Preston Plan*, p. 12 and pp. 23–5. See also updates of 1964 and 1966.

17. This and subsequent sections are based on the splendid series of local press

cuttings maintained by the Harris Reference Library.

18. *L.E.P.*, 22 December 1967.
19. Ibid., 7 October 1949.
20. Ibid., 9 June 1963.
21. *Daily Telegraph*, 29 January 1962; *L.E.P.*, 10 December 1966.
22. L.E.P., 27 September 1962.
23. *Sunday Times*, November 1964.
24. *L.E.P.*, 5 June 1964 and 20 April 1959.
25. Ibid., 9 December 1953; *Manchester Guardian*, 13 June 1956.
26. See Lancashire County Council, *A Preliminary Plan for Lancashire* (1952); Min. Housing, local govt., *Central Lancashire: Study for a City* (1967), hereafter *Study for a City*; N.W. Joint Planning Team, *Stategic Plan for the North West* (1974); C.L.N.T.C., *Outline Plan* (1974), hereafter *Outline Plan*. Many thanks are due to Rod Hamm, who kindly clarified many of the administrative points arising from my research.
27. *Dick Crossman Diaries*, 26 February 1965. Quoted in *The Guardian*, 10 June 1975.
28. *Study for a City*.
29. *Outline Plan*.
30. *Burnley Express*, 8 November 1974.
31. In the Commons, Edward Gardner, M.P.

for South Fylde, told Peter Shore that the New Town was 'one of the most unpopular developments ever to be imposed on an unwilling community'. *L.E.P.*, 4 April 1977 (Leyland Library Collection).
32. *L.E.P.*, 4 April 1977 and 6 April 1977.
33. For differing views of the C.L.D.C. see the following. Ibid., 22 February 1985, 25 November 1982 and 8 January 1987; *The Building Trades Journal*, 14 February 1975; *The Community Councils of Lancashire Newsletter*, March 1986; G. L. Woodcock, *Planning, Politics, and Communications: A Study of the Central Lancashire New Town* (1986), summarised in *L.E.P.*, 4 March 1986: 'an outstanding example of organisational survival when original goals disappeared or could no longer be achieved'.
34. R. Erikson, *A Survey of Ethnic Groups in Districts with Large Ethnic Populations in the County of Lancashire*.
35. This account is based on: Russell, op cit.; Berry and Allman, op. cit.; P. Agnew, *Finney – A Football Legend* (1989).
36. Agnew, ibid., p. 51.
37. Ibid., p. 159.
38. Ibid.

Note on the illustrations

The publishers are particularly grateful for the kind help of all the staff of the Harris Museum and Art Gallery during the picture research for this book. The Borough Council kindly gave permission for the use of material from the vast collections held there and Sally Coleman and Stephen Whittle in particular gave generously of their time in digging out useful and interesting material. Most of the photographs and illustrations used in this book are from the collections of the Harris Museum. We are deeply grateful.

Thanks also to the following depositors at the Lancashire Record Office for their kind permission to reproduce material held there: the proprietors of the *Lancashire Evening Post* for allowing us to reproduce the plan of the Market Place on page 17 (DDPr 141/20), the poster of the Corn Exchange on page 164 (DDPr 138/27) and the Lock-Out cartoon on page 189 (DDPr 138/87b); the Rt. Hon. the Earl of Derby, MC, DL for allowing us to reproduce Lang's Map of 1774 on page 32 (DDK 1549/6); the County Archivist, Lancashire Record Office, for allowing us to reproduce the map of the Battle of Preston in 1715 on page 115 (DDX 74/15); and the Rt. Hon. the Lord Hesketh for allowing us to reproduce Shakeshaft's Map of 1822 on page 153 (DDHe 122/31). Our thanks to the staff of the Lancashire Record Office, especially the County Archivist and Miss Barbara Sharp, for their help in arranging these illustrations and several others which unfortunately were omitted because of lack of space.

The re-drawn maps on pages 8, 13, 16, 35, 36, 38, 40, 42, 61, 81, 82 and 105 are the work of Ben Morgan, while the line drawings on pages 114, 117, 171, 176 and 203 are by Catherine Walker. The author provided several illustrations, which are reproduced on pages 144, 160, 196, 201 and 211. Many of the modern photographs were taken by Anna Goddard.

Index of people

Y

Index of places

A

B

C

D

F

G

R

Index of subjects